THE DEVELOPMENT OF IMPLICIT
AND EXPLICIT MEMORY

ADVANCES IN CONSCIOUSNESS RESEARCH

ADVANCES IN CONSCIOUSNESS RESEARCH provides a forum for scholars from different scientific disciplines and fields of knowledge who study consciousness in its multifaceted aspects. Thus the Series will include (but not be limited to) the various areas of cognitive science, including cognitive psychology, linguistics, brain science and philosophy. The orientation of the Series is toward developing new interdisciplinary and integrative approaches for the investigation, description and theory of consciousness, as well as the practical consequences of this research for the individual and society.

Series B: Research in Progress. Experimental, descriptive and clinical research in consciousness.

Volume 24

Carolyn Rovee-Collier, Harlene Hayne and Michael Colombo

The Development of Implicit and Explicit Memory

THE DEVELOPMENT OF IMPLICIT AND EXPLICIT MEMORY

CAROLYN ROVEE-COLLIER
Rutgers University

HARLENE HAYNE
University of Otago

MICHAEL COLOMBO
University of Otago

JOHN BENJAMINS PUBLISHING COMPANY
AMSTERDAM/PHILADELPHIA

TM The paper used in this publication meets the minimum requirements of American National Standard for Information Sciences — Permanence of Paper for Printed Library Materials, ANSI z39.48–1984.

Library of Congress Cataloging-in-Publication Data

Rovee-Collier, Carolyn K.
 The development of implicit and explicit memory / Carolyn Rovee-Collier, Harlene Hayne, Michael Colombo.
  p.   cm. -- (Advances in consciousness research, ISSN 1381-589X ; v. 24)
  Includes bibliographical references and index.
 1. Memory in children. 2. Implicit memory. 3. Explicit memory. I. Hayne, Harlene. II. Colombo, Michael. III. Title. IV. Series.
BF723.M4.R68   2000
153.1'3--dc21   00-034218
ISBN 90 272 5144 4 (Eur.) / 1 55619 724 1 (US) (Pb)

John Benjamins Publishing Co. • P.O.Box 75577 • 1070 AN Amsterdam • The Netherlands
John Benjamins North America • P.O.Box 27519 • Philadelphia PA 19118-0519 • USA

To our collective children, and to George

Table of Contents

Preface

This book evolved out of our concern that researchers who study memory in human adults have constructed a scenario of the ontogeny of memory in human infants without reference to empirical studies of infants themselves. This scenario is largely based on studies of brain-damaged adults and brain-lesioned animals and, because it fits neatly into a simple theoretical framework, is intuitively appealing — but it is wrong.

At the core of this scenario are two assumptions — the assumption that ontogeny recapitulates phylogeny and the assumption that the Jacksonian first-in, last-out principle applies to the development and dissolution of memory systems. In the first instance, evolutionary biologists have long recognized the error of designating species as "higher" or "lower" when the phylogenetic scale is tree-like and branching rather than linear. In the present context, this error has translated into the flawed conclusion that human newborns mirror lower animals and, over the course of development, come increasingly to resemble higher animals, namely, adult (or verbal) humans. In the second instance, studies with animals and human infants have failed to find support for the Jacksonian principle. Moreover, predicting the sequence of the normal dissolution of neural function from the sequence of its normal development is different from predicting the sequence of the normal development of neural function from the sequence of its normal dissolution. Taking this one step further, predicting the sequence of the normal development of neural function from the sequence of its *abnormal dissolution due to localized brain damage* is radically — and conceptually — different. In fact, some have even questioned whether the abnormal aging brain is an adequate model of the abnormal developing brain.

Finally, those of us who study infants for a living have come to realize the risk inherent in proclaiming that infants cannot do this or that. The study of human infants is itself in its infancy. It has become increasingly apparent that infants may do tomorrow what they seemed unable to do yesterday. Our new insights have resulted from the time-honored principle of "building a better mousetrap." As researchers discover new and better techniques for asking infants what they can and cannot do, we acquire new and ever-changing views of their capacities. That, in a nutshell, is what this book is all about.

For the title of this book, we selected the descriptive terms *implicit* and *explicit* memory because they refer to forms of memory and do not commit us to a particular memory-systems or processing approach. Our first aim in preparing this book is to provide a state-of-the-art exposition of the issues and facts surrounding the early development of implicit and explicit memory. Our second aim is to encourage young researchers to ask Big Questions — and to not be dissuaded by the current Zeitgeist from doing so.

The research reported in this book was supported by grant nos. R37-MH32307 and K05-MH00902 from the National Institute of Mental Health (CRC) and by Marsden grant nos. U00609 and U00703 from the Royal Society of New Zealand (HH, MC).

Carolyn Rovee-Collier, Piscataway, New Jersey, USA
Harlene Hayne, Dunedin, New Zealand
Michael Colombo, Dunedin, New Zealand

CHAPTER 1

Background of the Problem

This chapter reviews the origins of the popular notion that two, functionally distinct memory systems mature at different rates during the infancy period. Young infants are thought to share with amnesics an early memory system which supports implicit memory; the late memory system, which is damaged in amnesia and supports explicit memory, is thought to mature late in the first year. Recent evidence from preverbal infants, however, is inconsistent with this view.

How memory develops has been a topic of long-standing debate. Early theorists argued that the behavior of older infants and children is shaped by their earlier experiences (Watson 1930) and that adult personality is shaped by memories of events that occurred in infancy (Freud 1935). Their underlying assumption was that infants are endowed with a capacity for long-term memory — a means of preserving a relatively enduring record of their early experiences. Later theorists argued that infants younger than 18 months of age are incapable of representation (Piaget 1952), are not capable of forming enduring memories early in development (Kagan 1984), and cannot remember events over long periods before they are able to talk about them (Nelson 1990). These views are consistent with the assumption that young infants possess only a primitive memory system that mediates memories of procedures and simple learning (i.e., implicit memories) and lack the more advanced memory system that mediates memories of specific experiences (i.e., explicit memories) until relatively late in their first year (Nelson 1995; Schacter & Moscovitch 1984; Squire 1992a). The assumption that infants cannot retain information about their past experiences leads to fundamentally different conclusions about the importance of early experience.

Over the years, the debate over the development of implicit and explicit memory has been waged in the absence of data from infants themselves, largely because of the difficult problem of finding a task that could be used to study immature infants over an extended period of development. Now, this problem has been solved, enabling scientists to take a fresh look at the development of infant memory.

History of the problem

The notion that adults possess multiple memory systems is not new. As long ago as the late 1800s, philosophers, psychologists, psychiatrists, and neurologists proposed different typologies of long-term memory (for a listing, see Hermann 1982). What is new, however, is the notion that these memory systems develop hierarchically during the infancy period (Naito 1990; Schacter & Moscovitch 1984; Tulving 1983). How did this notion come about?

The origins of this belief are two-fold. For one thing, it seemed intuitively unlikely that organisms as immature and helpless as infants could have memories that in any way resemble our own. Over the years, this intuitive belief has been reiterated in countless general psychology and child development texts (e.g., Bjorklund, 2000). Secondly, the initial studies of infant memory suggested that young infants were incapable of retention longer than only a few seconds or minutes at most (e.g., Kagan & Hamburg 1981; Werner & Perlmutter 1979). These findings, however, were derived from measures of young infants' looking behavior in a task that is an analog of the delayed-matching-to-sample paradigm — the paradigm that researchers traditionally used to study short-term memory in rats (Roberts 1972a, 1974), pigeons (Grant & Roberts 1973; Roberts & Grant 1976; Shimp & Moffitt 1974; Zentall 1973), and monkeys (D'Amato 1973; Jarrard & Moise 1971; Jarvik, Goldfarb & Carley 1969). Findings that older infants can remember for longer periods of time came from motorically more demanding tasks, such as object search tasks, that very young infants are physically incapable of performing.

In the mid-1980s, the disparity between the memory performance of younger and older infants was attributed to two different and functionally distinct memory systems — the early memory system and the late memory system — that were hypothesized to mature at different rates during the infancy period (Schacter & Moscovitch 1984). The early memory system was thought to mediate *implicit memory* — a primitive form of memory for procedures or skills that is long-lasting and does not require conscious recollection or intentional retrieval, whereas the late memory system was thought to mediate *explicit memory* — the more advanced, adult-like form of memory for events that requires intentional retrieval and is accompanied by the conscious awareness of having experienced the event before.

The hypothesis that two distinct memory systems mature at different rates and mediate different forms of memory has been repeated so often that it is now generally regarded as a statement of fact. Most scientists, for example, believe that empirical evidence actually supports the widespread claim that very young infants are capable only of implicit memory and that the capacity for a qualitatively different form of memory does not appear until infants are much older — but no such evidence exists. In fact, until recently, the development of memory had not even been systematically studied with infants.

Origins of the developmental hypothesis

The notion that two, functionally distinct memory systems underlie memory performance initially arose when researchers found that amnesic and Korsakoff patients exhibited excellent performance on some memory tests but were severely impaired on others (Milner, Corkin & Teuber 1968; Scoville & Milner 1957; Warrington & Weiskrantz 1968, 1970). Subsequently, Tulving (1972, 1983) proposed that there were two types of memory systems — *the semantic memory system* and *the episodic memory system*, citing data from amnesics in support of this dichotomy. He characterized the semantic memory system as appearing early in development and the episodic memory system as appearing late in development. Schacter and Moscovitch (1984), however, were the first to draw a direct parallel between the memory abilities of infants and amnesics, suggesting that both possess only an early memory system. They assumed that the memory system that was lost in amnesia matured late in the first year of life. One year later, Graf and Schacter (1985) introduced the terms *implicit* and *explicit* memory, which were then applied to the forms of memory supported by the early and late memory systems, respectively. Since that time, the poor memory performance of brain-damaged amnesics has generally been accepted as the evidence that implicit and explicit memory emerge sequentially in infancy during the course of normal development.

Ironically, researchers have only recently begun to study memory development directly in infants. Two approaches are commonly taken to study the development of implicit and explicit memory during the infancy period. The first approach emphasizes conscious recollection as the defining characteristic of explicit memory. Researchers who follow this approach seek tasks that amnesics fail but that normal adults solve using conscious recollection. If preverbal infants can also solve them, then they are assumed to have solved them by using conscious recollection.

The second approach is strictly empirical and does not invoke the concept of conscious awareness one way or another. Researchers who follow this approach assess the functional relationships between various independent variables that affect adults' implicit and explicit memory performance differently on implicit and explicit tasks. If the variables that have a profound effect on explicit memory performance but have little or no effect on implicit memory performance in normal adults produce the same functional memory dissociations in preverbal infants, then infants' memory performance is assumed to reflect the operation of the same underlying memory systems.

The present exposition

In the following chapters, we review what is known about the development of implicit and explicit memory. In Chapter 2, we describe the general characteristics of implicit and explicit memory and the tasks that have been used with adults to measure them. In Chapter 3, we review what is known about the neural mechanisms that underlie implicit and explicit memory and discuss the classic studies of human amnesics that prompted researchers to search for different neuroanatomically-based memory systems in the first place. In Chapter 4, we describe the Jacksonian principle and the evidence for the development and dissolution of memory from studies with rats. We also consider the generality of the Jacksonian principle for the development of implicit and explicit memory in verbally competent children and its dissolution in human adults. In Chapter 5, we review the developmental evidence from nonhuman primates that is typically cited as support for the proposition that two different memory systems mature at different rates. In Chapter 6, we introduce the various memory tasks that have been used with human infants and evaluate what these tasks have revealed about the development of implicit and explicit memory. In Chapter 7, we consider the large number of experimental dissociations that are taken as evidence for implicit and explicit memory in adults and review evidence that corresponding functional dissociations also characterize the memory performance of preverbal infants. In Chapter 8, we review the major structural and processing accounts of memory dissociations in adults and consider their adequacy for describing infant memory performance. In Chapter 9, we consider the implications of data from infants for current concepts of implicit and explicit memory. Finally, in the Epilogue (Chapter 10), we summarize what recent studies with young, preverbal infants have revealed about the development of implicit and explicit memory and reflect on the lingering resistance in some quarters to the overwhelming amount of experimental evidence that implicit and explicit memory do not develop hierarchically.

CHAPTER 2

Distinctions between Implicit and Explicit Memory

In this chapter, we review the characteristics that distinguish implicit from explicit memory and describe the various tasks that have been used to measure them. Memory retrieval that is accompanied by conscious awareness of having previously experienced an event is widely regarded as the defining characteristic of explicit memory. Because animals and very young children are thought to lack the capacity for conscious recollection, they are also thought to be incapable of explicit memory. Therefore, we have focused particularly on the potential contributions of conscious and unconscious processes to memory performance, the means by which their contributions might be differentiated, and the significance of consciousness for memory research with infants. Finally, we consider whether implicit memory is a meaningful construct.

Popular support for two, functionally distinct memory systems initially arose from empirical dissociations in the memory performance of amnesic adults (Warrington & Weiskrantz 1968, 1970). Subsequently, similar dissociations were observed in the memory performance of normal adults who were administered different instructional sets (Graf, Mandler & Haden 1982; Graf & Schacter 1985). These memory dissociations have led to a number of important inferences about functional dissociations in the cognitive processes and neural mechanisms that might underlie them (see Chapter 3).

Experimental dissociations in adult memory performance

Tulving (1983) described the *rule of experimental dissociation* as follows:

> "Dissociation is said to have occurred if it is found that the manipulated variable affects subjects' performance in one of two tasks, but not in the other, or affects the performance in different directions in the two tasks. Thus,

dissociation refers to the absence of a positive association between dependent
variables of two different tasks" (p. 73).

He suggested that an analogous logic could be applied to studies of developmental or pathological dissociations by comparing the performance of groups
differing in age or pathology on two tasks.

In fact, one of the earliest reported dissociations was of the latter type.
Warrington and Weiskrantz (1970) administered free recall and recognition
tests as well as two priming tests (word-fragment completion involving degraded letters and stem-completion tests) to a group of brain-damaged amnesics
and a control group composed of patients without brain damage. They found
that amnesics' retention on the first two tests was impaired, but their performance on the priming tests was not. Since then, other researchers using a variety
of tasks have obtained similar results, namely, preserved learning on one
general type of task but not on another (Jacoby & Witherspoon 1982;
Moscovitch 1982; Shimamura & Squire 1984; for review, see Shimamura
1986).

Analogous dissociations were subsequently documented in normal adults,
who performed differently on recall/recognition tasks than on various priming
tasks as a function of a variety of independent variables after being instructed
to base their test response on a prior specific episode (e.g., the study episode)
or to respond with the first answer that comes to mind, making no reference to
a prior episode, respectively (Graf et al. 1982; Graf & Schacter 1985; Hintzman
1990; Schacter 1987; for review, see Richardson-Klavehn & Bjork 1988).
These findings suggested that amnesics were capable of initially encoding
information about a specific event but subsequently had difficulty in gaining
awareness of it (Crowder 1988).

Characteristics of implicit and explicit memory

Implicit and explicit memory are descriptive concepts that originally referred
to different forms of memory as well as to the memory tests that were used to
measure them (Graf & Schacter 1985). The type of memory tapped by priming
tests was referred to as *implicit memory*, whereas the type of memory tapped
by recall and recognition tests was referred to as *explicit memory*. Graf and
Schacter cited three lines of evidence supporting a distinction between implicit and explicit memory. First, healthy adults performed differently on

priming and recall/recognition tests in response to a variety of different experimental manipulations: Manipulations that affected their performance on recall/recognition tasks typically did not affect their performance on priming tasks. These performance differences are characterized as functional dissociations. Second, performance on recall/recognition tasks was stochastically independent of performance on priming tasks. Third, the memory performance of densely amnesic patients was impaired on recall/recognition tasks but not on priming tasks.

Although the terms *implicit* and *explicit* were not originally intended to refer to hypothetical memory systems, such as procedural and declarative memory (Squire 1987) or semantic and episodic memory (Tulving 1983), many researchers currently use these terms to refer to different underlying memory systems (e.g., Nelson 1998; see also Willingham & Preuss 1995) — a practice that has engendered increasing concern (e.g., Schacter & Tulving 1994). Moreover, the same evidence that Graf and Schacter (1985) originally cited as support for distinguishing between implicit and explicit forms of memory and the tests that measure them has also been cited as support for distinguishing between different memory systems. As *forms* of memory, however, implicit and explicit memory are equally amenable to explanation by various processing accounts that are based on a single memory system (see Chapter 8).

Generally speaking, what most laymen think of as everyday memory is what theorists have described as explicit memory. In contrast, the category of implicit memory is relatively new. It is commonly assumed that explicit memories are dated by the time and place that an event occurred; implicit memories are not. Thus, a woman may look familiar to an individual, but he may be unable to specify when or where he previously encountered her, which is the hallmark of explicit memory. Theorists frequently associate the term *remember* with explicit memories and the term *know* with implicit memories (Gardiner & Java 1993). The difference pertains to the rememberer's self-awareness of the time and/or place of a particular past happening versus the individual's general world knowledge.

The features that have been used to distinguish implicit memory from explicit memory are summarized in Table 2.1. These features include many of those that were originally proposed by Mandler (1985, p. 93) to distinguish between automatic and nonautomatic memories and by Tulving (1983, p. 35) to distinguish between semantic and episodic memory. Implicit memory is seen as a phylogenetically primitive form of memory, whereas explicit memory is thought to have appeared relatively late in phylogeny (Sherry & Schacter 1987). Also, whereas implicit memory is widely thought to become functional early in ontogeny, explicit memory is thought to become functionally mature much later in the infancy period (Schacter & Moscovitch 1984). Implicit memory is preserved after explicit memory has been impaired by the brain damage that is associated with various forms of organic amnesia.

Additionally, access to explicit memories tends to be effortful, deliberate (intentional or voluntary), and slow. A college student who tries to remember the name of his former biology teacher, for example, may end up recollecting a number of things about the teacher or the biology class before eventually remembering the sought-for name — if he ever does. Being able to retrieve some but not all aspects of an explicit memory for which one is searching is known as the tip-of-the-tongue phenomenon. Moreover, while trying to re-member the name, the student cannot readily engage in other mental activities.

Table 2.1. Frequently Cited Distinctions Between Implicit and Explicit Memory

Implicit Memory	Explicit Memory
phylogenetically primitive	phylogenetically more advanced
early maturing	late maturing
spared in amnesia	impaired in amnesia
unconscious	conscious
nonepisodic	episodic
general	highly specific
abstract	concrete
automatic	controlled
involuntary	voluntary
direct access	indirect access
fast access	slow access
all-or-none retrieval	partial retrieval
no capacity demand	limited capacity
weighted for object form	weighted for object function
perceptually-based	conceptually-based
context-free	context-dependent
incidental	intentional
nonassociative	associative
temporally persistent	time-limited
inflexible	flexible
know	remember

Thus, the capacity of explicit memory is limited. In contrast, access to implicit memories is noneffortful, incidental, and fast. An implicit memory simply pops into mind, uncontrollably and involuntarily. In fact, it may intrude into the individual's consciousness while he or she is doing something else. Its retrieval does not result from a time-consuming search process and requires no conscious capacity.

In fact, of the many characteristics in Table 2.1 that distinguish implicit from explicit memory, the distinction that is most often invoked is the role of *conscious awareness* in memory retrieval. Explicit memory requires that an individual be consciously aware of having previously had a specific experience (i.e., a sense of pastness), whereas implicit memory does not. Schacter (1989) enunciated this distinction clearly:

> "Explicit memory is roughly equivalent to 'memory with consciousness' or 'memory with awareness.' Implicit memory, on the other hand, refers to situations in which previous experiences facilitate performance on tests that do not require intentional or deliberate remembering" (p. 356).

Implicit and explicit memory tasks

The terms *direct* and *indirect* were introduced by Johnson and Hasher (1987) to refer to different types of memory tasks and are often used interchangeably with the terms *explicit* and *implicit*. Both explicit and direct tasks are generally thought to require conscious recollection of a prior experience, whereas both implicit and indirect tasks do not. Whereas memory performance on both explicit and direct tasks is impaired in amnesia, memory performance on both implicit and indirect tasks is not. The terms *explicit* and *implicit*, however, also refer to different forms of memory, whereas the terms *direct* and *indirect* do not.

The tasks that are used in studies of explicit memory are familiar to students of memory — recall, cued-recall, and recognition — and presumably require the explicit remembering of a specific, prior study episode. According to Mandler (1990), for example:

> "Recall is defined as accessing (bringing to awareness) information about something that is not perceptually present. By definition, recall is a conscious product" (p. 486).

The various tasks that are used in studies of implicit memory are less familiar (see Table 2.2). The implicit tasks that have figured prominently in studies of memory development are considered in more detail below. In these tasks, participants are shown an initial study list and are asked to report the first word that comes to mind during the ensuing memory test. Implicit tasks are described as *repetition priming tasks* (or, simply, as *priming tasks)* because the initial presentation of an item presumably primes or increases its accessibility, thereby facilitating the accuracy and rapidity of responding when the item is presented again during the test. (In all instances, an explicit version of these tasks can be constructed by showing participants the same study list but asking them to *recognize or recall* a specific item that had appeared on the original list.) Although verbal materials were originally used in explicit and implicit tasks, pictorial materials have been used more recently in some studies (e.g., Musen & Treisman 1990; Schacter & Cooper 1993; Schacter, Cooper & Delaney 1990; Schacter, Cooper, Delaney, Peterson & Tharan 1991a), particularly in memory studies with young children.

Table 2.2. Implicit Memory Tasks Used with Amnesics and Normal (Instructed) Adults

Task	Study
fragmented picture identification	Warrington & Weiskrantz 1968
word completion	Warrington & Weiskrantz 1970
short-term memory	Baddeley & Warrington 1970
free association of related information	Schacter 1986; Shimamura & Squire 1984
preference judgments	Kunst-Wilson & Zajonc 1980
perceptual identification (words)	Jacoby & Dallas 1981
word-stem completion	Graf, Mandler & Haden 1982
lexical decision	Moscovitch 1982
homophone spelling	Jacoby & Witherspoon 1982
shadow-face identification	Tulving 1984
anagram solution	Dominowski & Ekstrand 1967
word completion with new associates	Graf & Schacter 1985
serial reaction time	Nissen & Bullemer 1987
classical conditioning	Woodruff-Pak 1993
skill learning	Schwartz & Hashtroudi 1991
perceptual identification (objects)	Biederman & Cooper 1991, 1992
object decision	Cooper, Schacter, Ballesteros & Moore 1992
precuing serial order	Clayton, Habibi & Bendele 1995

Word-stem or word-fragment completion

In these tasks, adults are asked to study a list of words and are then presented with either word stems composed of the first three letters at the beginning of the words (*ass-*) or word fragments with several letters missing (*a - - a - - - -*). Their task is to complete the word stem or word fragment with the first word that comes to mind. Some or all of the word stems can be completed with words that previously appeared on the study list (*assassin*) or with a number of other words (*assiduous, assail, asset*), but each word fragment has a unique solution and can be completed only with a word from the prior study list. Subjects tend to use words from the previously studied list to complete both the stems or fragments.

Picture or picture-fragment completion

These tasks are like the word-stem or word-fragment completion tasks except that participants are tested with nonverbal materials. In these tasks, subjects study a set of pictures and then are asked to perceptually identify them from either fragmented or otherwise degraded versions of the same picture. In some studies, researchers present picture fragments at a number of different levels of perceptual completion, from most fragmented to most complete, via an ascending method of limits until the fragment is correctly identified (e.g., Mitchell 1993; Snodgrass & Feenan 1990). The priming effect is measured as the difference in accuracy of identifying old and new pictures.

Object and lexical decision tasks

In the object decision task, adults are shown line drawings of unfamiliar objects, some that can actually exist in three-dimensional space (*possible objects*), and some that cannot (*impossible objects*). During the initial exposure phase, subjects are asked to judge the direction that each object faces. During testing with some old and some new objects, they must decide as rapidly as possible whether the test objects are possible or impossible. Possible objects that have been seen before show priming effects, but impossible objects do not (Cooper, Schacter, Ballesteros & Moore 1992). The lexical decision task, an older verbal version of this task, is the same except that the study list contains either words or nonwords, and subjects must decide during testing whether a letter string represents a real word or a nonword (e.g., Moscovitch 1982).

Serial reaction time (SRT) task

This task was introduced by Nissen and Bullemer (1987) and has since been used with both normal and amnesic adults (for review, see Curran 1998) and children (Meulemans, Van der Linden & Perruchet 1998). In this task, a cue light is illumined on each trial under one of four keys that are arranged horizontally. The subject's task is to press the key above the light as rapidly as possible. When the response key is pressed, the cue light goes off and, after a brief delay, another cue light is illumined under a different key. The cue lights are illumined in either a repeating or a random sequence, but subjects are not informed when the sequence of lights is repeating. The RTs of subjects tested on a repeating sequence decrease over successive trials, suggesting that subjects are learning the sequence and anticipating which key will be signaled next. However, a decrease in RT per se is not sufficient for inferring sequence learning because subjects become practiced with nonsequential aspects of the task as well (e.g., mapping the response key to the corresponding stimulus). Therefore, the difference in RT on adjacent trial blocks on which the sequence is repeating (S) and random (R) is usually taken as the primary measure of sequence learning (R-S).

The clearest evidence that the SRT task measures implicit memory comes from a within-subjects study in which students were given scopolamine, a drug that induces temporary amnesia. Although the drug did not impair their retention of the repeating-sequence SRT task, they were unable to press the correct key when asked where the next light would appear — an explicit memory task (Nissen, Knopman & Schacter 1987).

Simple classical conditioning

In classical conditioning, an association is learned between two stimuli — an unconditional stimulus (UCS) that initially elicits an unlearned or involuntary reflex (the unconditional response, or UCR) and a conditional stimulus (CS) that does not initially elicit that reflex. In the classical conditioning paradigm, the CS is repeatedly paired with the UCS in close temporal contiguity until it elicits a reflex (the conditional response or CR) that is fundamentally the same as the unlearned reflex that the UCS had originally elicited. The percent of trials on which a CR occurred indexes how well the subject learned that the CS predicts the UCS. The development of the CR during acquisition can be measured by either its occurrence on successive UCS-omission trials (e.g., on every fifth trial, the CS is presented without the UCS) or its anticipatory production in the interval between the CS and the UCS over successive trials. In the latter case, the CR initially occurs immediately after the CS and then its latency becomes progressively longer until it immediately precedes and partially overlaps with the UCS. The gradual increase in the occurrence of the anticipatory CR over trials is usually classified as an instance of procedural memory or implicit memory. Retention is usually expressed in terms of savings during reacquisition. Because the two events that become associated need not be verbal, and verbal instructions are unnecessary for performing the task, classical conditioning can be used with nonverbal subjects.

Woodruff-Pak (1993) found that the amnesic H.M. exhibited savings in classical eyeblink conditioning to a tone 2 years after his original conditioning, reaching criterion in one-tenth the number of original acquisition trials, even though he could not remember them.

Problems with the implicit/explicit distinction: Consciousness and independence

Consciousness

Tulving (1985) distinguished three kinds of consciousness, each of which was associated with a different memory system. At one end of the continuum was *anoetic consciousness* or nonknowing consciousness, which characterized procedural memory — the most primitive memory system. Tulving associated this type of consciousness (or lack of consciousness) with the prewired or preprogrammed reactions of simple animals, plants, computers, and learning machines to external or internal stimuli (e.g., the expression of fixed action patterns, instinctive behavior, skill learning, classical and operant conditioning, and any gradually incrementing behavior that accrued with what came before). The intermediate level of consciousness, *noetic consciousness* or knowing consciousness, characterized semantic memory — a specialized subsystem that evolved out of procedural memory. Tulving described this type of consciousness as making possible the introspective behavior and factual world knowledge of lower animals, human infants, and brain-damaged individuals. Because they operate without conscious awareness, Tulving likened procedural and semantic memory to implicit memory.

At the other end of the continuum was *autonoetic consciousness* or self-knowing consciousness. Autonoetic consciousness characterized episodic memory — a specialized subsystem of semantic memory — and allowed individuals the subjective sense of self awareness that accompanies the autobiographical recollection of the past and the realization of future existence. By this account, consciousness at a particular level on the continuum could be impaired without affecting consciousness at a lower level. Amnesics and infants, for example, lack episodic memory and autonoetic consciousness but have procedural memory and noetic consciousness. Because it requires conscious recollection, Tulving likened episodic memory to explicit memory.

Obviously, Tulving's (1985) distinctions are untenable from both developmental and comparative perspectives. Whether an infant or an animal is consciously aware of having previously experienced an event or has a sense of pastness cannot be directly tested and will always remain in the sole domain of philosophical speculation (see also Shapiro & Olton 1994). Yet, this distinction has become the primary basis for assuming that memory in preverbal infants and animals is implicit only — an assumption that is shared by most memory researchers whether they posit multiple memory systems or only a single memory system with multiple processes (e.g., Bauer 1996; Mandler 1984, 1990; McDonough, Mandler, McKee & Squire 1995; McKee & Squire 1993; Naito & Komatsu 1990; Schacter & Moscovitch 1984; Tulving & Schacter 1990). Apparently, because it is impossible to demonstrate directly that preverbal infants and animals are capable of explicit memory, and perhaps because researchers also have little or no recollection of their own infantile or early childhood experiences, they have simply assumed that infants *lack* the capacity for explicit memory. To quote Olton (1989), however, "the absence of proof ... is not proof of absence" (p. 167).

Ironically, data from hippocampal lesion studies with rats and nonhuman primates, in whom conscious awareness also cannot be measured, are frequently cited as evidence for the distinction between implicit and explicit memory (e.g., Zola-Morgan & Squire 1984; for reviews, see Bachevalier 1990; Nadel 1994; Squire 1987, 1992b; Zola-Morgan & Squire 1985b). In addition, some investigators have developed animal models of human amnesia that use a delayed-nonmatching-to-sample task as a recognition test (e.g., Clower, Alvarez-Royo, Zola-Morgan & Squire 1991; Zola-Morgan & Squire 1985b, 1990b). Both of these practices were challenged by Olton (1989).

Willingham and Preuss (1995) concluded that because people cannot agree about what consciousness is, its role in memory cannot be defined and, as a result, the construct does not add to our understanding of memory. They argued that classifying memory into two fundamentally different types requires that they have two fundamentally different explanations, but question whether consciousness can be the critical attribute that distinguishes them. Because the role of consciousness is unknown, hence too are the ways in which conscious and unconscious memory systems would need to be different: "Consciousness, because we know nothing about it, implies nothing about why memories that have or do not have it might be different" (Willingham & Preuss 1995 [4.8]).

Dissociating Conscious and Unconscious Contributions to Memory Performance. A number of researchers have warned that performance on tests of implicit and explicit memory is rarely process-pure; that is, performance on implicit tests often reflects the contribution of an explicit component, and vice versa (e.g., Jacoby, Toth & Yonelinas 1993; Rajaram 1993; Snodgrass 1989). Jacoby (1991) wrote:

> "most past investigations of automatic (unconscious) influences of memory or perception assumed a one-to-one mapping between processes and tests. The drawing of conclusions, then, requires that tests be factor- or process-pure with regard to the type of processing they measure. A difficulty for identifying processes with tasks is that tasks are probably never process-pure....That problem is not fully solved by finding task dissociations between manipulations or between subject populations and type of test" (p. 531).

The problem of cross-contamination in interpreting data from implicit tests is compounded by the possibility that, after a few trials, some subjects may catch on to the fact that some of the items on the implicit test had been on the study list and intentionally recall information from the study session to perform the task. In this case, the implicit test would, practically speaking, be an explicit test (see also Richardson-Klavehn & Bjork 1988). The magnitude of this problem is illustrated in a study on implicit memory development by Russo, Nichelli, Gibertoni and Cornia (1995; see Chapter 4). Using the picture-fragment completion task, previous researchers had found that implicit memory performance improved with age (Parkin 1993; Parkin & Streete

1988). Because explicit memory performance typically improves with age, but implicit memory performance does not, these results raised the possibility that conscious recollection may have contributed to subjects' implicit test performance. When Russo et al. partialed out the influence of explicit recollection, however, they found that implicit memory performance was age-invariant.

As it became increasingly apparent that memory performance on implicit and explicit tasks was unlikely to reflect the exclusive operation of either an explicit or an implicit memory process, researchers struggled to find a way of splitting the relative contributions of conscious from unconscious processes to memory performance. The *retrieval intentionality criterion* solution was introduced to control for the effects of unconscious influences on explicit memory performance (Schacter, Bowers & Booker 1989). Schacter et al. (1989) proposed that before data are accepted as measures of explicit and implicit memory, they should meet a retrieval intentionality criterion. The criterion was necessitated by the fact that normal adults occasionally exhibited parallel effects on explicit and implicit tests when the manipulated variables produced memory dissociations on the same tests in amnesics. Based on the assumption that a memory dissociation on explicit and implicit tests cannot result if retrieval in both cases is intentional, the criterion provides an empirical means of ruling out the contribution of intentional retrieval on implicit tasks.

The retrieval intentionality criterion has two basic parts. Its first part requires that the study episode be the same for both types of test and that all of the nominal retrieval cues provided at the time of testing also be identical except the instructions given to the subject prior to each test. Instructions for implicit tests do not require subjects to think back to the study episode in order to respond, whereas instructions for explicit tests do. The latter stipulation was based on the original observation by Graf et al. (1982) that changing the instructions for normal adults altered the nature of their memory test from a priming to a cued-recall test. As a result, normal adults and amnesics exhibited the same memory dissociations on implicit and explicit memory tests. Its second part requires that the independent (manipulated) variable have a different effect on memory performance in implicit and explicit tests. In this way, differential performance on the test would presumably be attributable only to the retrieval processes associated with the instructions; that is, retrieval would be either intentional (explicit memory) or unintentional (implicit memory).

Graf and Schacter (1985) confirmed that the instructions that were used to induce memory performance affected the sensitivity of a test as a measure of implicit or explicit memory. In Experiment 1 of their study, they varied the instructions that were given to college students prior to performing implicit and explicit tests of memory for related word pairs. For the priming (implicit memory) test, they instructed students to complete word-fragments as quickly as possible with "the first word that [came] to mind." For the cued-recall (explicit memory) test, they reminded students of the word pairs they had previously studied, told them that the test words were the stimulus words from those pairs, and instructed them to recall the response word that had been paired with each stimulus word. As before, normal, healthy adults exhibited the same dissociation on explicit and implicit tests as amnesics if explicitly instructed to respond on the basis of the original study episode or not, respectively.

In a follow-up experiment, they gave a new group of students a list of unrelated word pairs and instructed them before both tests (word completion and cued-recall) that the cues were related to the word pairs they had studied and that they should use the cues to aid recall of the words from the study list. Their basic assumption was that if the instructions defined the form of memory that the test measured, then identical instructions would transform both tests into tests of explicit memory. In fact, this was their finding, confirming that the test instructions determine whether a particular test that is used with normal adults measures implicit or explicit memory.

The *process-dissociation procedure* was also introduced to disentangle the conscious and unconscious contributions to adults' memory performance but was in reaction to the concerns that had motivated the retrieval intentionality criterion, namely, that memory performance on indirect or implicit tasks might be contaminated by intentional or conscious influences. Jacoby et al. (1993) were concerned that memory performance on direct or explicit tests might be contaminated by unintentional or unconscious influences. The probability of recollection would be overestimated, for example, if automatic influences were to increase the probability of correct guessing on cued-recall tests.

To correct for such influences, Jacoby et al. pitted the probability of informed guessing or familiarity-based responding against the probability of genuine recollection-based responding. Thus, for example, on a word-stem completion test, unconscious influences would make subjects more likely to complete the word stems with previously studied words (i.e., words that automatically come to mind) than with new ones. Instructing subjects to complete the stems with words that were not presented earlier, however, would produce the opposite result. To the extent that responding was under their conscious control, Jacoby et al. assumed that subjects would select against old words that they could actually recollect. Should they respond with an old word, then their response would be attributed to unconscious influences, and the difference between responding with old and new words would be taken as the measure of conscious recollection. The probability of using a particular word as a completion for a stem when that word was not presented during study serves as a baseline against which the effects of prior study can be assessed. This baseline was subtracted from the calculated probability that a word would automatically come to mind.

Although this procedure has revealed that recollection and familiarity make statistically independent contributions to memory performance, there are at least two problems with using the process-dissociation procedure to assess the role of consciousness in memory processing. First, as Ratcliff and colleagues pointed out:

> "Process dissociation equations have two parameters (the probability of recollection and the probability of familiarity being above a threshold), and the equations are applied to only two data points in each experimental condition. This means that the method will always produce estimates of two components, even if the data were actually generated from a single process ... Furthermore, the interpretations of the components are valid only under the process dissociation assumptions....Therefore, what is learned about conscious versus unconscious processes [in recognition] is theory dependent, and process dissociation does not provide a theory-independent means of examining memory processes" (Ratcliff, Van Zandt & McKoon 1995, p. 359).

Second, the process-dissociation procedure cannot be used with nonverbal subjects, and it is probably also unsuitable for younger children, who would be likely to find the instructions about what to exclude from their responding confusing.

Are Infants and Other Nonverbal Organisms Consciously Aware? The question of whether organisms other than verbally competent humans possess conscious awareness has vexed philosophers since the time of the ancient Greeks. The issue was temporarily resolved in the 17th century by the Cartesian distinction between mind versus matter, or dualism. The recent introduction of the explicit versus implicit memory dichotomy with emphasis on conscious awareness, however, has reinvigorated advocates of dualism as well as its critics. In considering how conscious experience might be defined, the philosopher John Searle suggested adopting a common-sense rather than an analytic definition:

> "'Consciousness' refers to those states of sentience and awareness that typically begin when we awake from a dreamless sleep and continue until we go to sleep again, or fall into a coma or die or otherwise become 'unconscious'" (Searle 1995, p. 60).

Searle (1998) rejected dualism as obsolete. His conceptualization of consciousness is grounded in three basic principles: (1) Consciousness consists of inner, qualitative, subjective states and processes. (2) Consciousness cannot be reduced to third-person phenomena investigated in the neurosciences. (3) Consciousness is a biological process — a higher-order, natural feature of the organic brain. In concluding that brain processes cause consciousness, he echoed Hubbard's (1975) earlier conclusion that mental phenomena are direct consequences of neural activity. In arguing that conscious experience is an *emergent* property of neurobiological processes in the brain, Searle likened it to the solidity of a table, which is an emergent feature of the table's molecular structure: "mental states are both *caused by* the operations of the brain and *realized in* the structure of the brain" (Searle 1983, p. 265). In other words, he placed consciousness squarely in the realm of other, ordinary biological phenomena, such as physiological thermoregulation, mitosis, and digestive processes (Searle 1984, 1995).

In response to such arguments, however, Tulving (1987) argued that

> "the problem of consciousness and memory is different from problems of consciousness with which many generations of thinkers have wrestled ... problems such as what consciousness *is,* and how it emerges from the physical-chemical brain activity.... . [Instead it is] the selective but systematic occurrence of conscious awareness in remembering, as well as in other mental activities: Why are we — why must we be — consciously aware when we remember a recent event that we have witnessed, and why is the *same kind* of awareness missing when we use our stored knowledge, say, in solving a new complicated problem?" (p. 75)

Pointing to the literature on memory dissociations in amnesics, Tulving drew a sharp distinction between the form of memory in which amnesics express knowledge in behavior without any accompanying awareness that they possessed that knowledge (i.e., implicit memory) and the form of memory of which amnesics are incapable — the expression of knowledge which includes their introspective awareness of it (i.e., explicit memory). Although the dis-

tinction between consciousness and conscious awareness is intuitively appealing, Tulving did not offer an operational definition of conscious awareness
(see also Shapiro & Olton 1994, p. 108), nor did he suggest a way of
distinguishing it from consciousness or conscious experience.

Several decades ago, a similar issue arose in the field of animal communication. At that time, the common assumption underlying distinctions between
animal language and human language was that animals lack both conscious
awareness of their own mental experiences (if they had any) and a conscious
intent to communicate (e.g., Terwilliger 1968). Griffin (1976), however,
characterized this assumption as antagonistic to the "general principle of
evolutionary kinship and continuity" between animals and men and argued:

> "the hypothesis that some animals are indeed aware of what they do, and of
> internal images that affect their behavior, simplifies our view of the universe
> by removing the need to maintain an unparsimonious assumption that our
> species is qualitatively unique in this important attribute" (p. 101).

Like Searle, Griffin proposed that mental experiences are directly linked to
neurophysiological processes which, he noted, are highly similar in all multi-
cellular animals.

Independence

A major source of evidence supporting a distinction between two memory
systems is that memory performance on an implicit test is independent of
memory performance on an explicit test. Independence can take two forms —
stochastic independence (Graf & Schacter 1985; Tulving, Schacter & Stark
1982) and *functional independence* (Tulving 1985; Tulving et al. 1982).
Stochastic independence is demonstrated when the joint probability of memory
performance on implicit and explicit tasks is equal to the product of their simple
probabilities. Functional independence is demonstrated when an independent
variable affects memory performance on implicit and explicit tasks differently.
These two kinds of independence, however, need not coexist in the same data
set. Greene (1986), for example, failed to find *stochastic independence* between
memory performance on a word-stem completion task and on a recall task in
which word stems were used as explicit retrieval cues, but he did find *functional
independence* between memory performance on the two tests. A similar result
turned up in data obtained by Graf and Mandler (1984, Experiment 3), who had

compared memory performance on a word-stem completion test with memory performance on a cued-recall test in which word stems were the retrieval cues. Although Graf and Mandler reported evidence of functional independence between the tests, a reanalysis of their data found no evidence of stochastic independence between them (Greene 1986).

Stochastic Independence. One criterion for distinguishing two forms of memory is that memory performance on two different tests of the same items that presumably reflect the operation of different memory systems should be stochastically independent. This requirement means that subjects should be as likely to complete word-stems with old words or words they recognized as with new words or words they did not recognize. On the other hand, memory performance on two different tests that reflect the operation of the same memory system should be correlated, meaning that they measure the same thing — whatever it is. Tulving et al. (1982), for example, argued that if memory performance on the two tests were mediated by the same memory system, then subjects' memory for individual items on the two tests should have been correlated — but that also was not the case. He found that the joint probability of recognition and word-fragment completion was indistinguishable from the product of the simple probabilities of recognition and fragment completion, indicating that performance on one test was independent of performance on the other. Moreover, this effect was found four times — for both kinds of items (old, new) after two test delays (1 hour, 7 days).

In contrast, adults' memory for individual items on recognition tests is strongly correlated with their memory for individual items on recall tests (both tests of explicit memory). Ogilvie, Tulving, Paskowitcz and Jones (1980), for example, showed college students a list of familiar words and then gave them both a yes/no recognition test and a cued-recall test in which associatively related or rhyming words were the retrieval cues for words on the study list. Four outcomes were possible — list words could be recognized and recalled, recognized but not recalled, not recognized but recalled, and neither recognized nor recalled. They found that the conditional probability of recognition given recall was .90 for associative cues and .91 for rhyming cues. The fact that the proportion of recalled words that subjects also recognized was greater than the proportion of all words that they recognized indicated that the measures of recall and recognition were positively correlated.

Interpretations of stochastic independence between implicit and explicit tasks have been criticized because they are necessarily based on multiple measures of the same items. Thus, recognition is biased in the direction of independence by the fact that subjects previously saw the same items on a priming test hence experienced an additional "study" trial or exposure (Greene 1986; Shimamura 1985; Tulving et al. 1982). More recent advances in quantitative techniques hold promise for overcoming this problem. Using a linear structural modeling approach, for example, Nyberg (1994) tested the fit of a one-factor (i.e., one system) versus a two-factor model to students' memory dissociations on two types of memory tests (semantic and episodic) and rejected the one-factor but not the two-factor model. Nyberg noted that the notion of a unitary memory system was not rejected, however, if semantic and episodic memory were viewed as separate factors within the same memory system, for example, in the declarative memory system.

Functional Independence. Functional independence refers to the relation between two dependent variables that is found when a particular independent variable (e.g., the retention interval) or subject variable (age, amnesia) affects performance on one test but not the other (see Table 7.2). Functional independence is manifested as a dissociation in memory performance on an implicit and explicit test following the manipulation of a particular independent or subject variable. Tulving et al. (1982), for example, argued that if a single memory system had mediated adults' performance on a word-fragment completion (implicit memory) task and on a recognition (explicit memory) task, then either they should have exhibited forgetting of previously studied information over a 7-day retention interval on both implicit and explicit memory tasks or they should have exhibited no forgetting on both tasks over the same delay — but they did not. Instead, adults exhibited forgetting on the explicit memory task but no forgetting on the implicit memory task.

What is implicit memory? A second look

Although explicit (declarative) memory appears to be a fairly coherent form of memory that is associated with a fairly well-defined set of neuroanatomical structures (Shimamura 1990; Squire, Knowlton & Musen 1993; Squire & Zola-Morgan 1991), implicit (procedural) memory is not (Shimamura 1990; Willingham & Preuss 1995). One characteristic that supposedly sets implicit memories apart from explicit ones is their specificity or sensitivity to the physical conditions of encoding and retrieval: Implicit (nondeclarative) memories have been described as highly specific, whereas explicit (declarative) memories have been described as relatively flexible (Cohen & Eichenbaum 1993). Although evidence for specificity in rats and monkeys is compelling, evidence for specificity in humans on priming, motor skill, and other implicit memory tasks depends strongly on the conditions of testing (for review, see Willingham 1998a).

The *absence of conscious awareness* is also thought to distinguish performance on implicit memory tasks from performance on explicit ones, but researchers cannot agree on how to define *conscious awareness*. Neuropsychological data provide some basis for arguing that memories for which subjects evidence conscious recollection require the integrity of the medial temporal lobe and diencephalon, whereas memories that may not be associated with conscious recollection do not require these structures (Willingham 1994). As Willingham and Preuss (1995) pointed out, however:

> "The role of consciousness in memory parallels the neuroscientific data in another way. *Lack of awareness* as a characteristic does not really unify implicit memory; rather, *awareness* sets explicit memory apart from the others. Similarly, *not* relying on the hippocampus does not unify implicit memories; rather, *relying* on the hippocampus sets explicit memory apart [our italics]" (4.9).

Other researchers have expressed concern about the *grab-bag nature* of implicit memory (Johnson & Hirst 1993; Roediger 1990a; Roediger, Srinivas & Weldon 1989a; Schwartz & Hashtroudi 1991; Willingham & Preuss 1995). A major source of concern, for example, is the repeated finding of *parallels* in memory performance on tests of implicit memory and explicit memory and *functional dissociations* in memory performance on different tests of implicit memory. As reviewed earlier, theorists have attributed the parallels to the contribution of conscious recollection on implicit memory tests and to the contribution of unconscious influences on explicit memory tests. The finding of dissociations between tasks of implicit memory, however, is particularly problematic for the construct validity of implicit memory. On the surface, for example, word-fragment completion and perceptual word-identification tasks would seem to be highly related, but researchers have found that memory performance on these two tasks is not only uncorrelated (Perruchet & Baveux 1989) but is stochastically independent (Hayman & Tulving 1989; Witherspoon & Moscovitch 1989).

Some of the clearest evidence that different implicit tasks are functionally independent has surfaced in studies comparing performance on the serial reaction time (SRT) task with performance on other tasks of implicit memory. Healthy adults exhibit a decrease in RTs over successive trials when trained with a repeating sequence (Willingham, Nissen & Bullemer 1989), as do patients with Alzheimer's disease (Knopman & Nissen 1987) and Korsakoff syndrome (Nissen & Bullemer 1987). Like healthy adults, Korsakoff patients also retain their memory of the repeating sequence for 1 week (Nissen, Willingham & Hartman 1989). In contrast to their normal learning and memory on the repeating-sequence SRT task, however, Korsakoff patients' ability to learn a tactual style maze in which all blind alleys are blocked is significantly impaired (Nissen et al. 1989). Because both the maze task and the SRT task require the learning of a spatial sequence and, in normal adults, performance on these tasks is facilitated by prior training, both are thought to measure implicit memory. These data, then, reveal a memory dissociation *between* two tasks of implicit memory.

Schwartz and Hashtroudi (1991) similarly found a dissociation between implicit memory tasks. In Experiment 1 of their study, college students exhibited skill learning in partial-word identification and inverted reading tasks but not in a word-fragment completion task, but their amount of priming in all tasks was the same. In Experiment 2, they tested priming and skill learning with degraded words in the partial-word identification task. The amount of priming was the same whether students had acquired the skill of identifying degraded words or not. Importantly, the correlation between skill improvement over trials and priming performance was negligible whether subjects were tested immediately ($r = .01$) or after 1 week ($r = .06$). In Experiment 3 of their study, they hypothesized that students might be more skilled in learning to identify degraded words to which they had been preexperimentally exposed more often (high-frequency words) than words that occurred in language less often. If priming were unrelated to skill learning, however, then the frequency of occurrence of the words should not affect it. They found that skill learning was significantly affected by word frequency, but the amount of priming was not.

The large number of implicit memory tests that were functionally independent of each other prompted researchers to elaborate different mechanisms for explaining them. Schacter (1990), for example, proposed that priming effects in different implicit memory tasks are best understood in terms of a class of distinct memory modules or subsystems — the visual word form system, the structural descriptions system — comprising a perceptual representation system (PRS), which itself is a subsystem of semantic memory. Schacter argued that the effect of word- and object-priming on these tests was a presemantic phenomenon because performance was affected by perceptual changes in the surface features of visual stimuli independent of whether the study task required semantic processing or not. In representing the form and structure of words (word form system) and objects (structural descriptions system), these subsystems were thought to be functionally different from the episodic memory system, which represents information about meaningful events in space and time, but capable of interacting with it.

As an alternative to explaining memory dissociations in terms of separable memory systems or subsystems that represent different kinds of information, some researchers adopted a processing approach (e.g., Nelson, LaLomia & Canas 1991; see Chapter 8) or sought a single theoretical principle (e.g., Snodgrass & Feenan 1990) to explain them. In the latter instance, the results of a series of priming experiments with different levels of picture-fragment completion led Snodgrass and Feenan (1990) to propose the *perceptual closure hypothesis*. By this account, priming effects are explained by a process that operates at the time of retrieval: The minimal amount of information in the prime that can support perceptual closure will yield optimal priming. Presumably, the change that is induced in the perceived organization of the prime allows the prime to be identified and facilitates retrieval. Because the subject's attention is focused outward on the physical characteristics of the prime, the memory representation that is retrieved more or less perceptually matches the perceived prime and is devoid of self-referent information that would locate the prime in subjects' historical past.

On explicit memory tests, however, the perceptual characteristics of the retrieval cue are either deemphasized (recognition tests) or absent altogether (recall tests). Rather, explicit tests require subjects to interrogate their memory as to whether they previously encountered the target stimulus before. This interrogation focuses subjects' attention inward and necessitates the retrieval of autobiographical information pertaining to time or place. According to the perceptual closure hypothesis, therefore, *conscious recollection is not a fundamental feature of explicit memory but is simply a by-product of the attentional demands of explicit tests.*

Conclusions

Despite the large number of recent books devoted to implicit memory, this form of memory is still poorly understood. Willingham and Preuss (1995) argued that because implicit memories are not supported by common brain structures and do not use common processes and representations, implicit memory is not a coherent system. Moreover, there is no common attribute that links different implicit memory tasks such as priming, motor skill learning, classical conditioning, mirror reading, perceptual identification, and so forth. Johnson and Hirst (1993) made the same observation about procedural memory tasks, namely, that they share no obvious common characteristics except that amnesics cannot perform them. Changing the procedural/declarative nomenclature to nondeclarative/declarative (Squire 1992a) did not alter this basic problem. Nondeclarative memory remains a miscellaneous collection of tasks that are linked simply by the fact that they can be performed *without* the neural structures that are required to perform declarative memory tasks. In other words, nondeclarative tasks are, simply, *not declarative*.

Although the *absence* of conscious awareness is thought to characterize performance in implicit memory tasks, there is no agreement about how to define it. Moreover, because the *function* of conscious awareness is unknown, it is impossible to specify how a memory system that is based on conscious awareness differs functionally from one that is not (Willingham & Preuss 1995). As a result, any classification scheme that differentiates memory systems on the basis of the presence or absence of conscious awareness fails Sherry and Schacter's (1987) criterion, *the functional incompatibility of operations* (see Chapter 8), for establishing a new memory system.

CHAPTER 3

Neuroanatomical Basis of Explicit and Implicit Memory

We begin this chapter with an overview of the early studies of human amnesia that gave rise to the notion of two, dissociable memory systems. We review similar evidence for two dissociable memory systems in nonhuman animals — primarily, monkeys and rats. We then discuss evidence for the neural substrates that are believed to underlie implicit and explicit memory. We note that the concept of multiple memory systems emerged predominantly from studies in which damage to the medial temporal lobe impaired explicit memory but not implicit memory. Therefore, we present recent evidence that damage to the striatal system impairs implicit memory but not explicit memory and consider the implications of this evidence for multiple memory systems.

Studies of explicit and implicit memory in humans

The effects of MTL lesions

For quite some time, damage to the medial temporal lobes (MTL) in humans has been known to produce severe memory impairments. The classic and frequently cited example of the effects of such lesions is the patient H.M., who underwent bilateral resection of the MTL (hippocampus, amygdala, and surrounding tissue) in an effort to relieve intractable epilepsy that did not respond to conventional anticonvulsive medication (Scoville & Milner 1957). Although H.M.'s seizures were somewhat alleviated by the operations, he was left with a profound memory impairment that persists to this date (Corkin 1984; Gabrieli, Cohen & Corkin 1988; Milner 1972; Milner et al. 1968).

In the original 1957 paper, most of H.M.'s memory impairments were described anecdotally in terms of his postoperative failures to give accurate dates, his age, or to remember that he had been talking with a particular individual just minutes earlier. For example, H.M. was operated upon in September, 1953, when he was 27 years old. When asked during a psychological examination 19 months later (in April, 1955) for the current date and his current age, H.M. responded that the current date was March, 1953, and that he was 27 years old. His response suggested that he had no memory for events subsequent to his operation. In fact, so serious were his memory impairments that after the operation,

> "this young man could no longer recognize the hospital staff nor find his way to the bathroom, and he seemed to recall nothing of the day-to-day events of his hospital life" (Scoville & Milner 1957, p. 14).

According to Scoville and Milner, H.M. and patients with similar extensive damage to the medial temporal lobe appear to "forget the incidents of their daily life as fast as they occur" (p. 15).

Despite his profound memory impairment, H.M. performed normally on tests of intelligence, reasoning, and perceptual abilities (Milner et al. 1968). He was also able to remember a list of numbers and words if he was not distracted during the retention interval (Scoville & Milner 1957). Although his memory for events of his childhood appeared to be quite normal, H.M. did have difficulty remembering information that occurred within the 3 years prior to his surgery. In current terminologies, his memory deficits were characterized both by a severe *anterograde amnesia* (difficulty in forming new memories) and a limited *retrograde amnesia* (memory impairments for events prior to the operation). The characteristics of H.M.'s memory impairments have since been observed in many other patients with medial temporal lobe damage (Cummings, Tomiyasu, Read & Benson 1984; Victor & Agamanolis 1990; Victor, Angevine, Mancall & Fisher 1961). According to the convention we have adopted in this book, H.M. is said to suffer from impairments in *explicit memory*.

Some memories are spared

It soon became apparent that damage to the MTL did not produce a global amnesia because some memories were affected by the damage, but others were not. In particular, tasks that required certain motor skills were unaffected by MTL lesions. Milner (1962) made the first observation of one such spared memory. She noted that H.M. showed a steady improvement on a mirror-drawing task which required drawing within the outline of a double star while looking at a reflection of the star and his hand in a mirror (see Figure 3.1A).

Not only did H.M. show improvement within a session, but he also showed retention across sessions, beginning each day's session at roughly the level he had finished on the previous day. In spite of near-perfect retention that spanned 24 hours, he had no recollection of having performed this task on the preceding day.

The finding of spared memory with respect to the mirror-drawing task was the first of a series of such descriptions that ultimately formed the foundation for the idea of dissociable memory systems. Other motor skill tasks were soon described that also appeared unaffected by MTL lesions. For example, H.M. showed both improvement within a session and retention across sessions in the acquisition of a rotary pursuit task (see Figure 3.1B) in which he had to maintain a metal stylus pen in contact with a rotating metal disc (Corkin 1968). One advantage of this study over the mirror-drawing study was that H.M.'s performance was compared to that of a control group of normal subjects. Although his time-on-target score did improve steadily, his overall performance was inferior to that of the normal control group. Similar findings were reported for acquisition and retention of a bimanual tracking task and a bimanual tapping task, although his performance in the tapping task more closely approximated that of the normal control group (Corkin 1968).

Based on her early findings, Milner (1965) suggested that the types of memories spared by MTL damage were those that involved learning a motor skill. Subsequent studies, however, showed that MTL damage also spared performance on tasks in which a motor component was not the defining feature. Warrington and Weiskrantz (1968), for example, showed that patients with alcoholic Korsakoff's amnesia, a form of amnesia that produces memory impairments roughly similar to MTL amnesia, were able to learn the Gollin incomplete-pictures task. This task consists of a series of five pictures ranging from very fragmented to complete. Subjects are first shown the most fragmented rendition and then progressively less fragmented renditions until they are able to identify the picture. On the first exposure to the task, correct identification is likely to occur only when the complete rendition is shown. With practice, however, the subject is able to identify the picture from increasingly fragmented renditions. In line with the findings from motor skill tasks, amnesics improved their performance within a session and exhibited near-perfect retention across sessions (see Figure 3.1C). Also in line with their performance on other skill-based tasks, their overall error rate was significantly higher than that of the control group across the 3 days of testing.

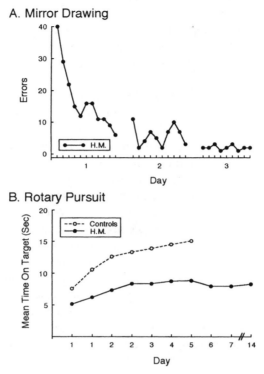

Figure 3.1. Spared memories in patients with medial temporal lobe damage or alcoholic Korsakoff's syndrome. (*A*) *Mirror drawing task.* The subject had to draw within the outline of the figure of a star (redrawn from Milner 1965). (*B*) *Rotary pursuit task.* The subject had to keep a metal pen in contact with a moving metal target (redrawn from Corkin 1968).

C. Gollin Incomplete Pictures

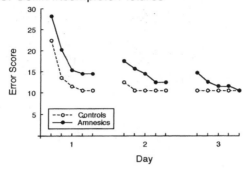

D. Mirror Reading

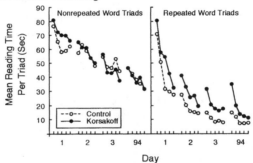

Figure 3.1 (continued) (*C*) *Gollin incomplete-pictures task.* The subject saw a series of five pictures that ranged from degraded to complete. The most degraded picture was presented first, followed by progressively less degraded pictures, until the subject could identify the picture (redrawn from Warrington and Weiskrantz 1968). (*D*) *Mirror reading task.* The subject read a list of three mirror-drawn words. Some words appeared more than once within a session (*repeated word triads*), whereas others did not (*nonrepeated word triads*) (redrawn from Cohen and Squire 1980).

Another example of a skill that is relatively spared by MTL lesions is performance on the Tower of Hanoi problem. In this task, the subject must learn to move a series of disks from a source peg to a goal peg while keeping in mind that only one peg can be moved at a time and that at no time can a large peg be placed over a small peg. Again, H.M. improved performance on this task within a session and exhibited excellent retention from session to session (Cohen & Corkin 1981). At no time, however, did he ever remember having performed the task. As described by the authors,

> "By the seventh and eighth days of training, despite near-perfect perfor-
> mance, his commentary during each trial always sounded as if he were
> solving the puzzle for the first time" (Cohen & Corkin 1981, p. 235).

A similar pattern of findings was reported for classical conditioning of an eyeblink response following MTL lesions (Weiskrantz & Warrington 1979).

Because the number of studies of spared memories following MTL lesions and the procedures that have been used to reveal them could fill a chapter by themselves, all will not be reviewed here. Two final studies, however, deserve special mention. Cohen and Squire (1980) tested amnesic patients of various etiologies, including alcoholic Korsakoff patients, a patient (N.A.) who had sustained a stab wound to the diencephalon, and patients being treated with electroconvulsive therapy, on a mirror reading task. All of these disorders and injuries produce impairments similar to that seen in MTL amnesia. Amnesic patients again showed improvement within a session and retention across sessions (see Figure 3.1D). Most interesting, however, was the finding that they still showed perfect retention of the task 3 months later. Despite these results, the amnesic patients performed very poorly on tests of recognition, had no recollection of having performed the task before, and could not even remember which words they had just read.

In the second study, Graf et al. (1984) showed that amnesics were impaired on free-recall and cued-recall tests but performed normally on word-stem completion tests. The most interesting comparison was between performance on the cued-recall test and on the word-stem completion test, which differed only in the instructions (see Chapter 2). In both cases, subjects were shown a list of words and then were presented with three letters. Prior to the cued-recall test, subjects were instructed to complete the three letters with a word they had seen on the prior study list, whereas prior to the word-stem completion test, they were simply instructed to complete the three letters with the first word that came to mind. This subtle difference in the type of instruction was critical to the outcome of the experiment. On the word-stem completion test, amnesics performed like normal controls, whereas on the cued-recall test, amnesics' performance was impaired relative to that of normal controls.

In summary, patients with MTL lesions and patients with disorders and injuries that damage structures related to the MTL suffer from severe memory impairments. Despite these impairments, they display a variety of forms of spared memories, ranging from normal motor skills to intact performance on perceptual and even some cognitive tasks. This simple dissociation led Cohen and Squire (1980) to distinguish between *knowing that*, which is impaired following MTL damage, and *knowing how*, which is spared following MTL damage. Over the years, this distinction has taken on many different labels. These are reviewed in Chapter 8. For our present purposes and for ease of exposition, we refer to *knowing that* as *explicit memory* and *knowing how* as *implicit memory*.

Studies of explicit and implicit memory in nonhuman animals

Memory tasks used with animals

Shortly after Scoville and Milner (1957) reported severe memory impairments in humans with MTL damage, attempts were made to develop an animal model of MTL amnesia. The main problem in this endeavor was expressed cogently by Orbach, Milner and Rasmussen (1960) when they stated:

> "the requirements of the tests applied to man are difficult to adapt to behavior that is within the repertoire of the monkey" (p. 248).

Nevertheless, over the years, numerous tasks have been used to study the effects of MTL lesions in nonhuman animals. Because later sections of this chapter rely heavily on an understanding of these tasks, a brief description of them is in order. What follows is not an exhaustive list of the tasks that have been used to assess the effects of brain damage in animals but, rather, descriptions of the tasks used most frequently.

Visual Discrimination. In a visual discrimination task, the animal must learn which of the two stimuli is associated with reward (see Figure 3.2A). In a typical session consisting of numerous trials, the same pair of stimuli is presented on each trial, and the same stimulus always serves as the rewarded

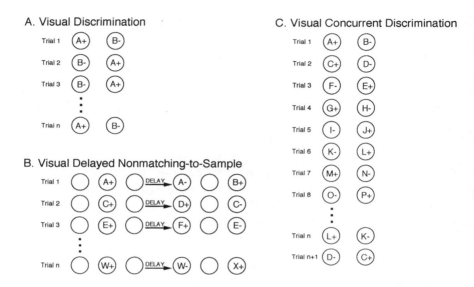

Figure 3.2. The three primary tasks that have been used with nonhuman animals to study the effects of damage to the medial temporal lobe on memory performance. (*A*) *Visual discrimination.* The same two stimuli are presented on every trial. The animal must respond to the same stimulus (*A*) to obtain a reward (+). Responses to the nonrewarded stimulus (*B*) result in punishment (–). (*B*) *Visual delayed nonmatching-to-sample (DNMS).* Each trial consists of two parts. The sample stimulus is presented and then is removed from view for a delay period. At the end of the delay period, two comparison stimuli are presented. The animal must respond to the novel stimulus to obtain a reward. Responses to the familiar stimulus are punished. (*C*) *Visual concurrent discrimination (CD).* The animal is trained with eight pairs of stimuli. Within each pair, the same stimulus is always rewarded, whereas the other stimulus is not. The animal must learn which stimulus of each pair is the rewarded stimulus. Each of the eight pairs of stimuli is presented a number of times within each session.

(positive) stimulus. Of all the tasks used in lesion studies, the discrimination task is the easiest for animals to learn. Although making the physical identity of the stimuli more similar increases both the difficulty of the task and the length of time required to solve it, the acquisition of discrimination tasks is typically measured in terms of days.

  Visual Delayed Nonmatching-to-Sample (DNMS). In a visual DNMS task, the animal must remember which stimulus it saw most recently. The

DNMS task has become a standard test of recognition memory in animals and is perhaps the most frequently used task in studies examining the effects of brain lesions on memory in monkeys. The procedure is quite simple (see Figure 3.2B). At the start of a trial, a stimulus is presented to an animal and then is removed from view for the duration of a delay interval. At the end of the delay, two stimuli are presented to the animal — one that is the same as the sample and one that is different. The animal must choose the stimulus that is different from the sample stimulus, that is, the *nonmatching* stimulus. Each session consists of numerous trials in this format. Although the task can also be structured so that the animal is required to choose the matching stimulus, the nonmatching task is the preferred version in lesion studies, most likely because it taps the monkey's predisposition for novelty (Mishkin & Delacour 1975).

Acquisition of the DNMS task takes considerably longer than acquisition of a visual discrimination task and is typically measured on a scale of weeks rather than days. The acquisition of the DNMS task, however, is not of primary interest in brain lesion experiments. The power of the DNMS procedure is that the delay between the sample and comparison stimuli can be varied, thereby allowing the experimenter to measure the effects of brain lesions on short-term retention. This is the context in which the DNMS procedure is used most often. With training, monkeys can eventually perform at above-chance levels with delays as long as 40 min between the sample and the comparison stimuli.

Visual Concurrent Discrimination (CD). The CD task is a complex version of the visual discrimination task described earlier. Recall that in a visual discrimination task, the animal obtains a reward by responding to the positive stimulus of one pair of stimuli that are presented repeatedly within a session. In the visual CD task, eight pairs of stimuli are presented repeatedly within a session, and the animal must learn which stimulus in each pair is associated with reward (see Figure 3.2C). Naturally, given so many pairs of stimuli, acquisition of a CD task takes longer than acquisition of a visual discrimination task and also longer than the acquisition of a DNMS task.

Radial Arm Maze. The radial arm maze task is one of the most frequently used procedures to study the neural basis of learning and memory in rats. Developed by Olton and Samuelson (1976), the task taps the amazing spatial abilities of rats. The maze consists of a central arena from which radiate eight arms (see Figure 3.3A). The rat is placed inside the arena and allowed to collect a piece of food placed at the end of each arm. The optimal strategy is to enter an arm once and then not revisit that arm. Revisiting an arm that has already been entered is scored as an error. Each session consists of a single trial in which the rat attempts to retrieve all eight pieces of food in the maze. Rats quickly learn to retrieve all the food after entering only eight (no errors) or nine (1 error) arms. They can achieve such levels of performance within 1 to 2 weeks.

Morris Water Maze. Like the radial arm maze, the Morris water maze (Morris 1981, 1984) also taps the spatial abilities of rats. Rats are placed in a circular pool filled with water rendered opaque by the addition of milk (see Figure 3.3B). Just below the water level in a constant position in the tank is a hidden platform. The rats are placed in the water in various quadrants of the tank and, in a short period, learn to locate and escape to the platform. A session consists of approximately 10 trials. Although rats will reach asymptotic levels of performance within a few days of testing, considerable learning occurs over the first 10 trials of the first session.

The effects of MTL lesions

Anterograde Amnesia. One of the earliest attempts to model human MTL amnesia was reported by Orbach, Milner and Rasmussen (1960), who tested monkeys with combined amygdala and hippocampal lesions — damage that was intended to approximate the lesion sustained by H.M. The monkeys were trained on a battery of visual and somesthetic discrimination problems. In tests designed to assess the effects of the lesions on postoperative retention, monkeys were trained on a task prior to lesioning and were tested for retention after the operation. In tests designed to assess the effects of the lesions on initial learning, monkeys were trained on a task after the operation.

Although monkeys with combined damage to the amygdala and hippocampus were impaired on both tests of postoperative retention and tests of initial learning of visual and somesthetic discriminations, three lines of evidence suggest that their impairments were not as profound as those suffered by humans with MTL lesions. First, all of the lesioned monkeys were eventually able to learn the visual or somesthetic discriminations. Second, although the monkeys showed postoperative retention impairments of preoperatively learned discriminations, they generally showed no postoperative retention impairment of postoperatively learned discriminations. Finally, in one test of

A. Radial Arm Maze

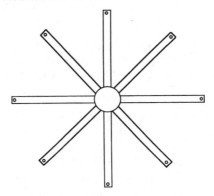

B. Morris Water Maze

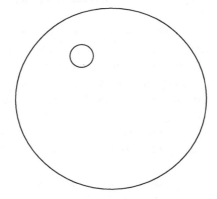

Figure 3.3. The two primary tasks that have been used with rats to study the effects of damage to the hippocampus on memory performance. (*A*) *Radial arm maze.* The apparatus consists of a central arena from which radiate eight arms. The rat is placed within the central arena and allowed to forage for food that is placed in a recessed well (*small circles*) at the end of each arm. The optimal strategy is to enter an arm once and then not return to that arm. (*B*) *Morris water maze.* The apparatus is a tank that contains water that has been rendered opaque by the addition of milk. Rats are placed in the tank at different positions against the wall and learn to escape to a hidden platform (*small circle*) that is submerged just below the water level.

initial postoperative learning with wide spacing between successive discrimination trials, operated monkeys acquired the task as fast as control animals. According to Murray (1996),

> "in the mid 1960s, replication of the lesions performed in H.M. did not yield convincing evidence for memory deficits in monkeys, and a role for the amygdala and hippocampus in stimulus memory looked doubtful" (p. 13).

In contrast to the relatively mild impairments reported by Orbach et al. (1960), Correll and Scoville (1965) reported that damage to the amygdala and the hippocampus (and probably to the tissue adjacent to these regions) in monkeys resulted in a serious postoperative retention impairment on a visual delayed matching-to-sample (DMS) task (see also Chapter 6). Prior to the operation, monkeys were initially trained on a simultaneous matching-to-sample task (i.e., the sample and comparison stimuli were presented concurrently), and then they were trained on a DMS task with delays as long as 5 s. Following surgery, all monkeys were impaired in relearning the simultaneous matching-to-sample task, and only one of four monkeys was able to perform the DMS task with a 0-s delay.

Despite the serious nature of these impairments, Correll and Scoville (1965) concluded that the deficits after MTL lesions in monkeys were "related to structural characteristics of the problem rather than to the rapid decay of a memory trace" (p. 366). Perhaps for this reason, Correll and Scoville are not generally credited with developing the first animal model of human MTL amnesia. This honor belongs to Mishkin (1978), who reported that combined — but not separate — damage to the amygdala and hippocampus and the tissue adjacent to these regions in monkeys produced serious impairment on a DNMS task.

Prior to the operation, the monkeys were trained on the DNMS task with a 10-s delay. After recovering from the lesion, they were tested for savings. Monkeys with damage to either the amygdala or the hippocampus were mildly impaired and required approximately the same number of trials to relearn the task postoperatively as they had required to learn the task originally. In contrast, monkeys with combined damage to the amygdala and the hippocampus required, on average, more than seven times as many trials to relearn the task postoperatively. Nevertheless, two of the three monkeys with combined lesions were able to relearn the DNMS task to criterion. The initial impairment and subsequent recovery is generally ignored in favor of the finding that the performance of monkeys with combined damage to the amygdala and hippo-campus was close to chance levels when tested after delays ranging from 30 to 120 s (see Figure 3.4A). In contrast, monkeys with damage to either the amygdala or hippocampus were only very mildly affected when tested after these same delays.

In addition to impairments on DNMS tasks, monkeys with damage to the MTL take much longer to learn an eight-pair CD task than unoperated control animals (Zola-Morgan & Squire 1985). Although impaired on the task, how-ever, the lesioned monkeys eventually do learn to solve this task to criterion. In rats, damage to the hippocampus impairs the learning of both the radial arm maze (Olton, Becker & Handelmann 1979) and the Morris water maze (Morris, Garrud, Rawlins & O'Keefe 1982). As is the case with monkeys, rats with damage to the hippocampus are able to relearn both tasks to criterion. The DNMS and CD tasks for monkeys and the radial-arm maze and Morris water-maze tasks for rats are generally regarded as equivalent to explicit memory tasks in humans.

Retrograde Amnesia. In addition to modeling aspects of anterograde memory loss, studies with animals have also modeled the retrograde amnesia that often follows MTL damage in humans. Recall that retrograde amnesia refers to a loss of memories for events that occurred prior to the damage. These memory impairments in humans are often temporally graded such that memory for recent events is usually much worse than memory for more remote events. Zola-Morgan and Squire (1990a) found that damage to the hippocampus and amygdala and the adjoining tissue in monkeys also causes temporally-graded retrograde amnesia. The monkeys were trained 16, 12, 8, 4, or 2 weeks prior to surgery with five different sets of 20 object discrimina-tions. An object discrimination task is similar to the visual discrimination task (see Figure 3.2A) except that the stimuli are objects instead of pictures. Half of the animals then received damage to the MTL, and half served as unoper-ated controls. Memory for the 100 discriminations was assessed following either recovery from surgery (operated animals) or a delay of similar length (unoperated control animals).

The results are also shown in Figure 3.4B. Control animals produced a standard forgetting function, remembering discriminations that they learned more recently (2 weeks prior to the surgery of lesioned animals) better than discriminations that they learned in the more remote past (16 weeks before-

A. Anterograde Memory Impairments

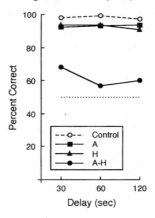

B. Retrograde Memory Impairments

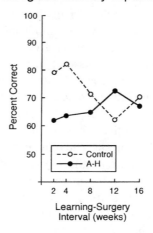

Figure 3.4. The effects of damage to components of the medial temporal lobe on antero-grade and retrograde memory in monkeys. (*A*) *Anterograde memory impairments.* The effects of damage to the amygdala (*A*), hippocampus (*H*), or combined amygdala-hippo-campus (*A-H*) damage on delayed nonmatching-to-sample performance in monkeys. The *dotted line* represents chance levels of performance (redrawn from Mishkin, 1978). (*B*) *Retrograde memory impairments.* The effects of combined amygdala-hippocampus damage on retention of visual discriminations that were learned prior to surgery (redrawn from Zola-Morgan and Squire, 1990).

hand). Like humans, however, monkeys with MTL damage showed the opposite effect, with greater forgetting of discriminations that had been learned in the recent past. Similar temporally-graded retrograde amnesia curves have been obtained in studies with rats (Bolhuis, Stewart & Forrest 1994; Cho, Kesner & Brodale 1995; Kim & Fanselow 1992; Ramos 1998; Winocur 1990). In summary, both anterograde and retrograde memory impairments that have been noted in humans with MTL damage have been replicated in monkeys and rats with similar lesions.

Some memories are spared

Recall that humans with MTL damage, although densely amnesic, are nevertheless able to learn certain motor, perceptual, and even problem-solving tasks. The same appears to be true for monkeys with MTL lesions. Malamut, Saunders and Mishkin (1984) showed that monkeys with combined damage to the hippocampus and amygdala were not impaired in the acquisition of a 24-hour CD task but were impaired on a DNMS task. The claim of spared performance on the 24-hour CD task was repeated frequently in numerous books and articles that followed the publication of this paper.

Recall that monkeys with MTL damage are impaired in the acquisition of an eight-pair CD task. The 24-hour CD task is procedurally almost identical to the eight-pair CD task with two main exceptions: First, in the 24-hour CD task, monkeys are trained with 20 pairs of stimuli instead of just eight. Second, in the 24-hour CD task, each pair of stimuli is presented only once in a session, whereas in the eight-pair CD task, the pairs of stimuli are presented numerous times within a session.

In the Malamut et al. (1984) study, seven monkeys with combined damage to the hippocampus, amygdala, and adjacent tissue and four unoperated controls were trained with 20 pairs of stimuli until they satisfied a criterion of 90 correct responses in 100 trials in five consecutive sessions. After they completed training with the first set of 20 pairs of stimuli (set A), they were trained in a similar fashion with a second set of 20 pairs of stimuli (set B). The lesioned monkeys were mildly impaired on the acquisition of the 24-hour CD task on set A but not on set B. Moreover, according Malamut et al., the monkeys who showed an impairment on either set A or set B had incidental damage to the visual association areas of the brain (area TE), which led the authors to discount damage to the amygdala and hippocampus as the source of the impairment.

Several aspects of this paper argue against the conclusion that MTL damage did not affect performance on the 24-hour CD task. Figure 3.5 presents data for the unoperated control monkeys on the left, for the operated monkeys that sustained no damage to area TE in the middle, and for the operated monkeys that sustained additional damage to area TE on the right. In Figure 3.5, data for monkeys that sustained damage to area TE are arranged from left to right in order of the increasing amount of damage to this area. Consider the acquisition of set A (see Figure 3.5A). Although monkey L2–3, who had the greatest damage to the visual areas, took the longest to learn the task, a closer inspection of this figure reveals that monkeys L2–2 and L3–2, who sustained *no damage* to the visual areas, also performed quite poorly. Furthermore, monkey L3–1, who learned faster than any other animal (including the unoperated animals), had considerable sparing of the amygdala and, most likely, of the tissue adjacent to the amygdala. In fact, researchers now recognize that the tissue adjacent to the amygdala — the perirhinal cortex — is critical for the successful performance of a number of visual memory tasks. Therefore, monkey L3–1, for whom this critical region was probably spared, should not be included with the animals that sustained combined damage to the amygdala and hippocampus.

Despite these problems, it is fair to say that the impairment in animals with amygdala-hippocampal damage that did not sustain damage to area TE was relatively mild, and they were eventually able to relearn the task to criterion. Furthermore, as the data for set B clearly show (see Figure 3.5B), there was very little difference between operated and control animals in terms of the number of sessions to learn the task. Therefore, this study has been used as evidence of spared memory following damage to the MTL in monkeys, especially because the same operated monkeys were seriously impaired on a DNMS task.

A second point, however, is also worth noting, namely, that the 24-hour CD task is easier for monkeys to learn than the eight-pair CD task. On average, monkeys require almost three times as many trials to learn an eight-pair CD task (i.e., 550 trials) than to learn a 24-hour CD task (i.e., 195 trials). The difficulty is even more apparent when one considers how many pairs the animal is required to learn in each task; monkeys require seven times as many trials to learn each pair in the eight-pair CD task (i.e., 69 trials) compared to

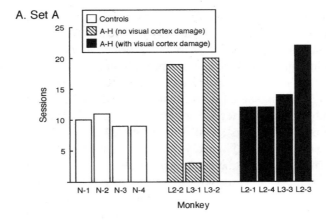

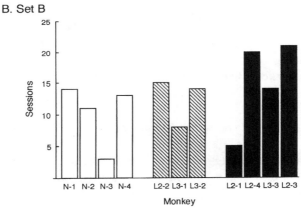

Figure 3.5. The effects of combined damage to the amygdala and hippocampus (A-H) on the 24-hour concurrent discrimination (CD) task. Animals with damage to the visual cortex are arranged from left to right in terms of increasing damage to the visual cortex (redrawn from Malamut, Saunders and Mishkin 1984). (*A*) *Set A*: Performance with the first set of 20 pairs of stimuli. (*B*) *Set B*: Performance with the second set of 20 pairs of stimuli.

the 24-hour CD task (i.e., 9.8 trials). For whatever reason, because the eight-pair CD task is more difficult for monkeys to learn than the 24-hour CD task, damage to the MTL might reasonably be expected to impair their performance on the eight-pair CD task before impairing it on the 24-hour CD task.

The effects of MTL lesions on monkeys' performance on motor tasks are more similar to the spared performance that has been seen following MTL lesions in humans, and they are certainly more convincing than the effects of MTL lesions on monkeys' acquisition of the 24-hour CD task. Zola-Morgan and Squire (1984) trained monkeys with medial temporal lobe lesions on both a Barrier motor-skill task and a Lifesaver task. In the Barrier task, the monkeys had to move a breadstick through three rows of a vertically arranged wooden barrier. In the Lifesaver task, monkeys had to remove a Lifesaver candy from a horizontal metal rod that contained a 90-deg bend. Monkeys with MTL lesions showed normal acquisition of both tasks (see Figure 3.6). Furthermore, in the case of the Lifesaver task, both control and lesioned animals showed similar levels of retention of the task following a 1-month pause in testing.

Thus, monkeys, like humans, do show some spared memories following damage to the MTL.

Parallel findings in humans and nonhumans

Humans have been tested on most of the tasks that are sensitive to MTL lesions in monkeys, and the results are generally consistent with the monkey data. Amnesic patients, for example, are impaired in performing the DNMS task and show the same accelerated delay-dependent decay rates as monkeys with similar damage (Sidman, Stoddard & Mohr 1968; Squire, Zola-Morgan & Chen 1988). Human amnesics are also impaired in the acquisition of an eight-pair CD task (Oscar-Berman & Bonner 1985; Oscar-Berman & Zola-Morgan 1980; Squire et al. 1988). The only inconsistency between the human and nonhuman data is in the acquisition of a 24-hour CD task: Monkeys are generally not impaired on this task, whereas humans are.

Problems with Tasks Used with Nonhumans. The primary problem with the tasks that are used with animals is that they tend to be defined as either explicit or implicit according to whether they are impaired by MTL lesions or not. The DNMS task, for example, is defined as an explicit memory task because it is sensitive to MTL damage, whereas the 24-hour CD task is defined

A. Barrier Task

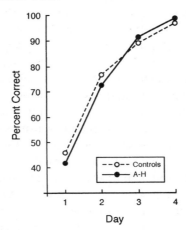

B. Lifesaver Task

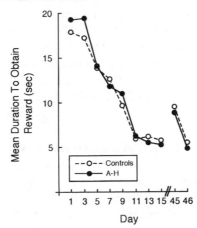

Figure 3.6. The effects of combined damage to the amygdala and hippocampus (*A-H*) on two motor skill tasks (redrawn from Zola-Morgan and Squire, 1984). (*A*) *Barrier task*. The monkeys were required to maneuver a breadstick through three rows of vertically arranged wooden pegs. (*B*) *Lifesaver task*. The monkeys were required to maneuver a Lifesaver candy off a metal rod that contained a 90-deg bend.

as an implicit memory task because it is either not impaired by these lesions or is less impaired by them. Numerous memory theorists have argued that such circularity does not apply to the tasks used with humans and that the memory distinctions between performance on different tasks in humans are process-driven (see Chapter 8). Although the extent to which this argument is true for tasks used with humans is debatable, it almost certainly is the case that process-driven accounts do not describe findings from memory research with monkeys. For example, it is difficult to reconcile the fact that procedurally identical or nearly identical tasks are often differentially sensitive to MTL lesions.

One example of this problem is animals' performance on an eight-pair CD task and their performance on a 24-hour CD task. Procedurally, the tasks are almost identical, and in both cases, the animal must learn which stimulus of a pair is consistently associated with reward. Yet, the effects of MTL lesions are quite different on the two tasks. A second example is animals' performance on a discrimination task. Zola-Morgan and Squire (1984) found that monkeys with MTL lesions are only mildly impaired when learning a difficult discrimination between 2-D stimuli. On the other hand, they found greater impairments on a procedurally identical discrimination task that used 3-D stimuli. The point here is that *the task per se* (CD or discrimination) cannot be classified as an implicit or explicit memory task on the basis of the procedure because the procedures are virtually identical. Rather, they are defined as an implicit or explicit memory task on the basis of whether or not task performance is impaired by MTL lesions, respectively.

Neural substrates of explicit and implicit memory

Neural substrates of explicit memory

Mishkin's Model. Although the MTL may be critical for normal memory, it is clear that memories are not stored in this area of the brain. This conclusion follows from the fact that H.M. and other patients with similar damage to the MTL, while suffering from severe anterograde amnesia and perhaps some retrograde amnesia, have some preserved memories for events that occurred prior to the operation or damage. What exactly, then, does the MTL contribute to the memory process? And how does it accomplish this feat? Mishkin (1982) proposed that recognition memory (i.e., *explicit memory*) is mediated by a cortico-limbic-diencephalic-cortico circuit (see Figure 3.7A). According to this model, memories are stored in higher-order sensory areas of the brain, but importantly, the storage of that information in cortex requires that the to-be-stored information course through limbic (hippocampus and amygdala) and diencephalic structures.

Consider the case of visual memories: Although visual information processing is far more parallel than Mishkin's model depicts, the basic premise of the model is still correct. Visual information from the eyes is projected to the primary visual cortex (*area OC*) in the posterior part of the brain. The information is then sent through a series of additional visual processing areas

A. Mishkin (1982)

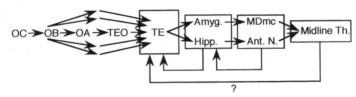

B. Petri and Mishkin (1994)

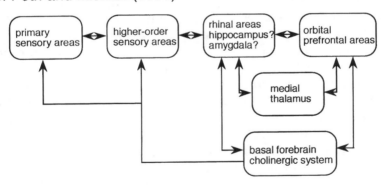

Figure 3.7. Neural substrates of explicit memory. (*A*) *Mishkin (1982) model.* In this model, both the amygdala and the hippocampus contribute equally to visual recognition memory (redrawn from Mishkin, 1982). (*B*) *Petri and Mishkin (1994) model.* In this revised model, the rhinal cortex is critical for visual recognition memory (redrawn from Petri and Mishkin, 1994).

in what today is referred to as the *ventral visual stream*. Each of these cortical areas (OB, OA, and TEO) is important for extracting and processing some aspect of a visual scene, such as color or form. The neurally most veridical version of visual information is represented and stored in the terminal regions of the ventral visual stream in the inferior temporal cortex, or area TE. Before that information can be stored in area TE, however, it must engage the limbic and diencephalic areas of the brain. By doing so, the information can then be *stamped in* to area TE.

According to the model, the memory is initially stored in area TE in a limbic-dependent fashion, that is, retrieval of the information requires the participation of the limbic system. Over time, however, the memory in area TE becomes so well established that it can be retrieved without the assistance of the limbic regions. At this stage, damage to the limbic system would not impair information that is already stored in area TE but would impair the future storage of information in area TE. This is believed to be what occurs in the case of MTL amnesia: Individuals with MTL damage are no longer able to form new memories because the limbic regions responsible for stamping in the memory are damaged. On the other hand, information that has already been stamped in, and is therefore limbic-independent, is spared following MTL damage.

Although this model was originally developed for visual memories, one of its strong features is its applicability to memories in any of the sensory systems by simply substituting the appropriate higher-order sensory area. For example, the same model would apply for the auditory system, with the exception that the auditory cortical areas TC→TB→TA would be substituted for the visual cortical areas OC→OB→OA→TEO→TE. Such substitution is justified on the grounds that the visual and auditory systems of the brain are anatomically similar in both their intrinsic and extrinsic projection patterns (Jones & Powell 1970; Pandya & Kuypers 1969). Furthermore, the behavioral consequences of damage to the auditory association cortex are virtually identical to the behavioral consequences of damage to the visual association cortex (Colombo, D'Amato, Rodman & Gross 1990; Colombo, Rodman & Gross 1996).

Modifications of the Model. Mishkin's basic scheme has remained essentially unchallenged since its inception, but its exact components and their contributions to memory have changed considerably (see Figure 3.7B). In his original formulation, both the hippocampus and the amygdala contributed equally to recognition memory performance, and both had to be damaged to cause an impairment in recognition memory. Mishkin (1982) acknowledged the "unusual practice that has been followed here of treating the amygdala and the hippocampus as a single functional unit" (p. 94). Nevertheless, this suggestion was reasonable given that damage to the amygdala or the hippocampus separately produced no appreciable DNMS impairments (see Figure 3.4A).

More than 10 years of research were required to understand why combined lesions of the amygdala and hippocampus are necessary to produce an impairment in memory. A schematic of the critical limbic structures and how they are arranged in the medial temporal lobe of the monkey's brain is shown in Figure 3.8. The amygdala and the hippocampus lie along the medial aspect of the temporal lobe, and the amygdala lies anterior to the hippocampus. The anterior portions of the perirhinal cortex and entorhinal cortex lie adjacent to the amygdala, and the posterior portions of these areas lie adjacent to the hippocampus. The parahippocampal gyrus is situated posterior to the perirhinal and entorhinal cortices and adjacent to the hippocampus.

In most lesion studies, damage to the hippocampus and amygdala is accomplished by subpial aspiration of the tissue. In addition, because the hippocampus and amygdala are located medially, but the surgical approach is often from the temporal aspect, damage to these structures invariably results in damage to the perirhinal cortex, entorhinal cortex, and parahippocampal gyrus. Therefore, in removing the amygdala and the hippocampus, Mishkin (1978) also damaged the tissue adjacent to these regions. As a result, it was unclear whether the DNMS impairments resulted from damage to the amygdala and

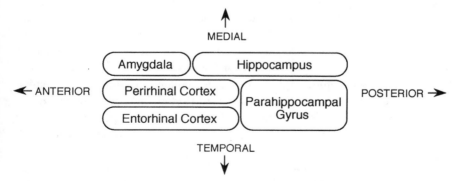

Figure 3.8. The spatial arrangement of the critical structures of the limbic system (adapted from Murray, 1996).

hippocampus or from damage to the perirhinal cortex, entorhinal cortex, or parahippocampal gyrus.

Studies by Larry Squire and Stuart Zola-Morgan throughout the 1980s and early 1990s helped clarify the contributions to memory made by the amygdala, hippocampus, perirhinal cortex, entorhinal cortex, and parahippocampal gyrus. In one of the earlier studies, Zola-Morgan, Squire and Amaral (1989a) noted that radiofrequency lesions of the amygdala, which did not damage the adjacent rhinal tissue, failed to worsen DNMS impairments that were seen after hippocampal damage. Thus, in contrast to the findings of Mishkin (1978, 1982), the amygdala appeared to play no role in DNMS behavior.

A second finding (see Figure 3.9) was that damage restricted to the perirhinal cortex and the parahippocampal gyrus and sparing the amygdala and hippocampus (the + + *lesion*) produced an impairment in DNMS behavior that was as severe as the impairment produced by damage that included the hippocampus (*the H++ lesion*) (Zola-Morgan, Squire, Amaral & Suzuki 1989b). This result not only served to emphasize that the amygdala was not a component of the recognition (*explicit*) memory circuit but also challenged the role of the hippocampus in this circuit. Nevertheless, these and numerous other studies that followed indicated that DNMS impairments were largely attributable to damage of the perirhinal cortex rather than to damage of the hippocampus.

The Role of the Hippocampus. But does damage to the hippocampus per se impair recognition memory? This question was difficult to answer because, unlike the amygdala, which is relatively small, the hippocampus is quite large and difficult to damage without incurring damage to adjacent tissue. Nevertheless, using a newly developed technique that combines stereotaxic surgery with magnetic resonance imaging (Alvarez-Royo, Clower, Zola-Morgan & Squire 1991), Alvarez, Zola-Morgan and Squire (1995) managed to selectively damage the hippocampus using radiofrequency lesions. Their results, also presented in Figure 3.9, revealed that restricted damage to hippocampus (the *H lesion*) produced only minor impairments in DNMS performance after the longest (10-min) delay (see also Zola-Morgan, Squire, Rempel, Clower & Amaral 1992).

The finding of an impairment after a long delay in the DNMS task was not replicated by Murray and Mishkin (1998), who used delays as long as 40 min. Furthermore, the monkeys in the Alvarez et al. (1995) study were not at

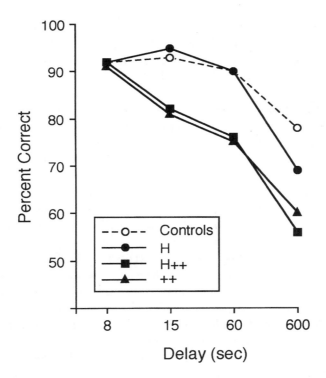

Figure 3.9. The effects of damage to the hippocampus (*H*), hippocampus plus perirhinal and parahippocampal cortex (*H*++), or only the perirhinal cortex and parahippocampal gyrus (++) on visual memory in monkeys (control animals: redrawn from Zola-Morgan, Squire, Rempel, Clower and Amaral, 1992; H animals: redrawn from Alvarez, Zola-Morgan and Squire, 1995; H++ animals: redrawn from Zola-Morgan, Squire, Clower and Rempel, 1993; ++ animals: redrawn from Suzuki, Zola-Morgan, Squire and Amaral, 1993).

all impaired in learning the eight-pair CD task. Recall that monkeys with hippocampal lesions that extended to the adjacent tissue were impaired in learning the eight-pair CD task. These findings suggest, therefore, that the visual memory deficit that follows damage to the hippocampus is transient at best. The same appears to be true in the case of rats (Mumby & Pinel 1994; Mumby, Wood & Pinel 1992).

Although these findings suggest that the hippocampus may not be a component of the explicit memory circuit, it is important to note that failures to observe memory impairments after hippocampal lesions are generally restricted to tasks that tap purely visual memory. In contrast, many experiments have shown that damage to the hippocampus in both mammalian and nonmammalian species reliably impairs performance on a number of tasks that require spatial memory (Angeli, Murray & Mishkin 1993; Colombo, Cawley & Broadbent 1997; Feigenbaum, Polkey & Morris 1996; Morris et al. 1982; O'Keefe & Nadel 1978; Olton et al. 1979; Parkinson, Murray & Mishkin 1988; Smith & Milner 1981). Thus, the hippocampus may indeed play a role in explicit memory, but one that is limited to the processing and retention of spatial information.

Other Views of Hippocampal Function. That the hippocampus is important for processing spatial information is not the only view of hippocampal function. A second possibility, related to the view that the hippocampus is important for processing spatial information, is that the hippocampus is important in processing contextual information (Hirsh 1974) or in the formation of context-dependent memories (Vargha-Khadem, Gadian, Watkins, Connelly, Paesschen & Mishkin 1997). According to this view, both the hippocampus and the perirhinal cortex are important for explicit memory, but the hippocampus is important for *context-dependent* explicit memory, whereas the perirhinal cortex is important for *context-independent* explicit memory. A third view is that the hippocampus is important for the *flexible or relational processing* of information across both spatial and nonspatial domains (Eichenbaum, Otto & Cohen 1994). In short, the exact role of the hippocampus in explicit memory is still being debated.

Neural substrates of implicit memory

Although the neural substrates of explicit memory are generally well defined, the neural substrates of implicit memory are not. In much the same way that the behavioral mechanisms of nondeclarative (implicit) memory are defined "not by any positive feature so much as by the fact that they are not declarative [explicit]" (Squire 1994, p. 233), the neural substrates of implicit memory seem to be defined as those areas of the brain that are *not* the neural substrates of explicit memory. According to Squire (1994),

> "the memory abilities that are not declarative are not of a single type and are not subserved by a single brain system [*but*] embrace several kinds of memory and depend on multiple brain systems" (p. 233).

Mishkin and colleagues proposed that a cortico-striatal-cortico circuit medi-ates habit (implicit) memory (Mishkin & Petri 1984; Mishkin et al. 1984). These pathways were elaborated by Petri and Mishkin (1994) and are illus-trated in Figure 3.10. Here, *habit memories*, like *recognition memories*, are stored in the highest-order cortical association areas of the brain. Forming a permanent trace of the habit memory in the association cortex, however, requires that to-be-remembered information be processed through the striatal system.

Why the striatal system was considered to be responsible for habit memory no doubt relates to the fact that many of the memories that were spared following MTL damage in humans were based on motor skills. The striatum consists of the caudate nucleus, which receives widespread connec-tions from higher-order cortical association areas, and the putamen. The caudate nucleus and the putamen project to the globus pallidus and, via the thalamus, to the motor cortex of the brain to effect movement. According to Mishkin et al. (1984),

> "this system of projections therefore provides a mechanism through which cortically processed sensory input could become associated with motor out-puts generated in the pallidum [*globus pallidus*] and so yield the stimulus-response bonds that constitute habits" (p. 74).

Petri and Mishkin (1994)

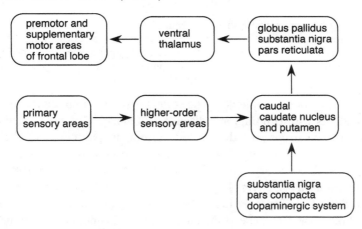

Figure 3.10. Neural substrates of implicit memory (redrawn from Petri and Mishkin 1994).

As we have previously noted, in addition to preserved motor skills such as mirror drawing, rotary pursuit, and bimanual tracking, patients with MTL amnesia also show preserved perceptual skills such as on the Gollin picture task (Warrington & Weiskrantz 1968), and preserved cognitive skills such as on the Tower of Hanoi task (Corkin & Cohen 1981). In addition, amnesics show normal priming such as on word-stem completion tasks (Graf et al. 1984), normal emotional memory (Bechara, Tranel, Damasio, Adolphs, Rockland & Damasio 1995), and normal classical conditioning (Weiskrantz & Warrington 1979).

A different neural system is held responsible for each of these forms of implicit memory (see Figure 3.11). The neural mechanisms underlying classical conditioning depend in large part on the cerebellum and its associated brainstem structures (Thompson 1990b), whereas the neural mechanisms underlying emotional memory depend on the amygdala (Adolphs, Tranel, Damasio & Damasio 1994; Scott, Young, Calder, Hellawell, Aggleton & Johnson 1997). The neural substrates of priming as well as of other perceptual and cognitive memories that are spared following MTL lesions, however, are still largely unclear. For the most part, they are said to be dependent on the neocortex — a term only slightly more informative than saying that they depend on the brain.

The general vagueness concerning the structures important for implicit memory performance has left the entire notion of implicit memory open to criticism. Wise (1996), for example, wrote,

> "One might suppose that such enthusiasm [*for the habit memory system*] stems from a wealth of empirical data and that the habit hypothesis had, being well and rigorously tested, withstood an onslaught of skeptical experimentation and testing. Examination of the published literature, however, reveals a less convincing body of data" (p. 39).

Most of the evidence implicating the striatal system in implicit memory comes from patients with Huntington's disease — a genetically transmitted disorder that results in atrophy of the striatal system, in particular, of the caudate nucleus. Patients with Huntington's disease are impaired on tests of implicit memory, such as rotary pursuit (Heindel, Butters & Salmon 1988), mirror reading (Martone, Butters, Payne, Becker & Sax 1984), and the Tower of Hanoi (Saint-Cyr, Taylor & Lang 1988), but they perform normally on tests of explicit memory. Evidence of the latter, however, is not at all convincing, and on some tests, they perform as poorly as patients with MTL-type amnesia

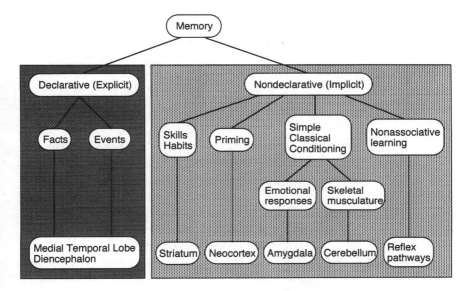

Figure 3.11. Diagram of the divisions of memory, the behaviors that underlie each division, and the candidate brain structures that support each behavior (redrawn from Milner, Squire and Kandel 1998).

(Butters, Wolf, Martone, Granholm & Cermak 1985). Furthermore, they *can* perform the implicit memory tasks, but they simply do so at a degraded level — a point that was also stressed by Wise (1996):

> "In the major clinical papers one can find evidence of procedural [implicit] learning that has often been neglected in favor of emphasizing statistically significant deficits" (p. 41).

Current issues in explicit and implicit memory research

Functional imaging studies of memory

Most of what we know about the neural basis of memory is based on lesion studies. The problem, of course, is that lesions rarely abide by functional boundaries. Even when they do, the consequences of a lesion can extend well beyond the intentionally damaged tissue. The task of ascribing function to a particular structure, therefore, will always be constrained by some degree of uncertainty regarding the extent of cortical damage. The solution to this problem has come in the form of imaging studies, which provide a window into the neural structures responsible for the processing and retention of information in the undamaged brain. According to Gabrieli, Brewer and Poldrack (1998):

> "progress in functional neuroimaging has broken the shackles of cognitive neuroscience memory research with humans" (p. 277).

The two most popular imaging techniques are *positron emission tomography (PET)* and *functional magnetic resonance imaging (fMRI)*. Neither technique directly measures neural activity. Rather, both rely on the fact that those areas of the brain that are neurally active are also those areas of the brain that are metabolically active. PET and fMRI are designed to detect changes in brain metabolism that follow naturally as a function of neural activity. Because the brain is always active, however, both techniques rely on the *method of subtraction*, in which activity during a baseline condition is subtracted from activity during an experimental condition.

Positron Emission Tomography (PET). PET produces a picture of the brain by measuring blood flow, oxygen consumption, or glucose metabolism. In all three cases, the subject is injected with a small amount of a lightly radioactive substance that decays and emits positively charged particles called *positrons*. When these positrons collide with electrons, which are negatively charged, they annihilate each other and produce energy in the form of two photons. The PET scanner records the level and origin of the photon activity. This information is then converted into a color-coded picture with a spatial resolution of approximately 5 mm and a temporal resolution of 1 min.

Functional Magnetic Resonance Imaging (fMRI). Like PET, fMRI measures brain metabolism in the form of blood oxygenation. In contrast to PET, which relies on the decay of an ingested radioactive substance, fMRI measures the magnetic properties of hemoglobin. Areas of the brain that are neurally very active are also undergoing greater amounts of blood oxygenation. Because oxygenated blood has more magnetic properties than deoxygenated blood, the fMRI scanner can detect this difference and convert this information into a color-coded picture of neural activity with a spatial resolution of 1 to 2 mm and a temporal resolution of 2 to 8 s (Ungerleider 1995).

Imaging Studies of Memory. Studies using PET and fMRI are being used with increasing frequency to chart the neural structures that are activated during memory performance (for reviews, see Gabrieli, Brewer & Poldrack 1998; Schacter 1997; Ungerleider 1995). Although a number of studies have imaged the brain during memory performance, only recently have studies begun to address the dissociation between explicit and implicit memory. One of the first studies of this type was conducted by Squire, Ojeman, Miezin, Petersen, Videen and Raichle (1992), who asked subjects to study a list of words. To ensure that they attended to each word, the experimenter asked them to rate how much they liked each word on a scale of 1 to 5. Their brains were then scanned using PET while they performed either a word-stem completion (*implicit memory)* task or a cued-recall (*explicit memory*) task. The explicit memory task activated the hippocampus and parahippocampal gyrus, whereas the implicit memory task led to a decrease in activity in the right posterior visual cortex. Unfortunately, the implicit memory task also activated the hippocampus and parahippocampal gyrus, although to a lesser extent.

The Squire et al. (1992) study fell short of providing the required double dissociation between memory task (explicit versus implicit) and neural structure (hippocampus versus posterior visual cortex) that would support the notion of multiple memory systems. The authors noted, however, that success on the word-stem completion task was uncharacteristically high (71.5%) and, more importantly, not that different from success on the cued-recall task (72.4%). It is possible, they argued, that performance on the word-stem completion task may have been contaminated by explicit memory influences (see also Chapter 2), and that the hippocampal activation that was seen during word-stem completion was a consequence of this contamination.

To address this possibility, Schacter, Alpert, Savage, Rauch and Albert (1996) repeated the word-stem completion task. Subjects were shown a list of words, but instead of rating them on a pleasantness scale, they counted the number of T-junctions in each word. This manipulation deemphasized the semantic nature of the task and encouraged them to process the words in a more incidental fashion. The experiment yielded the desired results: Subjects still showed priming effects, but they completed many fewer word stems than subjects in the Squire et al. (1992) study. Under these conditions, PET scans again revealed a decrease in activity in the posterior visual cortex. In contrast to the findings of Squire et al. (1992), however, no activation was seen in the hippocampus or parahippocampal gyrus.

One memory system or two?

There are a number of possibilities concerning the neural architecture of memory. The prevailing view is that there are at least two memory systems. According to this view, damage to one system impairs explicit memory but not implicit memory, whereas damage to the other system has the opposite effect. A second possibility is that there is only one memory system and that damage to this system impairs explicit memory tasks because they are more resource-demanding than implicit memory tasks.

Although the multiple-memory-systems view is by far the most prevalent today, in reviewing the literature on the effects of brain damage on memory, one is almost immediately struck by the fact that the vast majority of studies report impairments in explicit memory but not in implicit memory. In other words, the vast majority of evidence is based on *a single memory dissociation*. The same is true of evidence from studies with normal human adults who receive implicit or explicit test instructions (for review, see Chapter 7). The case for multiple memory systems would be stronger if damage to a second system could be shown to impair implicit memory while sparing explicit memory. Is there any evidence for such a double dissociation?

Double Dissociations: Nonhuman Animal Studies. Packard, Hirsh and White (1989) compared the effects of damage to the caudate nucleus and fornix (which is roughly equivalent to damage of the hippocampus) on the acquisition of two versions of the radial arm maze — one designed to measure implicit memory and the other designed to measure explicit memory. The explicit version was the standard radial arm maze task in which all eight arms of the maze were baited, and rats were required to enter an arm to obtain a reward. Because repeat visits to the same arm were considered an error, rats were trained to adopt a *win-shift strategy*. In the implicit version, a light at the entry to each of four baited arms was lit at the start of a session. The remaining four arms were neither baited nor lit. If a rat entered a lighted arm, then it was rewarded, and that arm was rebaited. Following a second entry into the same arm, the rat received another reward, and then the light was turned off. A third visit to an arm was considered an error. Thus, rats were trained to visit each of the four arms twice within a session — a *win-stay strategy*.

In the explicit version of the task, rats with fornix damage committed more errors than controls, but rats with damage to the caudate nucleus and unoperated control animals performed equivalently. In the implicit version of the task, rats with damage to the caudate nucleus were impaired relative to unoperated controls, but rats with damage to the fornix performed better than controls. (Note, however, that rats with caudate lesions were able to learn the task to above-chance levels.) In a follow-up study, Packard and White (1991) found that intracaudate injections of the dopamine (DA) agonist d-amphetamine improved performance on the win-stay version of the radial arm maze task, but intrahippocampal injections had no effect. Conversely, intrahippocampal injections improved performance on the win-shift version of the radial arm maze task, but intracaudal injections had little effect. These studies, then, revealed a double dissociation of function with respect to both the effects of lesions and dopaminergic activation.

Packard and McGaugh (1992), who trained rats on two versions of the two-platform Morris water maze task, provided more evidence of a double dissociation. In this task, one platform is stable and will support the rat, whereas the second platform is unstable and sinks when the rat stands on it. In the spatial (explicit) version of the task, the stable platform always resided in the same quadrant of the water maze, whereas the unstable platform shifted between the remaining three quadrants across trials. In the visual (implicit) version of the task, one visual cue indicated the correct platform, and another indicated the incorrect platform. Again, rats with fornix lesions were impaired on the explicit version of the two-platform task, but animals with caudate lesions performed as well as unoperated controls. Conversely, on the implicit version of the task, rats with caudate lesions were impaired in learning the task, but rats with fornix lesions performed no differently from unoperated controls.

McDonald and White (1993) uncovered evidence of a triple dissociation of function across the hippocampus, amygdala, and striatum. Unoperated control animals, as well as animals with damage to the amygdala, were trained on the win-shift and win-stay versions of the radial arm maze (see above) as well as on a radial arm maze version of a *conditioned cue preference (CCP)* task. In the CCP task, which used only two of the eight arms in the radial arm maze, one arm was lighted, and the second arm was not. For half of the animals, the lighted arm signaled reward, and the dark arm signaled no reward; for the remaining half, the cue-reward associations were reversed. During testing, rats' preference for the rewarded arm was measured. The experiments revealed a triple dissociation: Rats with damage to the fornix were impaired on the win-shift version but not on the win-stay or CCP versions; rats with dorsal striatum lesions were impaired on the win-stay version but not on the win-shift or CCP versions; and rats with amygdala lesions were impaired on the CCP version but not on the win-shift or win-stay versions.

Double Dissociations: Human Studies. Bechara et al. (1995) reported data from three patients — one with damage to the amygdala, one with damage to the hippocampus, and one with damage to both the hippocampus and amygdala. The patients were trained in a classical conditioning procedure in which the CS was either pictures or sounds, and the US was a very loud noise. The dependent measure was the skin conductance response. The patient with lesions of the amygdala showed no conditioning but could describe facts about the task, such as the stimuli. The patient with hippocampal damage exhibited conditioning but was unable to describe facts about the task. The patient with damage to both the hippocampus and amygdala showed neither conditioning nor the ability to describe facts about the task. Thus, this study shows a double dissociation between conditioning *(implicit memory)* performance and declarative *(explicit memory)* knowledge with respect to the functions of the amygdala and the hippocampus.

A second study demonstrating a double dissociation was conducted by Gabrieli, Fleischman, Keane, Reminger and Morrell (1995). In this study, a patient with damage to the right occipital lobe received a perceptual identification *(implicit memory)* test with 24 old and 24 new words. Initially, the stimuli were presented very briefly, and then the duration of each word presentation increased until the subject correctly identified the word. In the recognition test, the patient was presented with 48 words and asked to judge if each word had been seen before. The patient was no faster at identifying old words than new words but performed as well as the controls on the test of recognition memory. According to the authors, this patient, along with amnesics who showed the opposite pattern of results,

> "provides the first neuropsychological evidence for [*a double dissociation*] that illuminate[s] the functional neural architecture of human memory: A memory system mediating visual implicit memory…is separable from the memory systems mediating explicit memory for words" (p. 81).

In another example of a double-dissociation study in humans, Knowlton, Mangels and Squire (1996) tested amnesics and patients with Parkinson's disease, who have damage to the substantia nigra — a component of the system thought to support implicit memory. Two tasks were used — a probabilistic classification learning task (*implicit memory*) in which subjects had to learn whether a visual pattern predicted rain or shine, and a multiple-choice test that assessed their declarative (*explicit*) memory for the first task. Both amnesic and control patients learned the probabilistic classification task at the same rate, but the performance of patients with Parkinson's disease was impaired. However, both the Parkinson and control patients did well on the multiple-choice test, but amnesics performed poorly. The authors concluded that probabilistic classification learning depends on the integrity of the caudate nucleus and the putamen, whereas declarative memory depends on the integrity of the medial temporal lobe.

Two points are worth mentioning: First, with extended training, the Parkinson patients were able to perform the implicit task at an above-chance level, but they simply did not perform it at the same levels in the same number of trials as amnesic patients. Second, because the Parkinson patients also had frontal lobe dysfunction, their memory impairment may have resulted from this damage instead of from damage to the system thought to underlie implicit memory. The authors addressed this issue by also testing patients with circumscribed frontal impairments. They found that these patients' scores on the probabilistic classification task were intermediate between the scores of patients with amnesia and Parkinson's disease. Therefore, the possibility that some frontal damage may have contributed to the impairment on the probabilistic classification task is difficult to dismiss.

Conclusions

In this chapter, we have reviewed the effects of damage to the medial temporal lobe on explicit and implicit memory performance in humans and nonhuman animals. We have also reviewed the neural substrates of explicit and implicit memory. Finally, we have tackled the question of whether this evidence points to a single memory system or a multiple memory system.

There is ample evidence to suggest that explicit and implicit memory are mediated by two distinct neural systems — one that taps structures in the medial temporal lobe, and the other that taps structures in the striatal system. This view, however, is not without problems. It is hard to escape the fact, for example, that the vast majority of studies have reported impairments in explicit but not implicit memory performance. Furthermore, although a few studies have noted impairments in implicit but not explicit memory performance after damage to structures that are believed to support implicit memory, it is usually the case that some learning on implicit tasks is still possible. For that matter, some learning on explicit tasks is also possible after damage to structures that are believed to support explicit memory. With respect to multiple memory systems, there seems to be ample support for the soft definition of a double dissociation in memory performance but very little support for the hard definition of a double dissociation.

CHAPTER 4

The Jacksonian Principle and Memory Development

The Jacksonian principle states that the nervous system is organized hierarchically and that the development and dissolution of function follow a first-in, last-out sequence. The general finding that implicit memory is spared in brain-damaged human amnesics but explicit memory is not, encouraged the application of the Jacksonian principle to the development and dissolution of memory systems. This principle attributes implicit memory to a primitive memory system that matures quite early in development and explicit memory to a late-maturing memory system. This chapter reviews the Jacksonian principle and evidence of its applicability to the hierarchical development and dissolution of memory in animals and children.

The Jacksonian principle

In 1884, John Hughlings Jackson introduced the concept that the nervous system — and the behavior that it controlled — was vertically and hierarchically organized. By this account, the neural functions that appeared first in evolution are also those that appear first in development and disappear last in disease. This progression reflects the fact that earlier-appearing neural elements are overlaid or suppressed by new functions under higher levels of neural control as the nervous system continues to develop. The later-appearing neural elements are increasingly more fragile or susceptible to disruption by disease or other challenges. As a result, adverse conditions can reverse the stages of evolution and the development of the nervous system such that the neural control of behavior reverts to that of a more primitive stage. This account is referred to as *the Jacksonian principle of the development and dissolution of function*. In brief, the Jacksonian principle states that the last functions to develop are the first to disappear after brain damage from injury, disease, or aging, whereas the first functions to develop are the last to be affected when the organism undergoes demise.

Classic examples of the Jacksonian principle come from studies of reflexive development. The first objective reports of fetal reflexive development were by Hooker (1952), who filmed exteriorized, prevital foetuses in a temperature-controlled water bath as they underwent anoxia. Hooker reported that the first foetal response to tactile stimulation at 7½ postmenstrual weeks was a contralateral reflex in which the head and upper trunk bent away from the site of stimulation. Contralateral reflexes are referred to as *avoiding reactions* because they move the stimulated region away from the stimulating source (Angulo y Gonzales 1932; Coghill 1916, 1929). Beginning at 11½ postmenstrual weeks, contralateral reflexes began to be replaced by ipsilateral reflexes. The earliest appearing reflexes were total-pattern reflexes. Later appearing reflexes were increasingly specific to the site of stimulation and progressed cephalocaudally with age: Stimulated head movements preceded stimulated hand movements, which preceded stimulated plantar movements, which preceded integrated hand-mouth reflexes (Humphrey 1969). This same sequence was subsequently observed in spontaneous activity by de Vries, Visser and Prechtl (1984), who recorded foetal activity longitudinally over the course of gestation.

Critical support for the Jacksonian principle was Hooker's finding that as the foetus progressively underwent anoxia, stimulated reflexes disappeared in the reverse order of their original appearance, with the most primitive reflexes being preserved the longest. As one example, ipsilateral reflexes were replaced by contralateral reflexes. A reversion in the sequence of reflexes accompanying anoxia was also reported by Angulo y Gonzales (1932). Hooker attributed this reversion to the fact that the reflexes that appeared first in development required less oxygen to perform:

> "The low oxygen capacity of the early embryo is evidently without untoward effect upon the activity of the primary reflex arcs. They have developed in a still lower oxygen environment and the greater supply at the time of their beginning function is entirely adequate. This is not the case, however, with newer neural mechanisms which become active later. It is particularly not the case in connection with those centers which have their synapses at higher levels of the central nervous system...all newer neural components which develop find a decreasing increment in oxygen supply....As a result, there is a tendency for newer neural mechanisms at higher levels to succumb relatively early to the effects of anoxia and asphyxia. This causes a reversion in the

behavior pattern to an earlier type of activity in young fetuses" (Hooker 1952, pp. 104–105).

Humphrey (1969) reported that the developmental sequence of the appearance of prenatal reflexes was recapitulated postnatally during the transition from elicited to voluntary activity. She hypothesized that the postnatal repetition of fetal activity sequences was similarly due to the lower oxygen requirement of more primitive fetal reflex arcs. That is, those reflexes that were mediated by reflex arcs that had functioned the longest required less oxygen to be initiated than reflexes that were mediated by reflex arcs that had matured more recently. However, the sequence in which the postnatal reflexes appeared, like the sequence of prenatal reflexes previously observed by Hooker, was reversed when the organism underwent challenge:

> "Thus when the oxygen supply is decreased or conditions are unfavourable for other reasons, the reflexes that develop earliest are the most readily elicited. Since recently developed centres require a higher oxygen level, motoneurones that have been active for a longer time are more easily fired than newly functioning motor nerve cells, and so become regulated earlier by descending fibre systems than do those that mature later" (Humphrey 1969, p. 67).

In other words, the developing organism always reverts to earlier maturing reflexes if the oxygen supply is not good because the reflexes that matured more recently require more oxygen in order to be elicited. Thus, for example, if the neonate is stressed, then primitive contralateral reactions reappear (Humphrey 1969). Likewise, following some kinds of brain injury (Willis & Grossman 1973), adults exhibit the Babkin reflex — a very rudimentary reflex that consists of opening the mouth or gaping, returning the head to midline, and raising or flexion of the head (Babkin 1960). It has been observed in premature infants as early as 14 weeks of gestational age but is suppressed between the third and fourth postnatal month (Humphrey 1969). Also, during advanced stages of senility, adult patients often exhibit primitive foetal and infantile reflexes (Paulson 1977). For example, infantile sucking and grasping reflexes reappear in patients with advanced senile dementia (Paulson & Gotlieb 1968).

Support for the Jacksonian principle has also been found in the domain of sensory function. This was described by Gottlieb (1971), who reviewed the development of sensory function in a variety of avian and mammalian species, including man. He found that the sequential onset of function was the same in all species — tactile, vestibular, auditory, and visual. Alberts (1978) extended this sequence to the developing rat, finding that the thermal and chemical (olfaction, gustation) senses were the last to develop prenatally — after vestibular and tactile sensation; audition and vision began functioning postnatally. In the course of normal aging in humans, these functions (olfaction, thermal sensitivity, audition, and vision) decline in the reverse order of their onset.

The Jacksonian principle and animal memory

The Campbell, Sananes, and Gaddy study

One of the first attempts to apply the Jacksonian principle to the development and dissolution of memory function in animals was undertaken by Campbell, Sananes and Gaddy (1984, 1985). Given evidence that developing animals typically exhibit poorer memory than adults (Campbell & Spear 1972), these investigators asked if the Jacksonian principle describes the sequential appearance of various memory abilities in infant animals and the sequential decline of the same memory abilities in aging animals. To answer this question, Campbell et al. (1984) conducted a major review of the studies of memory performance on tasks that had been used in common with infant, young adult, and aged rats. This section reviews their basic assumptions, the relevant findings, and their final conclusions.

The Basic Assumptions. In order to provide a compelling test of the Jacksonian principle, Campbell et al.'s analysis was based on four assumptions. First, they required that the tasks that were used with normal adult and aged rats had to be solved sequentially during development by the preweanling rat. Three representative tasks for which infants exhibited sequential development of long-term memory were *conditioned taste aversion*, which infants learn at the youngest age; the *auditory conditioned emotional response*, which infants learn when they are slightly older; and *visually-based passive avoidance*, which infants learn when they are older yet. The rate at which rat pups acquired these three tasks mirrored the sequential development of the sensory systems on which they depended (Alberts 1984) — gustation, audition, and vision, respectively. A fourth task, *spatial learning*, also relies heavily on visual cues and appears quite late in infancy. Animals' performance on this task will be considered separately below (*"Final Conclusions"*).

Second, Campbell et al. required that a common metric be used to compare retention of the various tasks across the different ages. For this, they used percent retention scores, defining 100% retention as the terminal training score or the preset ceiling level, and 0% retention as either the score on the first training trial or the test score of an untrained control group. Third, they required that young adults exhibit a relatively low rate of forgetting in order that greater forgetting on the part of younger and older subjects could be seen. And fourth, as evidence for the Jacksonian principle, they required that aged adults exhibit a sequential loss of memory in the reverse order from that exhibited by infants.

The Findings. The corresponding percent retention data for preweanlings, normal adults, and aging adults as a function of the retention interval are presented in Figure 4.1 for the three tasks. The studies from which these data were drawn are listed in Table 4.1. The data of infants (in the left panel of each figure) show that they forgot each of the three tasks rapidly. The data of young

Table 4.1. Studies that Assessed the Memory Performance of Infant, Young Adult, and Aged Adult Rats on Conditioned Taste Aversion, Auditory Conditioned Emotional Response, and Passive-Avoidance Tasks (Cited in Campbell, Sananes & Gaddy 1984)

Task x Age	Study
Conditioned Taste Aversion	
Infants	Campbell & Alberts, 1979; Gregg et al., 1978; Schweitzer & Green, 1982
Young Adults	Campbell & Alberts, 1979; Cooper et al., 1980; Guanowsky & Misanin, 1983; Klein et al., 1977; Steinert et al., 1980
Aged Adults	Cooper et al., 1980; Guanowsky & Misanin, 1983
Auditory Conditioned Emotional Response	
Infants	Dean et al., 1981
Young Adults	Campbell & Campbell, 1962; Campbell et al., 1980
Aged Adults	Campbell et al., 1980
Passive Avoidance	
Infants	Schulenberg et al., 1981; Stehouwer & Campbell, 1980
Young Adults	Bartus et al., 1980; Campbell et al., 1980; Dean et al., 1981; Gold et al., 1981; Jensen et al., 1980; Schulenberg et al., 1981
Aged Adults	Bartus et al., 1980; Campbell et al., 1980; Dean et al., 1981; Gold et al., 1981; Jensen et al., 1980

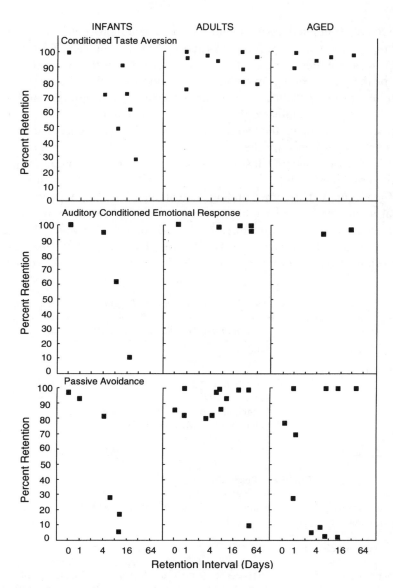

Figure 4.1. Scatterplots of transformed retention data from differently-aged rats in conditioned taste aversion tasks (*top panel*), auditory conditioned emotional response tasks (*middle panel*), and passive-avoidance tasks (*bottom panel*). From left to right, panels contain data from infants, young adults, and aged adults, respectively. Each point represents an independent observation from one of the studies listed in Table 4.1.

adults (in the middle panel of each figure) reveal that they exhibited little or no forgetting of any task after any retention interval, thereby meeting Campbell et al.'s third requirement. The sole exception occurred in a passive-avoidance study in which the researchers had used a single training trial, a weak shock, and a very long retention interval (Gold, McGaugh, Hankins, Rose & Vasquez 1981). The data of old adults are presented in the right panel of each figure.

As shown in Figure 4.1, the pattern of retention across tasks reveals no consistent relation between forgetting by the aged rats and forgetting by the infants. Whereas infants exhibited rapid forgetting in the conditioned taste aversion and auditory conditioned emotional response tasks, for example, aged rats exhibited almost perfect retention in the same tasks over the same delays. Recall, however, that the passive-avoidance task is the last task to be learned during development, and only in some studies using this task did the aged adults forget as rapidly as infants — in several other studies, they exhibited near-perfect retention after very long delays.

Only one task provided support for the Jacksonian hypothesis. Preweanlings exhibited no spatial learning prior to 20 days of age whether they were tested in an eight-arm radial maze (Rauch & Raskin 1984) or in a Morris water maze (Schenk, Inglin & Morris 1983). Likewise, old adults failed to attain the final level of performance of young adults in the eight-arm radial maze even after extensive training (Davis, Idowu & Gibson 1983; Wallace, Krauter & Campbell 1980); similar results were found in the Morris water maze when the hidden platform was moved (Gage, Dunnett & Bjorklund 1984). These data, then, yield the inverted U-shaped function of acquisition and retention that is predicted by the Jacksonian hypothesis. (The extent to which age-related deficits in perception, motivation, or motoric competence contributed to these results is not known.)

Final Conclusions. Campbell et al. asked whether the Jacksonian hypothesis predicts the development and dissolution of memory in animals. They found that rats' memories for the two tasks that were acquired sequentially *early* in ontogeny (conditioned taste aversion, the auditory conditioned emotional response) were completely spared in aged rats. Aged rats exhibited no evidence of sequential loss. Although memory for the spatial learning task, which is acquired *late* in ontogeny, was consistently impaired in aged rats, their memory for the passive-avoidance task, which also is acquired late in ontogeny — and after the taste aversion and conditioned emotional response tasks, was not. In fact, in some passive-avoidance studies, aged rats exhibited near-perfect retention. Again, then, aged rats exhibited no evidence of sequential loss. Based on these studies, Campbell et al. concluded that there was no compelling evidence for extending the Jacksonian hypothesis to the development and dissolution of memory in animals.

The Jacksonian principle and pathology in human memory

Extending the Jacksonian principle to human memory also requires evidence that the sequential appearance and disappearance of memory capabilities follow an inverted U-shaped function. This function has long been documented in cases of human pathology. Ribot (1882) anticipated the Jacksonian principle in cognitive functioning and cited extensive anecdotal evidence that more recent memories are more vulnerable. The temporally organized dissolution of memory is illustrated in an anecdote that Ribot (1882) obtained from a physician in Philadelphia:

> "Dr. Scandella, an ingenious Italian who visited this country a few years ago, was a master of the Italian, French, and English languages. In the beginning of the yellow fever, which terminated his life...he spoke English only; in the middle of the disease, he spoke French only; but, on the day of his death, he spoke only in the language of his native country" (Ribot 1882, p. 182).

Modern data on the phenomenon of retrograde amnesia suggest that although most amnesics forget memories of at least some events that occurred before the onset of their pathology, they continue to remember events that occurred earlier in their lives. Using a questionnaire consisting of multiple-choice questions about television programs that had been broadcast for only 1 year at different times in the past, for example, Squire and Slater (1975) found that amnesics' memory for programs within the 5 to 10 years that preceded testing was poor relative to their memory for programs from the more distant past. Another example of the development and dissolution of human cognitive functioning was reported by Ajuriaguerra, Rey-Bellet-Muller and Tissot (1964), who observed that the sequence in which Piagetian abilities emerged in childhood (Piaget 1952) disappeared in the reverse order as the cognitive abilities of senile adults progressively degenerated. In general, the capacities that children acquired last over the course of development dropped out first when adults became senile.

Retrograde amnesia can also accompany more temporary amnesic states.

Scoville and Milner (1957), for example, described a middle-aged doctor (D.G.) who was densely amnesic for events that immediately followed his temporal-lobe surgery but had clear and detailed memories of his childhood and medical training. Finally, even benign senescence can be accompanied by a loss of memories for events from the recent past and the preservation of memories from childhood. In both of these cases, however, adults' preserved memories of childhood events do not include events from the early childhood period that is typically characterized by infantile amnesia (Rozin 1976).

The Jacksonian principle and multiple memory systems

Memory studies with adults

Many scientists have argued that the order in which memory systems fail in elderly and amnesic adults predicts the order in which they appear in infancy (Nadel 1990; Naito & Komatsu 1993; Parkin 1993; Schacter & Moscovitch 1984; Tulving & Schacter 1990). Nadel (1990), for example, proposed that the hippocampal system is essential for the formation of cognitive maps and that, during development, an increasingly greater proportion of it becomes functional until a threshold level of connectivity is passed and the structure as a whole can function. Invoking the Jacksonian principle, he wrote:

> "[This view] seems to provide a handle not only on the up-side of life (development), but also on the down-side (senescence, or brain damage). It is well known that many brain functions undergo what 'connectionist' modelers have come to call 'graceful degradation' with aging/damage. That is, the progressive removal of functional elements from the system has little impact until some critical extent is reached, at which point the system rapidly deteriorates. This phase transition is really the *mirror image of what is seen during early life* [italics ours]…" (p. 621).

In fact, that part of the Jacksonian principle that applies to the *hierarchical dissolution* of multiple memory systems has met with some success. Most research on the effects of age on the memory performance of healthy individuals has found that elderly adults are inferior to young adults on explicit memory tasks but perform as well as young adults on implicit memory tasks (for reviews, see Graf 1990; Light & Lavoie 1993). In particular, age-related memory deficits have been found on tests of recognition and cued recall, but age differences on various single-item priming tests have been small or absent altogether (e.g., Isingrini, Vazoiu & Leroy 1995; Java & Gardiner 1991; Light & Albertson 1989; Light & Singh 1987; Mitchell, Brown & Murphy 1990).

Mitchell and Schmitt (1992, cited in Mitchell 1993), for example, compared the memory performance of young adults, healthy older adults, and older patients with Alzheimer's disease on two explicit memory tasks (cued recall and free recall) and an implicit memory task (priming). They found that performance on the free-recall task was worse for both groups of older adults than for the younger adults, performance on the cued-recall task was the same for the younger and healthy older adults but was impaired for older adults with Alzheimer's disease; in contrast, performance on the priming task (picture-naming latencies) was equally excellent for all groups. They concluded that the brain damage associated with Alzheimer's disease hastened the dissolution of the memory system responsible for performance on the free-recall task but spared the memory system responsible for performance on the priming task.

Developmental changes in healthy young and older adults' ability to recognize specific item, location, and color information in isolation was examined by Chalfonte and Johnson (1996). Participants studied a particular feature of a set of line-drawn objects (from Snodgrass & Vanderwart 1980) that were arranged on a grid and were not in their original color. They then received a recognition test for one type of feature. For the item recognition test, they saw old and new black and white objects; for the location recognition test, they saw black Xs in old and new locations on the grid; and for the color recognition test, they saw old and new colors on rectangles. Young and older adults recognized item and color information equivalently, but older adults' recognition of location information was impaired.

Although healthy elderly adults perform more poorly than young adults on tasks that require them to retrieve factual knowledge that was presented earlier (Radvansky, Zacks & Hasher 1996), they perform as well as or better than young adults on tasks that require subjects to exhibit more global levels of understanding, for example, the ability to understand what is being referred to by the presented information (Radvansky 1999). Thus, although the decline of memory functioning in elderly adults is consistent with the Jacksonian principle, their excellent-to-superior performance on some higher-level cognitive tasks is not.

Memory studies with children

That part of the Jacksonian principle that applies to the *hierarchical development* of multiple memory systems in childhood has yielded findings that, on the surface, appear to be consistent with the Jacksonian hypothesis. When analyzed more carefully, however, the findings appear to be more inconclusive. The issue is whether or not implicit memory performance, as measured in these studies, remains stable over age. Most research on the effects of age on the performance of children on explicit and implicit memory tasks has reported that performance on recall and recognition tests improves with age, while performance on priming tests remains stable (e.g., Carroll, Byrne & Kirsner 1985; DiGiulio, Seidenberg, O'Leary & Raz 1994; Greenbaum & Graf 1989; Naito 1990; Parkin 1989; Parkin & Streete 1988). Based on this pattern, most researchers concluded that implicit memory develops earlier than explicit memory in childhood. Parkin (1993), for example, attributed the earlier appearance of implicit memory to phylogenetic influences. In doing so, he invoked Jackson's (1880) argument that the neural systems that are evolutionarily more primitive (e.g., those that mediate the organism's perceptually-based responding) are more localized than the neural systems that appeared later in evolution (e.g., those that mediate higher-level neural functions) and are more widely distributed throughout the brain. Assuming that ontogeny recapitulates phylogeny — an assumption that the noted evolutionary biologist Steven Jay Gould has vigorously disputed (Gould 1998), Parkin concluded that the phylogenetic system that is more primitive and mediates perceptually-based memory performance (i.e., implicit memory) appears earlier in development and is less susceptible to insult in old age than the phylogenetic system that mediates higher-level memory performance (i.e., explicit memory).

Studies of children's memory performance on implicit and explicit tests have increased in frequency over the last decade. Their general finding is that memory performance on implicit tests is invariant over age, whereas memory performance on explicit tests increases with age. A pervasive interpretative problem in studies of children's memory development, however, is the ready tendency of researchers to attribute age-related changes in memory performance to maturational changes in the brain. Although such changes are just as likely to reflect age-related differences in experience or language development, this possibility is rarely considered.

In a typical study (Naito 1990), groups of first-, third-, and sixth-grade children and college students were shown a list of 32 words, one per page, in a study booklet and were asked whether a word contained a particular letter and what the word's category name was. The study list was followed by a 4-min distractor task. In Experiment 1 of this study, children received a word-fragment completion test of implicit memory consisting of the original 32 words and 16 new ones. All age groups completed old items more accurately than new items, and adults completed more items than the other age groups, who did not differ; there was no interaction. In addition, whether encoding was orthographic (shallow) or elaborative (deep) did not differentially affect memory performance at any age, and the magnitude of proportional repetition priming on the implicit test was approximately the same at all ages.

In Experiment 2 of the same study, Naito repeated the preceding procedure but this time asked children to recall the words that had been on the study list — an explicit memory test. The number of words correctly recalled increased with age, and all children except the first graders recalled more words in the elaborative than in the orthographic encoding condition. Taken together, these experiments revealed that performance on implicit memory tests is stable over age and is insensitive to encoding condition, whereas performance on explicit memory tests increases with age and is affected by the conditions of encoding.

These studies, however, like most studies of children's memory development, have used verbal materials — the practice commonly followed with adults. Unfortunately, this practice has introduced a major confound into the memory data from children in terms of age differences in verbal competence. Some researchers have sidestepped this problem by testing children with pictorial stimuli. Not only is children's memory performance better when they are tested with pictures than with words (Madigan 1983), but also pictures can be used in memory tests with all ages and species (e.g., Cornell 1974; Wright, Santiago, Sands, Kendrick & Cook 1985). Mitchell (1993) performed a meta-analysis over nine developmental studies that had used pictorial stimuli and had compared at least two age groups of children or adults on both an explicit and an implicit memory test. All studies in his analysis met the retrieval intentionality criterion for distinguishing between intentional and unintentional retrieval on explicit and implicit tests, respectively (Schacter et al. 1989; see Chapter 2). In addition, all studies used recognition tests of explicit memory except two, which used cued-recall tests. The implicit memory tests that they used were picture naming, picture-fragment completion, object decision, and category exemplar generation.

Mitchell found no significant age differences in accuracy or latency on implicit tests. On the explicit tests, however, he found large age differences in accuracy that were described by an inverted U-shaped function, with older children performing significantly better than younger children (age range = 3 to 12 years) and older adults performing significantly worse than younger adults (age range = 18 to 71 years). Moreover, the memory dissociation on implicit and explicit tests was just as robust between 3 and 5 years of age as between 18 and 71 years of age. He concluded that memory performance on tasks using pictorial materials was similar to memory performance on tasks using verbal materials: Performance on explicit memory tests changes over the course of normal aging, whereas performance on implicit memory tests does not. Characterizing memory development over the life span in traditional Jacksonian terms, he wrote:

> "As the most specialized system, episodic memory is the last to develop fully in childhood. Its unique specialization, however, may also make it the most fragile, and therefore it is the first to go in the course of normal aging. Procedural memory...seem[s] to be hard-wired from the start and...[is] very hardy in surviving the effects of aging" (Mitchell 1993, p. 173).

Snodgrass (1989), however, was concerned that correct identification on picture-completion tests could arise from one or more of three sources — *pure guessing*, when subjects actually cannot identify a test item; *learning a specific association between an unrecognized fragment and its name during test trials*, so that the fragment itself actually becomes the retrieval cue; or *true perceptual learning at the time of priming*, which results from phenomenologically reexperiencing the previously studied event and retrieving it automatically and effortlessly from semantic memory. She hypothesized that true perceptual priming may reflect how correct identification is measured. Typically, researchers measure correct identification as the savings in accuracy of identifying old versus new pictures, but this could be expressed as either the *absolute difference* between the number of old and new pictures correctly identified (e.g., Jacoby & Dallas 1981; Roediger & Weldon 1987) or as the *relative difference* (the absolute difference divided by the maximum possible difference). The absolute measure disregards initial baseline performance, whereas the relative measure takes into account the total number of pictures that subjects had an opportunity to learn during testing. Using both measures to analyze a prior data set, she and her colleagues found that the relative measure provided a better fit to the data (Snodgrass, Smith, Feenan & Corwin 1987).

The particular savings measure that is used has major consequences for conclusions about whether priming changes with age. Mitchell's meta-analysis, for example, included a study by Parkin and Streete (1988) with subjects ranging from 3 years of age to young adults. When they expressed savings as the absolute difference in correct identifications of old and new items, they found that priming increased with age, but when they calculated the difference proportionally to take baseline differences into consideration (i.e., the number of items correctly identified on trial 2 minus the number of items correctly identified on trial 1/the number of items correctly identified on trial 2), they found that priming was age-invariant (see also Graf 1990). When Parkin (1993) recalculated the amount of priming in the original data set using Snodgrass's (1989) measure of relative difference, however, he again found that priming increased significantly with age.

In a subsequent study using pictorial stimuli, Russo et al. (1995) attempted to exclude potential explicit memory influences from the final estimate of implicit memory (for discussion, see Jacoby et al. 1993; Russo & Parkin 1993) and to eliminate age differences in baseline responding. In an initial experiment, preschoolers between 4 and 6 years of age and a group of young adults participated in two tasks — a picture-completion (implicit memory) task and a cued-recall (explicit memory) task. Two sets of pictures were used for the implicit task and a third set was added for the explicit task. During the study phase of both tasks, children were asked to name the objects that appeared in 12 pictures.

In the picture-completion test, children were shown up to eight versions each of the old pictures and 12 new ones and were asked to identify the objects in the pictures as quickly as possible. The most fragmented version of all objects was presented first, followed by the next most fragmented version of all objects, and so forth until the whole object was presented. Once an object was correctly identified, it was not tested further. Scoring was based on the level of fragmentation at which an object was correctly identified. For the cued-recall test, children were shown the fragmented versions of the old objects and asked to use them as cues to try and remember what they had seen during the study phase. The two ages did not perform differently on the priming test, but 6-year-olds were superior on the cued-recall test.

In a follow-up experiment, Russo et al. repeated the preceding procedure but included a group of young adults and asked all subjects to recall the pictures they had previously named before performing the picture-completion test. All age groups exhibited equivalent priming, but the number of pictures recalled increased with age. To determine whether prior recall on the explicit test had contaminated performance on the ensuing repetition priming test, separate proportional priming scores were calculated for the objects that had been recalled and for those that had not. Adults' priming scores were significantly higher for previously recalled objects, but children's priming scores were the same regardless of whether they had initially recalled the object. These data reveal that when researchers are careful to control for the potential contribution of explicit influences on implicit memory performance, implicit memory is age-invariant from at least 4 years of age (the age of the youngest children in the present study), whereas explicit memory improves with age.

More recently, researchers have used the serial reaction time (SRT) task (see Chapter 2) to study the development of implicit and explicit learning and memory (Meulemans et al. 1998; Thomas 1997). Using a within-subject design, for example, Meulemans et al. (1998) trained 6- and 10-year-olds and adults for either one session or two sessions separated by 1 week and tested their retention immediately after their last (or only) session. On each trial, subjects saw four arrows on a computer screen with a star underneath one of the arrows. They were instructed to press the button on the computer keyboard (X, C, N, M) that corresponded to the starred arrow as quickly as possible but to try to make as few mistakes as possible. Alternating blocks of 10 trials were programmed so that the sequence of starred spatial positions was either random or repeating. Immediately before the recognition test, subjects were told that one of their study sequences had been repeating. During the test, they saw eight sequences of four stimuli from the repeating-sequence condition (old) and eight sequences that they had never seen (new) and were asked to rate on a scale from 1 to 5 ("I am sure I never saw it," "I believe I never saw it," "I don't know," "I believe I saw it," "I know I saw it") whether each four-item test sequence had been part of the repeating sequence or not. As expected, RTs decreased over successive trial blocks and were faster for older subjects and on repeating than on random sequences. The pattern of RTs on the two types of sequences, however, was the same at all ages. In addition, more errors were made by children than adults and on random than on repeating sequences; this effect did not change over blocks.

One week later, RTs were significantly faster at the outset of session 2 than they had been at the end of session 1 for both 6- and 10-year-olds but not for adults, whose RTs could not decrease further. Although adults responded that they had seen a test sequence before more often than children whether it was old or new, the most frequent response was "I don't know," and performance on the recognition test was unrelated to performance during the sequence-learning task. These data, then, are consistent with prior evidence that performance on implicit tasks does not change over development and is statistically independent of performance on explicit tests of the same information.

Pictures have also been used to assess the basic features of an object that children of different ages recognize. Using exactly the same line-drawn stimuli that had been used with healthy adults (Chalfonte & Johnson 1996), Gulya,

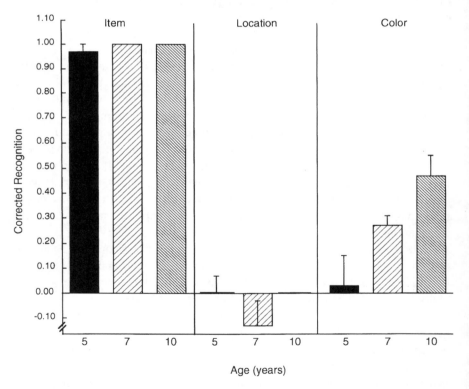

Figure 4.2. Mean corrected recognition scores for 5-, 7-, and 10-year-old children on three nonverbal feature recognition tests.

Rossi-George, Hartshorn, Rovee-Collier, Johnson and Chalfonte (submitted) obtained recognition data for the identity, color, and location of objects from 4-, 5-, 7-, and 10-year-olds and analyzed them with the data previously obtained from 19- and 70-year-olds on identical feature tests. These analyses revealed that memories for different types of features develop at different rates over the childhood period and that their decline in old age approximates the reverse order of their acquisition. As shown in Figure 4.2, item recognition was already excellent by 4–5 years of age, whereas color recognition improved significantly between 5 and 10 years of age and peaked at 10 years of age. Children's memory for location was poor at all ages, but location memory peaked at 19 years of age (see Figure 4.3). Conversely, by 70 years of age,

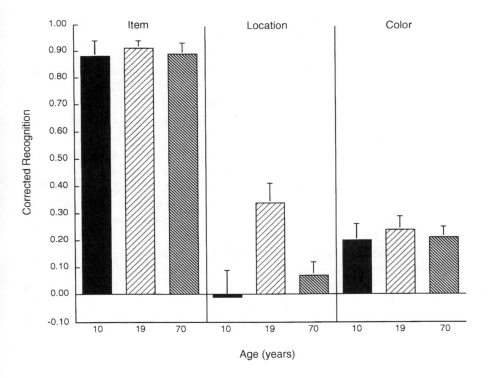

Figure 4.3. A comparison of the mean corrected recognition scores of 10-year-old children 19-year-old (*young*) adults, and 70-year-old (*elderly*) adults. An identical pencil-and-paper version of the feature recognition task with identical study and test stimuli was used with children and adults.

adults' memory for location had significantly worsened, and their color recognition had begun to decline as well, predictive of an even greater decline at older ages. Nonetheless, elderly adults' item recognition was excellent and at the same high level as that of the youngest children. This inverted U-shaped function is consistent with Jackson's first-in, last-out principle and suggests that the Jacksonian principle describes the development and dissolution of memory for individual features.

Conclusions

The Jacksonian principle states that the development and dissolution of function follow a first-in, last-out sequence. The present chapter reviewed evidence that this principle also describes the development and dissolution of memory. Studies of memory function with infant, young adult, and aged animals failed to support the Jacksonian principle. In all but one instance, the tasks that were acquired earliest in ontogeny were not learned or remembered better at other ages than the tasks that were acquired later in ontogeny. Studies with young adults and healthy elderly adults, however, found that normal memory performance declines late in adulthood on explicit but not implicit tests, and studies that were free of age confounds in verbal competence or base rates of responding found that memory performance improves during childhood on explicit tests but not implicit tests. The combined results of these studies portray explicit memory performance as an inverted-U shaped function of age and implicit memory performance as age-invariant over the major portion of the life span.

These studies, however, assessed developmental changes in implicit and explicit memory performance in individuals for whom both types of memory were already functional. They did not ask whether the onset of implicit and explicit memory function is hierarchical, which is the first half of the Jacksonian principle. To answer this question, we next will consider studies of implicit and explicit memory in infants (Chapters 5, 6, and 7).

CHAPTER 5

Development of Implicit and Explicit Memory in Nonhuman Primates

In this chapter, we review the evidence for a developmental dissociation between implicit and explicit memory in nonhuman primates. We begin with the classic study conducted by Bachevalier and Mishkin (1984) in which monkeys were shown to master one memory task substantially earlier than another during development. We then describe the neural mechanisms that are thought to underpin this age-related change in memory performance. Finally, we reconsider the notion that there is a developmental dissociation between two memory systems in nonhuman primates.

As described in Chapter 3, studies with both human and nonhuman adults have shown that damage to the medial temporal lobe results in a syndrome of global amnesia. What is particularly intriguing about this phenomenon is that adults with temporal lobe damage exhibit profound impairment on some memory tasks but little or no impairment on other memory tasks. This dissociation in memory performance has been the cornerstone for the claim that memory is not a unitary phenomenon but, rather, is comprised of at least two functionally distinct systems with different underlying neural pathways.

A second line of evidence often marshaled in support of the multiple-memory-systems view is that these systems are dissociable during the course of normal development as well, with one system emerging substantially earlier than the other (Bachevalier 1990, 1992; Nadel & Zola-Morgan 1984; Nelson 1995; Rudy 1991; Rudy & Sutherland 1989; Schacter & Moscovitch 1984). The underlying assumption here is that the neural pathways that support implicit memory mature earlier in ontogeny than the neural pathways that support explicit memory. In the present chapter, we review the empirical literature behind the claim that two memory systems emerge independently during the course of normal development in nonhuman primates. We then discuss the revisions to this claim that are required in light of recent findings. In Chapters 6 and 7, we address the issue of a developmental dissociation in the memory performance of human infants.

Historical background

The notion that there is a developmental dissociation in the memory performance of nonhuman primates began with a hallmark study by Bachevalier and Mishkin (1984). In that study, the authors traced the development of monkeys' performance on two memory tasks over the first 3 years of life. As described in Chapter 3, prior work with adult monkeys had shown that damage to the medial temporal lobe impaired performance on the delayed-nonmatching-to-sample (DNMS) task, but the same damage had no effect on performance on

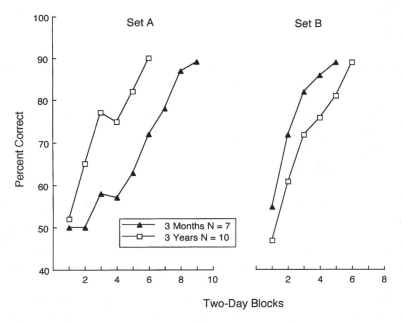

Figure 5.1. Acquisition of the 24-hour concurrent discrimination (CD) task by 3-month-old and 3-year-old monkeys. The monkeys were trained first on set A and then on set B. Each set contained 20 different pairs of stimuli (redrawn from Bachevalier and Mishkin 1984).

the 24-hour concurrent discrimination (CD) task (e.g., Malamut, Saunders & Mishkin 1984). Based on these findings, Bachevalier and Mishkin (1984) hypothesized that monkeys' ability to solve these tasks might emerge independently during development if the neural systems that supported performance on each task matured at different rates.

To test their hypothesis, Bachevalier and Mishkin (1984) compared the performance of 3- and 36-month-old monkeys on the 24-hour CD task and the performance of 3-, 6-, 12-, and 36-month-old monkeys on the DNMS task. In the CD task, monkeys were trained successively with two sets of 20 pairs of stimuli (set A, set B). On both sets, one stimulus of each pair was designated as correct, and choosing that stimulus was rewarded. The other stimulus in the pair was designated as incorrect; choosing that stimulus was not rewarded. Within each daily session, a pair of stimuli was presented only once. Acquisition of the CD task is shown in Figure 5.1. Although 3-month-olds were slower than 3-year-olds to learn the task when trained with set A (see Fig-

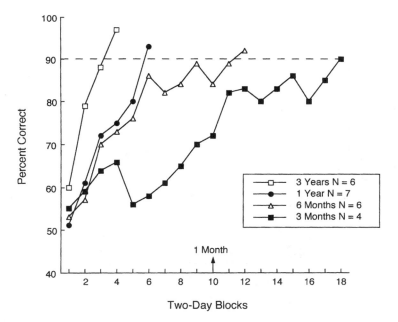

Figure 5.2. Number of days required by 3-, 6-, 12-, and 36-month-old monkeys to learn the delayed-nonmatching-to-sample (DNMS) task. The dashed line represents criterial levels of performance (redrawn from Bachevalier and Mishkin 1984).

ure 5.1, *left panel*), there was no age-related difference in the number of sessions required to learn set B (see Figure 5.1, *right panel*).

In contrast to performance on the CD task, Bachevalier and Mishkin (1984) documented a significant age-related difference in the number of days required for monkeys to learn the DNMS task. Three-year-old monkeys reached criterion (90% correct) on the DNMS task after only 8 days of training, whereas 3-month-olds required 36 days of training to achieve the same level of performance (see Figure 5.2). The performance of 6- and 12-month-olds was intermediate between these two age extremes. When tested after a 15-day retention interval, there was an inverse relation between age and the number of trials required for animals to relearn the task (see Figure 5.3). Furthermore, younger animals were more impaired than older animals when the delay between the sample and the test stimuli was increased from 10 to 120 s (see Figure 5.4) and when the list length was increased.

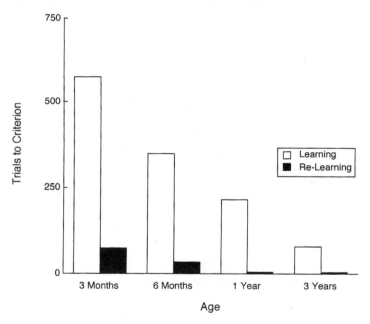

Figure 5.3. Number of trials required by 3-, 6-, 12-, and 36-month-old monkeys to learn (*open columns*) the delayed-nonmatching-to-sample (DNMS) task and to relearn (*shaded columns*) the same task after a 15-day rest period (redrawn from Bachevalier and Mishkin 1984).

On the basis of these findings, Bachevalier and Mishkin (1984) drew two conclusions. First, given that the monkeys succeeded on the CD task long before they succeeded on the DNMS task, Bachevalier and Mishkin concluded that one neural system, which they called *the habit system*, emerged earlier in development than the other neural system, which they called *the memory system*. Using the terminology adopted in the present book, *the habit system* is roughly equivalent to *implicit memory*, and *the memory system* is roughly equivalent to *explicit memory*. Second, given that adult monkeys with lesions of the medial temporal lobe (including the hippocampus) are impaired when tested on the DNMS task but not on the 24-hour CD task, Bachevalier and Mishkin (1984) attributed the delayed development of DNMS performance to the delayed maturation of the hippocampus.

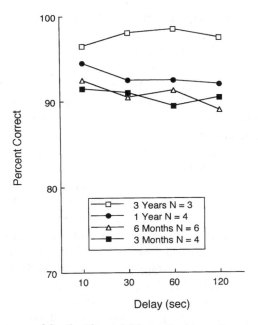

Figure 5.4. Performance of 3-, 6-, 12-, and 36-month-old monkeys on the delayed-non-matching-to-sample (DNMS) task with delays of 10, 30, 60, and 120 s (redrawn from Bachevalier and Mishkin 1984).

The impact of Bachevalier and Mishkin's (1984) study cannot be overestimated. Since its publication, this paper has been used as *prima facia* evidence of a developmental dissociation of memory function in nonhuman primates. Subsequent research by Bachevalier, Mishkin, and others, however, has challenged the original conclusion that maturation of the hippocampus is responsible for the emergence of DNMS performance. Research with adult monkeys, for example, has suggested that the hippocampus plays little or no role in DNMS performance (see Chapter 3). Furthermore, recent behavioral research has shown that successful memory performance on a response-to-novelty task that is procedurally similar to DNMS emerges very early during development. In fact, a careful review of Bachevalier and Mishkin's (1984) original data raises fundamental questions about the issue of a developmental dissociation between the two putative memory systems of nonhuman primates per se.

Maturation of the hippocampus and DNMS performance

Bachevalier and Mishkin (1984) originally assumed that the slow emergence of DNMS performance was due to the late development of the hippocampus. Subsequent research, however, has shown that the time-table for hippocampal maturation does not match the time-table for mastery on the DNMS task in nonhuman primates. Bachevalier and Mishkin's original assumption that the hippocampus matured late in ontogeny was based primarily on anatomical studies that had been conducted with rodents (Nadel & Zola-Morgan 1984). Similar studies with nonhuman primates, however, have revealed that the hippocampus matures relatively early in development (Bachevalier, Ungerleider, O'Neill & Friedman 1986; Diamond 1990a). Although only 15% of the neurons in the dentate gyrus (a component of the hippocampus) are present at birth in the rat, 80% of these neurons are present at birth in the monkey (Rakic & Nowakowski 1981). Furthermore, the opiate and muscarinic receptor-binding sites in the hippocampus of the nonhuman primate brain at birth are virtually identical to those found in the adult brain (Bachevalier et al. 1986; O'Neill, Friedman, Bachevalier & Ungerleider 1986).

Studies using lesion techniques have also challenged links between the development of DNMS performance and hippocampal maturation. The rationale behind these studies was that lesions of the hippocampus during infancy should be less disruptive than the same lesions performed during adulthood if the hippocampus did not mature until late in ontogeny. Contrary to Bachevalier and Mishkin's original hypothesis, however, neonatal lesions of the medial temporal lobe have been found to severely impair performance on the DNMS task (Bachevalier & Mishkin 1994; Malkova, Mishkin & Bachevalier 1995). As shown in Figure 5.5, infants who received bilateral lesions of the medial temporal lobe during the first month of life were impaired on the DNMS task when they were tested for the first time at 10 months of age (Bachevalier & Mishkin 1994), and they continued to be impaired when they were retested at 4 to 5 years of age (Malkova et al. 1995). In fact, the effect of neonatal lesions on DNMS performance is virtually identical to the effect of adult lesions on performance in the same task (Mishkin 1978; Mishkin & Philips 1990).

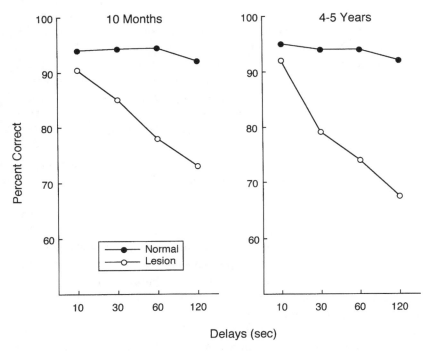

Figure 5.5. The delayed-nonmatching-to-sample (DNMS) performance of rhesus monkeys following neonatal lesions of the medial temporal lobe and of normal controls (redrawn from Malkova et al. 1995).

Finally, the involvement of the hippocampus in DNMS performance per se has recently been challenged by studies with both nonhuman primate adults and infants. Although lesions of the entire medial temporal lobe produce severe impairments in DNMS performance by adult monkeys, lesions restricted to the hippocampus alone produce little (Alvarez et al. 1995) or no (Murray & Mishkin 1998) effect. Similarly, although neonatal lesions of the entire medial temporal lobe produce severe impairments in DNMS performance by juveniles and young adults (see Figure 5.5), neonatal lesions that are restricted to the hippocampus do not (Bachevalier, Beauregard & Alvarado, in press). Taken together, these findings suggest that maturation of the hippocampus is not requisite either for DNMS performance by adults or for the emergence of DNMS performance during development.

In light of these findings, Bachevalier (1992; Bachevalier, Malkova & Beauregard 1996) has revised her view of the neural basis of the development of visual recognition memory. She has recently proposed that maturation of brain area TE, rather than maturation of the hippocampus, may underlie the development of DNMS performance. In a series of experiments, Bachevalier and her colleagues have shown that, in contrast to adult lesions of area TE, neonatal lesions of the same area have only a mild and transitory effect on DNMS performance (Bachevalier, Brickson, Hagger & Mishkin 1990). These data suggest that, unlike the medial temporal lobe, area TE exhibits a high level of plasticity during infancy, indicating that this region of the primate brain is still functionally immature for some time after birth.

Although Bachevalier's more recent data suggest that maturation of area TE, rather than maturation of the medial temporal lobe, may influence age-related changes in DNMS performance, this finding does not address the issue of a developmental dissociation between the memory systems of nonhuman primates per se. Although neonatal lesions of area TE have no effect on DNMS performance (i.e., *the explicit memory task*), for example, they also have no effect on CD performance (i.e., *the implicit memory task*) (Bachevalier 1992; Bachevalier & Mishkin 1994; Malkova et al. 1995). Furthermore, adult lesions of area TE impair performance on both the DNMS and CD tasks (Bachevalier 1992). Given that lesions of area TE do not produce a dissociation in performance on the two tasks, the finding that area TE is immature at birth has no bearing on the issue of a dissociation in the development of the habit and memory systems.

DNMS performance as a measure of explicit memory

Bachevalier and Mishkin's (1984) original conclusion regarding the developmental dissociation of two memory systems was based exclusively on monkeys' performance on two tasks — 24-hour CD and DNMS. Subsequent research that has used another recognition memory procedure has challenged the view that explicit memory is a late-developing system. The *visual paired-comparison (VPC) task* was originally developed for use with human infants (see Chapter 6). In this task, participants are familiarized with a given stimulus for a brief period of time. Following a delay, they are simultaneously presented with two stimuli — the familiar one and a novel one, and their visual behavior toward both is recorded. If subjects spend proportionally more time looking at the novel stimulus during the test, then the researcher infers that they recognized the familiar one (Fagan 1970, 1973).

Gunderson and her colleagues were the first to use the visual paired-comparison task with nonhuman primates (Gunderson & Sackett 1984; Gunderson & Swartz 1985, 1986). In the first study of this kind, infant pigtailed macaques were tested using a VPC procedure similar to that used with human infants (Gunderson & Sackett 1984). During familiarization, monkeys were exposed to a black-and-white patterned stimulus for 60 s. Following a 30-s delay, infants were tested simultaneously with the familiar stimulus and a novel one. Each infant received five familiarization and test trials. Infants who were 4 weeks old (*middle*) or older (*old*) at the time of testing exhibited a significant novelty preference, but infants who were younger (*young*) did not (see Figure 5.6). Subsequent research has shown that infants as young as 6 weeks of age can exhibit a novelty preference after a 30-s delay after as little as 5 s of familiarization time; infants of the same age can exhibit a novelty preference after a 24-hour delay after as little as 45 s of familiarization time (Gunderson & Swartz 1986).

Bachevalier (1990) has also used the VPC task to study the development of visual recognition memory in infant rhesus monkeys. In her experiment, infants were familiarized and tested with three-dimensional objects. During the familiarization phase of each trial, the infant was shown a pair of identical objects for 30 s. Following a 10-s delay, the familiar object and a novel one were presented together during a 10-s paired-comparison test. After an intertrial interval of 20 s, the infant was familiarized with another object, and so forth, for a total of 10 trials. The amount of time that infants fixated the

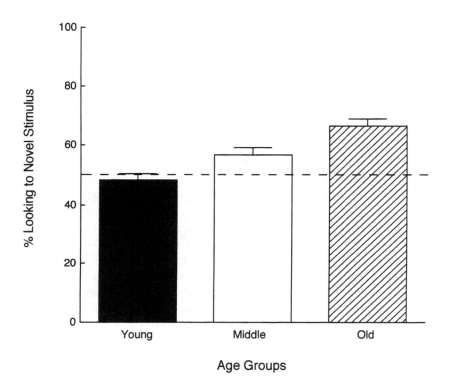

Figure 5.6. Mean percent fixation time to the novel test stimulus in younger (Young: 1 to 2 weeks old), intermediate-aged (Middle: 4 weeks old), and older (Old: 13 weeks old) infant pigtailed macaques tested in a visual paired-comparison task (redrawn from Gunderson and Sackett 1984).

familiar and the novel objects during the test was recorded.

The novelty-preference scores (percent time spent looking at the novel stimulus) obtained by Bachevalier (1990) are shown in Figure 5.7 as a function of age and gender. Clearly, novelty preference increased as a function of age. Although 5-day-old monkeys did not exhibit a reliable preference for the novel stimulus during the test, 30-day-old monkeys did. Furthermore, 15-day-old females — but not 15-day-old males — also exhibited a preference for the novel stimulus during the test.

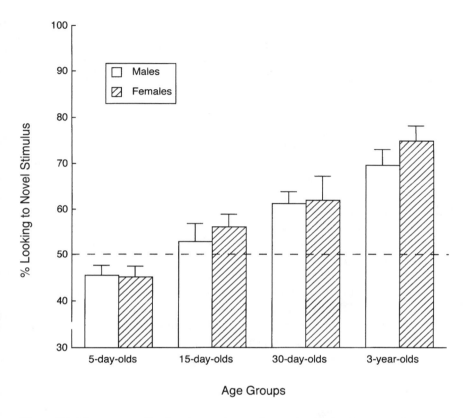

Figure 5.7. Mean percent fixation time to the novel test stimulus by rhesus monkeys tested in a visual paired-comparison (VPC) task as a function of age and gender (redrawn from Bachevalier 1990).

The developmental time course for visual recognition memory as assessed by the VPC task stands in stark contrast to the developmental time course for visual recognition memory as assessed by the DNMS task and originally reported by Bachevalier and Mishkin (1984). It is important to bear in mind that the VPC task is *conceptually identical* to the DNMS task. In both tasks, subjects are initially exposed to a single stimulus and then select the novel stimulus during the test phase. The two tasks differ only in the test phase: In the DNMS task, the subject *reaches* for the novel stimulus, whereas in the VPC task, the subject *looks* at the novel stimulus. In addition to their procedural similarity, the underlying neural mechanisms that are required to solve both tasks are similar. Lesions of the medial temporal lobe, for example, disrupt memory performance on the VPC task (Bachevalier, Brickson & Hagger 1993), just as they disrupt memory performance on the DNMS task (Bachevalier 1992).

Because the VPC and DNMS tasks are so similar, the findings obtained by Gunderson (Gunderson & Sackett 1984; Gunderson & Swartz 1985, 1986) and Bachevalier (1990) challenge the proposal that recognition memory (i.e., *explicit memory*) does not emerge in nonhuman primates until 4 months of age (Bachevalier & Mishkin 1984). Obviously, the ability of nonhuman primates to remember a stimulus even after a 24-hour delay is present substantially earlier than is predicted by findings obtained using standard DNMS procedures (see also Bachevalier et al. 1993). Researchers now recognize that some ability other than the development of explicit memory contributes to the relatively late emergence of DNMS performance (Diamond 1990a, 1995; Diamond, Churchland, Cruess & Kirkham 1999).

At least one possible explanation for the discrepancy in performance on tasks of VPC and DNMS is that an inability to inhibit a previously rewarded response contributes to young infants' persistent failure on the task. Recall that in the DNMS procedure, subjects are reinforced for displacing the sample stimulus during the first phase of the experiment, but they are reinforced for displacing the *other* stimulus during the test. Thus, within the same trial, responding to the sample stimulus is correct in one phase but is incorrect in the other. The recent finding that lesions of the frontal lobe impair performance on the DNMS task in adult monkeys provides some support for the conclusion that inhibition is required for success on the DNMS task (Malkova, Bachevalier, Webster & Mishkin, in press). Furthermore, recent studies with human infants have shown that if infants are not reinforced for displacing the sample stimulus during the initial phase of the trial, then they can succeed on the DNMS task at the same early age as they succeed on the VPC task (Diamond 1995; see Chapter 6).

In conclusion, despite the seductive nature of Bachevalier and Mishkin's (1984) original findings, it is now clear that age-related changes in performance on the DNMS task are due in large part to processes other than memory. As such, the emergence of DNMS performance during development should not be used as a yardstick for the emergence of a fundamentally different memory system.

The developmental dissociation revisited

Bachevalier and Mishkin's (1984) seminal paper set the stage for more than a decade of research on the developmental dissociation of memory systems. More recent research has challenged both the underlying neural mechanism thought to be responsible for their findings as well as the notion of the developmental dissociation per se. In fact, Bachevalier and Mishkin's original data foreshadowed questions regarding a developmental dissociation between memory systems.

Consider first the original Bachevalier and Mishkin (1984) finding that younger animals were not impaired relative to older animals in the acquisition of a 24-hour CD task. Recall that the monkeys were actually trained in succession on two 24-hour CD tasks, each using a different set of stimuli (set A, set B). Although there was no age-related difference in the speed with which the monkeys learned set B, younger monkeys learned set A more slowly. This procedure may have contributed to early success on the CD task. With this in mind, it is possible that had the younger animals also been given a second exposure to the DNMS task (with new stimuli), they might have learned the second task as quickly as adult monkeys.

In addition, although the older monkeys clearly learned the DNMS task faster than the younger monkeys (see Figure 5.2), it is important to keep in mind that even the youngest monkeys *eventually* learned the DNMS task to the same 90% level of performance. Although the authors argue that the infants were not able to learn the task until they were at least 4 months old, even at 3 months of age, infants performed above chance and showed a steady improvement in performance across their first month of training. Furthermore, although the younger animals required more trials than older animals to relearn the DNMS task after a 15-day retention interval (see Figure 5.3), even the youngest animals exhibited substantial savings. Finally, although performance by the infants was inferior to that of the 3-year-olds when the delay between the sample and the test was increased, even the youngest animals were approximately 90% correct when tested after a 120-s delay (see Figure 5.4). Taken together, these findings demonstrate that although infants' performance on the DNMS task was statistically poorer than that of adults, by all accounts, they still performed remarkably well.

Conclusions

The hypothesis that two or more memory systems develop independently and at different rates in nonhuman primates is no longer tenable. When monkeys were tested on the VPC task, for example, they exhibited long-term (i.e., 24-hour) recognition memory as early as 1 month of age — well before they could even be tested in either the CD task or the DNMS task. Although monkeys clearly master some tasks earlier in life than others, these differential rates of mastery do not reflect the emergence of different memory systems, but the emergence of different processes other than memory that are required to perform the tasks. Although successful performance on the 24-hour CD and DNMS tasks requires the same degree of perception, attention, and motivation as well as the same target response (i.e., reaching), the two tasks differ on a number of other dimensions that may contribute to infants' differential rate of success on them. One process that is likely to contribute to the protracted development of DNMS performance is inhibition. When infants are not required to inhibit responding to a previously rewarded object (as, for example, in the VPC task), visual recognition (explicit) memory emerges very early in development.

Perhaps the best test of the hypothesis that age-related changes in inhibition rather than in memory underlie the late emergence of successful performance on the DNMS task would be to compare performance on the DNMS task with performance on the delayed-matching-to-sample (DMS) task. In the DMS task, monkeys are rewarded for choosing the test stimulus that is the *same* as the sample stimulus. In other respects, however, the DMS task is identical to the DNMS task with the exception that monkeys are not required to *inhibit* responding to a previously rewarded stimulus. If inhibition is the basis for the late emergence of successful DNMS performance, then monkeys should succeed on the DMS task considerably earlier than on the DNMS task. We are currently exploring this possibility.

CHAPTER 6

Development of Implicit and Explicit Memory in Human Infants

In this chapter, we review some of the experimental procedures that have been used to study memory in human infants. We then outline the classic claims that have been made regarding the similarity of memory in human infants and adult amnesics and consider the challenges that recent data have presented for these claims. Finally, we evaluate the adequacy of the analogy between infants and amnesics by discussing the problems associated with inferring conscious recollection on the part of preverbal infants.

The view that memory is comprised of two independent and functionally distinct systems has had a profound influence on theories of infant memory development. Psychologists from a number of different theoretical persuasions have postulated that these two memory systems mature at different rates during the infancy period (Mandler 1990; McKee & Squire 1993; Naito & Komatsu 1993; Nelson 1995; Parkin 1989, 1993; Schacter & Moscovitch 1984; Tulving 1983; Tulving & Schacter 1990). Specifically, all claim that young human infants possess only an implicit memory system prior to approximately 9 months of age, after which time they gain access to the more advanced explicit memory system. In this chapter, we evaluate the validity of this claim.

Not surprisingly, the empirical study of memory in preverbal human infants has been fraught with both procedural and interpretive problems. As in studies with rats and monkeys, for example, memory must be inferred from nonverbal behavior alone. Furthermore, although age differences in task performance are typically attributed to differences in memory, subsequent investigation has often revealed that these differences actually reflect age differences in the task demands, the degree of motor coordination that the particular version of a task requires, or particular task parameters.

Memory tasks used with preverbal infants

Below we describe some of the tasks that have been used in studies of memory with preverbal infants. Our review is selective (for a complete review, see Rovee-Collier & Hayne, 2000) and focuses on tasks with direct implications for the development of implicit and explicit memory.

Response-to-novelty tasks

The two classic response-to-novelty tasks that have been used to study infant visual recognition memory are the *paired-comparison task* and the *habituation task*, which exploit the young infant's propensity to look at novel stimuli. Conceptually, both tasks are based on Sokolov's (1963) model of habituation of the orienting reflex. In this model, each time a stimulus is encountered, an internal representation or *engram* of it is established. Over successive encounters with the same stimulus, the initial representation is gradually fleshed out by new information that the subject notices about the stimulus. As the representation becomes progressively more complete, subjects attend to the external stimulus less and less; once the representation is complete (i.e., no new information remains to be added to it), then subjects no longer orient to it. As the representation decays over time (i.e., *forgetting*), subjects renew orienting to the extent that the internal representation and the external stimulus no longer match. In most response-to-novelty studies conducted with human infants, the primary dependent variable is visual attention. The measure of retention of a previously encountered visual stimulus is inferred from the extent to which an infant does not look at it but directs attention elsewhere, exhibiting a *novelty preference*.

Paired-Comparison Task. Fagan (1970) was the first to study infant memory using a novelty-preference procedure, which he adapted from Fantz's (1956) original pioneering work on infants' visual preferences. In this procedure, infants are initially exposed to a particular stimulus for a fixed duration or until they have accumulated a specified amount of time looking at it. Immediately afterward, infants are tested with two stimuli presented simultaneously for two trials (counterbalancing for the side of the novel stimulus) (see Figure 6.1). One stimulus is the previously exposed one (i.e., familiar), and one is novel.

Figure 6.1. The paired-comparison response-to-novelty task with a 6-month-old infant. The infant was previously shown two identical pictures (e.g., of the woman's face). Immediately afterward, the infant received a paired-comparison test, shown here, with the previously exposed picture (the woman's face) and a novel one (the man's face). Proportionally longer looking at the novel picture — a novelty preference — is taken as evidence that the infant recognized the preexposed one. (Test photographs courtesy of J.F. Fagan, III.)

The proportion of time that infants spend looking at the novel member of the test pair is statistically compared with chance (50% of total looking time). Proportionally longer looking at a novel stimulus than at the preexposed one is taken as evidence that infants recognize the preexposed stimulus. Some researchers have argued, however, that proportionally longer looking at the preexposed stimulus also indicates that infants recognize that stimulus because a familiarity preference represents nonchance attention (Cohen & Gelber 1975; Colombo & Bundy 1983; Hunter & Ames 1988; Weizmann, Cohen & Pratt 1971). For infants of all ages, proportionally equivalent looking at the novel and the preexposed stimulus is taken as evidence of forgetting.

Habituation Task. In the habituation task, a stimulus is repeatedly presented until infants' attention to it has declined to some absolute (e.g., McCall,

Kennedy & Dodds 1977) or relative (e.g., Cohen, DeLoache & Pearl 1977) level. At this point, some infants are presented with a novel stimulus, whereas others are again presented with the original one. Greater looking at the novel stimulus is again taken as evidence that infants remember the preexposed (habituation) stimulus. As the delay increases between the last habituation trial and the test with the original stimulus, infants increasingly respond to it. At some point, the infant's responding returns to the level that was seen at the outset of the habituation trials. Because the original stimulus is physically absent when infants are tested with the novel one, the habituation procedure incurs a greater memory load than the paired-comparison procedure.

Infants' response to novelty in paired-comparison and habituation tasks is usually measured within a single brief session, and the novel stimulus is presented within seconds of infants' prior exposure to the other stimulus. Under these conditions, the task provides a measure of short-term memory. When familiarization with the preexposed stimulus occurs over multiple daily sessions (Fagan 1970, 1973) or when testing occurs across sessions that are separated by days or weeks (Bahrick & Pickens 1995; Bahrick, Hernandez-Reif & Pickens 1997; Pascalis & DeSchonen 1994), then long-term memory is implicated.

Long-Term Familiarization Task. Long-term familiarization is procedurally similar to habituation except that infants are preexposed to a stimulus over a period of 1 or more days before the final test. During the initial preexposure phase, the experimenter does not record responding and often is not even present. In a sense, the long-term familiarization procedure provides a degree of ecological validity to formal laboratory studies in which stimulus exposure is highly controlled and typically very brief.

Hunt and his colleagues (Hunt 1970; Hunt & Uzgiris 1964; Kaplan 1967; Uzgiris & Hunt 1970), for example, used a long-term familiarization task with infants in their classic studies of the development of visual attention. Kaplan, for example, exposed infants twice daily between 8 and 14 weeks of age to a nonmoving mobile, a continuously moving mobile, or a mobile that moved in response to their own activity. Every 2 weeks, she gave them a 4-min paired-comparison test with the familiar and a novel mobile (both nonmoving) 24 hours after their last exposure. Until infants were 12 weeks old, they showed no differential fixations to novel and familiar mobiles, when they fixated novel mobiles longer. However, the type of movement infants saw during familiarization interacted with stimulus novelty: Infants familiarized with continuously moving mobiles showed no novelty preference, those familiarized with a nonmoving mobile showed a slight novelty preference, and infants familiarized with the responsive mobile looked twice as long at the novel mobile. This result revealed that, after long-term familiarization, young infants could exhibit 24-hour retention.

Newborns can also retain information about speech stimuli to which they were exposed in utero. DeCasper and Fifer (1980), for example, tested newborns in an operant procedure in which high-amplitude sucking on a nonnutritive nipple turned on a tape-recording of either their own mother's voice or the voice of another mother. During testing 33 hours after birth, newborns displayed an operant preference, sucking more to hear the voice that they had heard *in utero*. In another study, pregnant women recited aloud a passage from a Dr. Seuss book twice daily during their last 6 weeks of pregnancy, and their newborns were tested approximately 56 hours after birth (DeCasper & Spence 1986). During testing, infants could suck to present either the preexposed passage or a novel Dr. Seuss passage that was read by either their own mother or another mother. A control group that was not prenatally exposed to the target passage could also listen to the mother read both passages. Again, both prenatally-exposed groups sucked more to hear the familiar Dr. Seuss passage (the one to which they were exposed *in utero*) than the novel one, irrespective of who read it, revealing that speaker familiarity did not account for their operant preference. In contrast, the control group displayed no operant preference. These studies clearly reveal that memories for both the speaker and a complex pattern of speech sounds can be established *in utero* and can be retained for at least 2 days after birth.

Using a long-term familiarization procedure, other investigators have found that infants can recognize their mother's face and discriminate it from the face of another woman within 3 to 4 days after birth (Field, Cohen, Garcia & Greenberg 1984; Pascalis, DeSchonen, Morton, Deruelle & Fabre-Grenet 1995).

Delayed-nonmatching-to-sample (DNMS) task

The standard DNMS task that has been used with human infants is procedurally identical to the standard DNMS procedure that has been used with nonhuman primates (see Chapter 3 and 5). Briefly, infants participate in two kinds of trials. On sample trials, the sample object is placed over a well that contains a reward. After the infant removes the sample and finds the reward, a screen is lowered between the infant and the sample object. After a delay, the screen is raised revealing the sample and a novel object. On these test trials, the reward is always hidden under the novel object. If the infant responds correctly by displacing the novel object, then he or she is allowed to retrieve the reward. If the infant responds incorrectly, then the experimenter reveals the reward under the novel object but does not let the infant have it. Typically, a new pair of objects is used on every trial (i.e., trial-unique stimuli). The maximum delay after which an infant responds correctly is the measure of memory.

Human infants do not succeed on the standard version of the DNMS task until midway through their second year of life. In most studies, they do not reliably choose the novel stimulus until approximately 15 to 21 months of age, even when the delay between the sample trial and the test trial is only 5 to 10 s (Diamond, Towle & Boyer 1994; Overman, Bachevalier, Turner & Peuster 1992). Even after younger infants have mastered the task at these short delays, their performance is still disrupted by delays of 30 s and longer.

The prolonged time course for the development of DNMS during the infancy period is surprising in view of the procedural similarity between this task and the visual paired-comparison task. In both tasks, the infant is required to respond to the novel stimulus during the test. Subsequent research has shown that minor changes in the behavioral requirements of the DNMS task can dramatically alter its developmental time course (Diamond 1995; Diamond et al. 1999). In the traditional version of the DNMS task, for example, infants are required to displace the novel test stimulus in order to retrieve a reward that is placed beneath it. Alternatively, when the infant's reward is simply the opportunity to play with the novel test stimulus (i.e., stimulus = reward), infants solve the task at 6 months of age and perform significantly above chance after delays as long as 10 min (Diamond 1995). Their performance on the modified version of the DNMS task is virtually identical to their performance on the standard response-to-novelty paired-comparison task. Similarly, infants' performance on the task is also enhanced when verbal praise of the correct choice is used as a reward (Diamond et al. 1999). Taken together, these findings have led Diamond (1990b, 1995; Diamond et al. 1999) to conclude that some ability other than memory contributes to the developmental lag in DNMS performance on the standard task.

Object search task (A-not-B)

The A-not-B search task was originally introduced by Piaget (1954) and has resurfaced as another method for studying memory development in infants and young children (Diamond 1985; Fox, Kagan & Weiskopf 1979; Gratch & Landers 1971). In the standard version of the task, the infant is seated between two identical wells (A, B) where an object can be hidden. The experimenter shows the infant an object, places it in well A as the infant watches, and simultaneously covers both wells. After a delay, the infant is permitted to reach. Infants reaching to the empty well are shown the object in the other well but are not given it. The experimenter continues to hide the object in well A until criterion is achieved (e.g., a correct response on two consecutive trials), at which point the procedure is repeated with the object hidden in well B. After the hiding well is reversed, infants often continue to search in well A, despite having watched the experimenter place it in well B. This behavior is called the *A-not-B error*.

When infants are tested in this version of the object search task, the frequency of the A-not-B error increases as a function of delay, and older infants tolerate increasingly longer delays between hiding and reaching. Diamond (1985), for example, found that infants who were tested cross-sectionally tolerated delays of 1 to 2 s at 7 months, 5 s at 9 months, and 10 s at 12 months, whereas infants tested longitudinally tolerated slightly longer delays. Irrespective of the experimental design, however, the delay at which the A-not-B error occurred increased gradually and continuously at the rate of approximately 2 s per month.

As in DNMS studies, seemingly minor variations in the task parameters produce dramatically different estimates of retention (for review, see Diamond 1990a). These variations have included the use of multiple wells (Diamond, Cruttenden & Niederman 1989) and the substitution of a different object for the object that infants either saw hidden or heard named (Ramsay & Campos 1978). Considered in the light of similar findings obtained with the DNMS task, these results suggest that developmental improvement on object search tasks is due not only to age-related changes in memory ability but to nonmemorial factors as well.

Delayed response task

The delayed response task was introduced by Hunter (1913) as a measure of "sensory thought" in animals and children. In the original study, Hunter hid a food reward behind one of three doors. A light over the door signaled the location of the reward. After the light was turned off, a delay was imposed before subjects were allowed to respond. The maximum delay tolerated was 50 s (after 507 trials) at 30 months of age and 25 min (after 15 to 46 trials) at 6 to 8 years of age; however, all children initially encountered difficulty after delays of 4 to 6 s. Subsequently, Hunter (1917) used delays ranging from 3 to 35 s with a child between 13 and 16 months of age who lacked vocal language. Here, the child watched the experimenter hide an object in one of three hinged boxes. During the delay, which was timed from when the lid was shut, the child was distracted. Between 13 and 15 months of age, the child tolerated a 12-s delay; at 16 months, she tolerated a 24-s delay.

The procedures used in the delayed response task and the object search task, described above, are almost identical. They differ in that the hiding location is randomly determined across trials in the delayed response task, whereas hiding at B occurs only after infants have learned to search successfully at A in the object search task. Not surprisingly, infants' performance on these tasks is also almost identical (Diamond 1990b; Diamond & Doar 1989). Across ages, the length of the delay that was tolerated in both tasks increased gradually (see Figure 6.2); within a given age, the maximum delay that was tolerated in both tasks was the same.

In studies using visual behavior instead of reaching as the dependent measure, infants have exhibited retention at a younger age and after much longer delays. In a series of experiments conducted by Baillargeon and her colleagues (Baillargeon & Graber 1988; Baillargeon, DeVos & Graber 1989), for example, 8-month-olds were presented with an object at one of two locations on a portable stage. Identical screens were then placed in front of each location; behind one screen was the object, and behind the other, there was nothing. After a 15-s delay, infants watched a hand retrieve the object either from behind the screen where it had originally been hidden (the *possible event*) or from behind the other screen (the *impossible event*). Infants looked significantly longer at the impossible event, suggesting that they remembered the location of the original object and were surprised when they saw it retrieved from the other location.

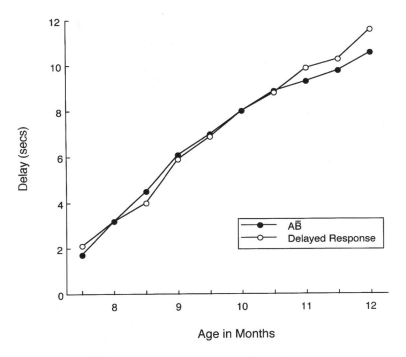

Figure 6.2. Developmental progression in the delay that human infants can tolerate in the delayed response and A-not-B tasks (redrawn from Diamond 1990b).

Even younger infants succeed in reaching versions of the delayed response task if they are required to reach for the object directly rather than to remove a cover to retrieve it. In an experiment with 5-month-olds — the youngest age at which infants reliably engage in visually-guided reaching — Hood and Willatts (1986) showed infants an object at one of two locations and then turned off the lights and removed the object. After the lights were turned back on, infants reached more to the side where the object had been. Goubet and Clifton (1998), also using a cover of darkness, similarly found that young infants could remember an object's prior location. In their study, a noisy ball rolled down one of two Plexiglas tubes on either the left or right of midline before landing silently in a tray, where infants could retrieve it. When tested in the dark, 6½-month-olds who had previously practiced in the light reaching directionally reached significantly more to the correct side and corrected their search errors significantly more often than controls who had practiced reaching to midline in the light.

Classical conditioning tasks

Most of the early studies of classical conditioning (Pavlov 1927) with infants were single-subject studies, and those that tracked an individual's conditioning performance over substantial periods of time provided evidence of long-term memory. In a hallmark study of this kind, Watson and Rayner (1920) sounded a loud gong (the *unconditioned stimulus*, or UCS) which produced crying and withdrawal (the *unconditioned response*, or UCR) when an 11-month-old infant named Albert touched a white rat (the *conditioned stimulus*, or CS). This procedure occurred twice. One week later, Albert still withdrew his hand when tested with the rat (the *conditioned response*, or CR); in this session, he also received five more CS-UCS pairings. Five days later, Albert exhibited CRs when tested with the rat as well as with previously neutral stimuli that resembled it in some way (a rabbit, a dog, a fur coat, a Santa Claus mask, and cotton wool) but not to perceptually different stimuli (wooden blocks). Ten days later, his CR to the rat had become so muted that it was freshened with another CS-UCS pairing. Also at this time, the UCS was explicitly paired once each with the rabbit and the dog. One month later, Albert still exhibited strong CRs to the rat, dog, mask, and fur coat.

In another early study of classical conditioning, Jones (1930) exposed a 7-month-old infant to repeated pairings of a tapping sound (the CS) and an electrotactual stimulus (the UCS) for five sessions over consecutive days. The CR, an anticipatory galvanic skin reflex, was established midway through session 1. Jones found that the infant still exhibited the CR 6 weeks later despite receiving no additional conditioning trials in the interim. Moreover, the CR had not completely disappeared 7 weeks after training was over. Later, Kantrow (1937) reported that an infant less than 10 days old still exhibited a conditioned leg flexion (CR) to a tone (CS) 18 days after the final conditioning session.

The most widely studied response in the classical conditioning literature, irrespective of species or age, is the eyeblink response — a protective reflex. When the UCS is a corneal air puff, the CR that immediately anticipates the UCS is also a functional avoidance response. Many of the early failures to establish a conditioned eyelid reflex in infants undoubtedly resulted from use of a nonoptimal interstimulus interval (ISI). Little (1970) found that the optimal interval for eyelid conditioning in newborn infants is three to four times longer than the 500-ms ISI that is optimal for eyelid conditioning in studies with human and nonhuman adults (Kimble 1961; Solomon, Pomerleau, Bennett, James & Morse 1989). Similar evidence that younger organisms require longer ISIs was also found with nonprimate infants (Caldwell & Werboff 1962).

The finding that more immature organisms actually require *longer* ISIs in order to exhibit classical conditioning is at odds with Schacter and Moscovitch's (1984) original conclusion that,

> "the absence of a functioning late memory system may create difficulty even in simple conditioning tasks when reinforcement is delayed or the intertrial interval is lengthened" (p. 196).

Apparently, the longer ISIs required to produce classical conditioning in immature subjects reflects an age-related change in synaptic efficacy. Kandel and Hawkins (1992), for example, found that the 500-ms interval that promotes classical conditioning of the gill-withdrawal reflex in *Aplysia* is related to:

> "the time during which calcium is elevated in the presynaptic terminal and binds to calmodulin so as to prime the adenylyl cyclase to produce more cyclic AMP in response to serotonin" (p. 84).

Their conclusion that cyclic AMP is critically implicated in classical conditioning at the molecular level has been supported by genetic evidence from fruit flies with single-gene mutations. In these mutants, the genetic defect impairs both the stimulation of adenylyl cyclase (which is otherwise enriched in the part of the normal fly brain that is implicated in associative learning) and their classical conditioning (Kandel & Hawkins 1992).

Little, Lipsitt and Rovee-Collier (1984) demonstrated robust acquisition and retention of the conditioned eyeblink response in very young infants using the nonoptimal 500-ms ISI as the control condition and the optimal 1500-ms ISI as the experimental condition. Infants were trained for a single session at either 10, 20, or 30 days of age with a tone (CS) paired with an air puff (UCS) and were tested in a second session 10 days later. Only infants in the 1500-ms condition learned the association, doing so at every age, and infants who were first trained at 20 and 30 days of age exhibited significant savings (see Figure 6.3). The percentage of CRs increased with age, and the oldest group attained a higher

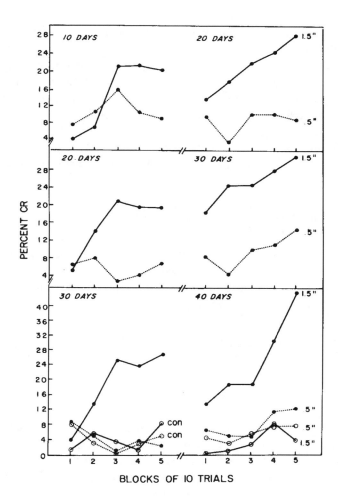

Figure 6.3. Percentage of responses on CS-UCS trials by infants who were initially conditioned at 10, 20, or 30 days of age (*left panels*) to blink their eyes to a tone (CS) that was paired with an air puff (UCS) and were retrained in a second session 10 days later (*right panels*). The CS and UCS were separated by either a 1500-ms or 500-ms interstimulus interval (ISI).

level of conditioning than the youngest group. In addition, infants who were trained at 20 days of age and tested at 30 days of age performed significantly better than 30-day-olds being trained for the first time. The finding that infants exhibited significant retention after 10 days is particularly impressive in view of the small number of reinforced presentations (50), the small percentage of reinforced trials (71%), the brevity of the training session (20 min), and the age at which the youngest infants were trained (10 days).

Solomon, Groccia-Ellison, Levine, Blanchard and Pendlebury (1990) found that the optimal CS-UCS interval increases during early to late adulthood. Whereas young adults conditioned more rapidly with an ISI of 400 ms than with ISIs of 650 and 900 ms, elderly adults conditioned more *slowly* with the 400-ms ISI. Their rate of conditioning was equivalent to that of young adults who were trained with a 900-ms ISI. Solomon et al. concluded that their facilitated conditioning at the longest ISI was not a result of age differences in sensory acuity or motor function but probably reflected age differences in synaptic efficacy. Taken together, the infant and adult data reveal that the temporal relationships in classical conditioning are an inverted U-shaped function of age (see also Chapter 4).

The heart-rate response was successfully conditioned in premature hydraencephalic and decerebrate infants via a *UCS-omission procedure* (Berntson, Tuber, Ronca & Bachman 1983; Tuber, Berntson, Bachman & Allen 1980). Omitting the UCS when it was expected to occur elicited a *what-is-it reflex* (Pavlov 1927), which was reflected in the heart-rate CR. The preceding result is consistent with evidence that amnesics (Warrington & Weiskrantz 1979; Woodruff-Pak 1993), hippocampally-damaged adult animals (O'Keefe & Nadel 1978), and even *Aplysia* (Kandel & Hawkins 1992) can be classically conditioned. Because of such data, many scientists have concluded that all conditioning tasks — both classical and operant — require only a primitive memory system, regardless of whether they take a multiple-memory-systems approach (Mandler 1984, 1998; Schacter & Moscovitch 1984) or a processing approach (Roediger et al. 1990; Roediger & Srinivas 1993).

Operant conditioning tasks

In operant conditioning, an association is learned between a response and the outcome it produces. This learning is manifested by the voluntary production of that response and is measured in terms of an increase in either response rate (number of responses per unit of time) in a *free-operant procedure* or the number of correct responses in a *discrete-trials procedure*. The classification of operantly conditioned responses, however, is ambiguous with respect to the type of memory it reflects. In humans, for example, spoken language is a product of operant conditioning (Skinner 1957). In most of the early studies that used operant conditioning tasks, infants were trained for multiple sessions. Although designed to study learning, these studies also revealed retention from one session to the next (e.g., Sameroff 1968; Watson 1984). An early study of conditioned vocalizations with 3-month-olds is typical (Rheingold, Gewirtz & Ross 1959). In this study, infants' baseline vocalizations to the expressionless experimenter were recorded on days 1 and 2, their vocalizations were socially reinforced by the experimenter on days 3 and 4, and the original baseline condition was reinstated on days 5 and 6 (i.e., extinction). Infants responded appropriately to all changes in the contingency and vocalized more on day 4 than on day 3, revealing 24-hour savings.

The majority of operant studies of infant long-term memory, however, have used the mobile conjugate reinforcement procedure (Rovee & Rovee 1969) with infants between 2 and 6 months of age. During the baseline period and all retention tests, a mobile is merely hung over the infants from one suspension bar, and an ankle ribbon is connected to another (see Figure 6.4a). During the acquisition period, which is interpolated between baseline and retention testing, infants learn to kick to move a particular mobile via a ribbon that is strung from one ankle to an overhead suspension hook (see Figure 6.4b). Typically, they have to meet a learning criterion, which is responding at 1.5 times their baseline rate. During the long-term retention test, infants are either exposed to the original training mobile or one that differs in some way. If they recognize the test mobile, they kick above their baseline rate; otherwise, they do not. Because the ribbon is not connected to the mobile during the long-term test, infants' test performance reflects only what they remember of their prior training experience and not new learning or savings at the time of testing.

Because the mobile task is inappropriate for use with infants older than 6 months, a second operant task was developed for infants between 6 and 18 months of age. In this task, infants learn to press a lever to move a miniature train around a circular track (see Figure 6.5). During the long-term retention test, the lever is deactivated. Otherwise, all aspects of the two tasks are identical. Because 6-month-olds exhibit identical memory performance in

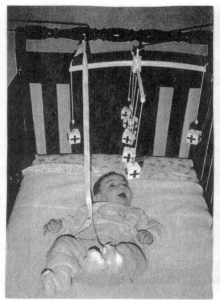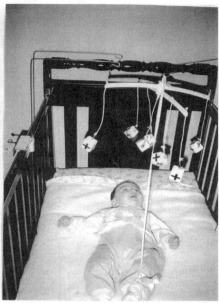

Figure 6.4. The mobile task. (*a*) The experimental arrangement during baseline and the delayed recognition test. Here, the ankle ribbon is attached to an empty stand while the mobile is suspended from a second stand. In this arrangement, the infant's kicks cannot move the mobile. (*b*) The experimental arrangement during acquisition. Shown here is a 3-month-old who is moving the mobile via a ribbon that is strung from his ankle to the same stand as the mobile.

both tasks (Hartshorn & Rovee-Collier 1997; Hildreth & Rovee-Collier 1999), the train task can be viewed as an upward extension of the mobile task.

The first systematic evidence of 24-hour cued-recall in infants was found using the mobile task (Rovee & Fagen 1976). In this study, groups of 3-month-olds were trained for 3 consecutive days with the same mobile. On day 4, the experimental group was presented with a different mobile, whereas the control group continued to receive the original one. During delayed recognition tests at the outset of sessions 2 and 3, both groups responded at the same level at which they had ended the previous day's session, indicating that they recognized the mobile after a 24-hour delay. At the outset of session 4, however, the control group again responded to the original mobile at their terminal rate of the day before, but infants in the experimental group did not

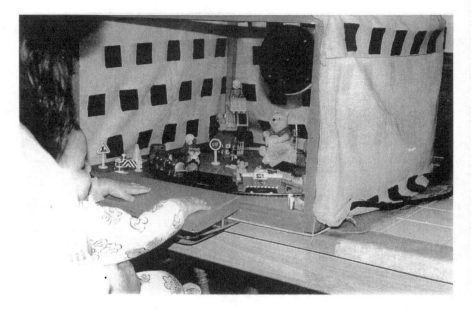

Figure 6.5. The train task. Shown here is a 6-month-old pressing the lever below the Plexiglas window to move the train inside the box during an acquisition phase. During the delayed recognition test, the lever is deactivated so that lever presses do not move the train.

recognize the novel mobile, failing to respond above their baseline level. Their behavior was taken as evidence that they discriminated the test mobile as different from the training mobile they had seen 24 hours earlier.

Subsequent studies using the mobile and train tasks have found that retention increases linearly between 2 and 18 months of age (Hartshorn, Rovee-Collier, Gerhardstein, Bhatt, Wondoloski et al. 1998b; see Figure 6.6). When infants are tested in the mobile conjugate reinforcement paradigm, for example, 2-month-olds exhibit retention for 1 or 2 days, 3-month-olds exhibit retention for 5 or 6 days, and 6-month-olds exhibit retention for 14 or 15 days. When 6-month-olds are tested in the operant train task, their maximum retention is identical to their maximum retention in the mobile conjugate reinforcement task. Furthermore, as in the mobile task, retention in the train task increases with age: 6-month-olds exhibit retention for 2 weeks, 9-month-olds exhibit retention for 6 weeks, 12-month-olds exhibit retention for 8 weeks, 15-month-olds exhibit retention for 10 weeks, and 18-month-olds exhibit retention for 13 weeks.

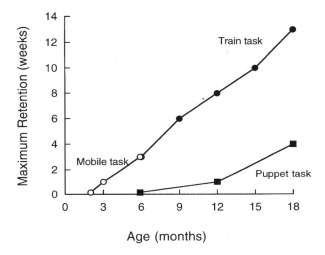

Figure 6.6. The maximum duration (in weeks) of delayed recognition of independent groups of infants who were trained and tested in the mobile task (2 to 6 months of age) and the train task (6 to 18 months of age). At 6 months of age, infants were trained and tested in both tasks, and their long-term retention in both tasks was the same. Also shown is the maximum duration (in weeks) of retention of independent groups of infants who were tested in the puppet task (6 to 18 months of age). Although the absolute duration of retention in the operant conditioning and deferred imitation paradigms is different, the pattern of retention in the two paradigms is identical.

Deferred imitation tasks

Deferred imitation is another task that can be used to study memory during infancy and early childhood. Simply put, this task incorporates a "monkey see, monkey do" procedure in which an adult models a behavior, and the infant is then given the opportunity to imitate it after a delay. Deferred imitation played an important role in Piaget's (1962) theory of the emergence of mental representation during infancy. In tasks that are based on Piaget's original conception of deferred imitation, infants do not practice the target behavior(s) prior to the test. In this way, their memory performance is based exclusively on a representation of the originally modeled event and not on a memory of their own prior actions.

According to Piaget (1962), deferred imitation does not emerge until infants are approximately 18 to 24 months of age. Although a number of studies initially supported Piaget's developmental time-table (e.g., Abravanel, Levan-Goldschmidt & Stevenson 1976; McCall, Parke & Kavanaugh 1977), many lacked essential control groups, making conclusions regarding the first appearance of deferred imitation uncertain. Meltzoff subsequently challenged Piaget's fundamental assumptions and examined deferred imitation under highly controlled experimental conditions (for review, see Meltzoff 1990). He demonstrated that 9-month-olds can imitate an experimenter's unique actions after a 24-hour delay (Meltzoff 1988) and that 14-month-olds can exhibit deferred imitation after a 4-month delay (Meltzoff 1995).

For more than a decade, 9 months was considered to be the youngest age at which infants could exhibit deferred imitation. Recently, however, a number of studies have reported that infants as young as 6 months can exhibit deferred imitation after delays of 10 min (Heimann & Nilheim 1999), 24 hours (Barr, Dowden & Hayne 1996; Collie & Hayne 1999; Hayne, Boniface & Barr 2000a), and even 14 days (Barr & Vieira 1999). In one of the tasks commonly used with 6-month-olds, infants watch an experimenter remove a mitten from a hand-puppet, shake it to ring a bell inside, and replace the

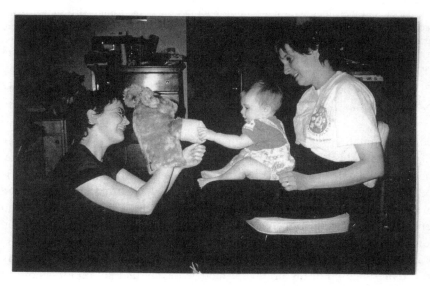

Figure 6.7. The experimental arrangement used with 6- to 24-month-old infants in deferred imitation studies. Shown here is a 6-month-old removing a mitten from the puppet's hand — an action the experimenter had modeled 24 hours earlier.

mitten. The infant's ability to imitate these target actions is then assessed after a delay (see Figure 6.7). Six-month-olds can imitate these actions 24 hours later if the demonstration lasts 60 s but not if it lasts only 30 s (Barr et al. 1996). This latter result suggests that failures to document deferred imitation by young infants are as likely to reflect the choice of an inappropriate task or task parameters as the infants' fundamental inability to imitate what they saw an adult do earlier.

In a modified version of the deferred imitation procedure, infants are allowed to practice the target behaviors prior to the retention interval (e.g., Bauer, Hertsgaard & Dow 1994). Using this procedure, Bauer and Shore (1987) reported that 1- to 2-year-olds exhibited retention after 6 weeks. Infants' imitation is also influenced by the structure of the target event (Bauer & Mandler 1989; Bauer & Shore 1987). Without exception, infants' imitation of actions that can only be performed in a specific temporal order (*causal or enabling events*; e.g., making a rattle by placing a ball in a container, putting a lid on it, and shaking it) is superior to their imitation of actions that can be performed in any order (*arbitrary events*; e.g., dressing a teddy bear by putting a ring on its finger, a scarf around its neck, and a cap on its head). The finding occurs even when the enabling and arbitrary events have been matched on the basis of target actions and event goals (Barr & Hayne 1996) and is identical to findings with older children (Fivush, Kuebli & Clubb 1992) and adults (Ratner, Smith & Dion 1986).

The range of behaviors that infants can imitate after a delay expands with age from facial and body movements (Meltzoff & Moore 1994), to specific actions on a specific object and then on similar objects (Barr et al. 1996; Hayne, MacDonald & Barr 1997; Hayne et al. 2000a), to intended actions and social goals (Meltzoff 1995). This developmental progression is thought to reflect developmental increases in infants' motor competence and cognitive abilities as well as age changes in their social niche.

Memory parallels between infants and amnesics?

Schacter and Moscovitch (1984) were the first to suggest a direct analogy between the memory performance of infants younger than 9 months of age and the memory performance of amnesic adults. In their view, infants and amnesics possess only an *early memory system* that supports unconscious or *implicit memory* and lacked *the late memory system* that supports conscious recollection or *explicit memory.* These conclusions were based on the extant literature on infant memory development.

A closer review of Schacter and Moscovitch's (1984) arguments, however, indicates that many of their conclusions were not supported either by the data that they originally reviewed or by data that have been collected since their seminal chapter was published. Below we outline four of the parallels that they drew between the memory performance of amnesics and the memory performance of human infants younger than 9 months of age. In addition, we review the evidence for and against each claim.

Effects of retention interval

A number of studies have shown that although adults' memory performance on explicit memory tasks such as recognition and recall decreases as a function of the delay between study and test trials, their performance on implicit memory tasks such as perceptual identification and word-stem completion does not. After reviewing infants' response-to-novelty data, Schacter and Moscovitch concluded that the forgetting function exhibited by infants in this task is flat and resembles the forgetting function typically obtained on tests of implicit memory with adults. Their conclusion was based on the finding that 5-month-olds exhibit little or no forgetting after a 24-hour delay in response-to-novelty tasks (Fagan 1973). This result, however, is not typical of studies using this experimental procedure. In general, infants exhibit extremely rapid forgetting in response-to-novelty tasks, and the amount of forgetting increases as a function of the delay. Stinson (1971, cited in Werner & Perlmutter 1979), for example, obtained the first systematic forgetting function using this procedure. In a study with 4-month-olds, he introduced delays of 0, 15, 30, or 75 s between the final habituation trial and a test trial with the original stimulus and found that forgetting increased linearly over the delays. After delays longer than 15 s, infants' response to the original stimulus was the same as on the first habituation trial, suggesting that they had forgotten within 15 s — a duration of retention typical of short-term memory. Other single-session studies using the paired-comparison task have similarly found retention within the span typical of short-term memory at 4 months of age (Diamond 1990a). Although the duration of retention in paired-comparison tasks increases slightly with age, it rarely exceeds more than a minute or two (e.g., Cohen & Gelber 1975;

Rose 1981). Even when infants exhibit retention across sessions, however, their memory performance is delay-dependent (Bahrick et al. 1997; Bahrick & Pickens 1995).

Delayed-nonmatching-to-sample

Schacter and Moscovitch also proposed that infants' performance on the DNMS task is analogous to that of amnesic adults. As described in Chapters 3 and 5, performance on the delayed-nonmatching-to-sample (DNMS) task has been taken as a hallmark of explicit memory. When the delay between the sample and the test stimulus is more than 15 to 60 s, the memory performance of human adults with temporal lobe amnesia (Squire, Zola-Morgan & Chen 1984) and nonhuman primates with temporal lobe damage (Mishkin 1978; Zola-Morgan, Squire & Mishkin 1982) is close to chance. Schacter and Moscovitch (1984) used the late maturation of DNMS performance in human infants (Brody 1981) to draw parallels between the memory performance of infants and amnesics. As described earlier in this chapter, however, human infants as young as 6 months of age can solve this task even when tested after a 10-min delay if only minor task modifications are made (Diamond 1995). Given this result, there is no empirical basis for drawing an analogy between infants' and amnesics' performance on the DNMS task.

A-not-B errors

Schacter and Moscovitch (1984) also cited data from object search tasks to argue that the performance of infants and amnesics is the same. The data they cited for amnesics originated in a study with six severely amnesic patients and six control patients who exhibited mild cognitive deficits but no significant memory loss and who did not differ from the amnesics in age, education, or IQ. When tested in an object search task analogous to the traditional tasks that had been used with infants, the amnesic patients — but not the controls — committed the A-not-B error. Amnesic patients successfully found the object when it was hidden at location B if they were tested after no delay, but they unsuccessfully searched at location A — where the object was previously found — after a delay.

The corresponding data that were cited for infants came from a study conducted by Fox et al. (1979). In that study, infants were tested in a standard object search task in which they first learned to search at location A, and then the object was hidden at location B. Although 8- and 9-month-old infants searched successfully at B when there was no delay between hiding and searching, they committed the A-not-B error when there was a 7-s delay. In contrast, 10-month-old infants successfully searched at B irrespective of whether the delay was 0 or 7 s. On the basis of these data, Schacter and Moscovitch (1984) concluded that the search performance of 8- and 9-month-olds and adult amnesics was analogous.

More recent data, however, have refuted this analogy. Subsequent research using the standard task has shown that the search performance of infants of all ages declines as the delay between hiding and finding increases and that the maximum delay that infants will tolerate increases as a function of age (see Figure 6.2). As such, conclusions regarding the stage-like effect of age on A-not-B errors from the Fox et al. (1979) study cited by Schacter and Moscovitch (1984) are limited by the fact that the maximum delay after which infants were tested was only 7 s. Furthermore, age-related gains in the maximum delay that infants tolerate increases at a relatively constant rate between 7½ and 12 months of age (Diamond 1985). This latter finding does not support the view that infants suddenly gain access to the late memory system after 9 months of age. Finally, the finding that infants can solve object search tasks much earlier in development when looking rather than searching manually also suggests that their failure on the standard task is due to some process other than memory (Baillargeon & Graber 1988; Baillargeon et al. 1989).

Recall of specific prior episodes

Under some circumstances, amnesics do learn from prior experience; however, they are generally unable to recall the specific prior episodes that contributed to their learning. On the basis of these findings, Schacter and Moscovitch (1984) attributed the ability to recall specific prior episodes to the late-maturing system. At the time when their chapter was published, virtually no data were available from infants that addressed their ability to recall specific prior episodes from their past experience. Over the past 10 years, however, infants' ability to exhibit deferred imitation is often used to argue that they have the ability to recall a specific prior episode (Bauer & Hertsgaard 1993; Mandler 1988, 1990; McDonough, Mandler, McKee & Squire 1995). In deferred imitation tasks, the experimenter typically demonstrates the target actions during a single session, and the infant's ability to reproduce those actions is then assessed after a delay. In this task, infants can only respond to the test stimuli on the basis of their memory for the single demonstration episode. Given that infants as young as 6 months have been shown to exhibit deferred imitation, we would conclude that, at least by this age, infants can recall a single prior episode.

Deferred imitation is not the only task in which infants have exhibited memory for a single prior episode. Research using the mobile conjugate reinforcement paradigm has shown that at least by 3 months of age, infants exhibit retention of an event that occurred on a single prior occasion (Greco et al. 1990; Hayne, Greco-Vigorito & Rovee-Collier 1993; Rovee-Collier et al. 1993b). In a prototypic study, 3-month-old infants learned to kick to activate a series of different yellow-block mobiles displaying alphanumeric characters on each block (see Figure 6.8, *bottom*) and were subsequently provided with information that a stained-glass and metal windchime (see Figure 6.8, *top*) was movable. This information was provided to the infant during a 3-min passive-exposure procedure during which the experimenter hung the wind-chime from the mobile suspension hook and jiggled it while the infant merely watched. This event occurred on *only a single occasion* 4 days after training. When infants were shown the stationary windchime during a delayed recognition test 1 day later (5 days after training), they kicked vigorously, apparently attempting to move it by using the response that they had previously used to move the yellow-block mobiles. The infants kicked, however, only if they had been provided with information that the windchime could move; infants who had previously viewed the windchime while it was motionless did not attempt to move it during the test (Greco et al. 1990; Rovee-Collier et al. 1993b). Also, because infants had *not* moved the windchime themselves on that occasion, they obviously had neither *practiced* kicking to move it nor been *reinforced* for kicking to move it.

In another study demonstrating memory for a single prior episode, 3-month-olds were trained for three sessions with a series of yellow-block mobiles (Hayne et al. 1993). During *session 3 only*, a blue- and red-striped cloth was draped around the sides of the crib. At the end of session 3, the ankle ribbon was detached from the overhead suspension hook, the mobile was removed, and the stationary windchime was suspended over the infant for 3 min in the presence of the blue- and red-striped context. The next day, infants received a delayed recognition test with the stationary windchime. Even

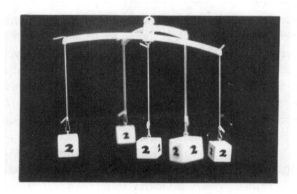

Figure 6.8. (Top) The stained-glass and metal butterfly windchime to which 3-month-olds were briefly exposed on a single occasion. (Bottom) One of the three mobiles with which infants were initially trained; the blocks on all mobiles were yellow and displayed the same figure (A or 2) in the same color, but the color of the figures differed from one mobile to the next.

though the blue- and red-striped context *was not present* during the test, infants kicked robustly, apparently trying to move the windchime — even though they had never before seen it move. A control group was treated exactly like the experimental group except that the distinctive blue- and red-striped cloth was not present either during their third session or when they saw the stationary windchime immediately afterward. This group did not kick during the delayed recognition test. These data indicated that the shared session-3 context had linked the representation of the windchime with the representation of the training event. This study offers unambiguous evidence that the delayed recognition performance of the experimental group during the 24-hour test resulted from the retrieval of their memory for a single prior episode — session 3. Moreover, although the training event and the stationary windchime had been integrated by means of the common context, like a catalyst, that context was unnecessary for infants' subsequent test performance once the integration had occurred.

Unfortunately, many researchers have summarily dismissed infants' memory performance in the mobile conjugate reinforcement task without understanding how the task has actually been exploited to study infants' memory abilities (e.g., Nelson 1995; Mandler 1998; Schacter & Moscovitch 1984). Because the initial response in this procedure is established by conditioning, for example, they think that studies using this procedure tap only implicit memory that is acquired gradually or incrementally through reinforced practice (e.g., Bauer 1995, 1997; Bauer & Hertsgaard 1993; Mandler 1984, 1990, 1998; Schacter & Moscovitch 1984).

On the contrary, the experimental procedures described above are remarkably similar to the procedures commonly used in deferred imitation tasks — tasks that these same individuals argue tap explicit memory (Bauer 1995, 1997; Bauer & Hertsgaard 1993; Mandler 1984, 1990; Nelson 1995, see below). As in deferred imitation, for example, the target action and its consequence were *not physically present* at the time of the delayed recognition test with the windchime in the mobile task. Also, in both the deferred imitation and mobile tasks, the experimenter provides the subject with a prop (e.g., a mobile) in lieu of instructions, thereby creating an occasion for cued recall, but the specific action to be performed is *not externally cued*. Finally, as in studies of deferred imitation, infants acquired information about the windchime through *observation alone*; during the test, infants merely applied an action that was already in their behavioral repertoire upon the test object in order to make it function as they had learned it could — even though *perceptual information about its function was not available* at the time of testing.

The analogy revisited

Although the analogy between infants and amnesics originally put forward by Schacter and Moscovitch has not withstood empirical scrutiny, their argument has been reiterated by others who still contend that the memory processing by infants and amnesics is the same. In fact, the current strategy used by these investigators resembles that of Schacter and Moscovitch (1984) in fundamental ways. Consistent with Schacter and Moscovitch, a common approach to infant memory development has been to find tasks that amnesics fail and then determine whether or not infants fail the same tasks (Mandler 1990; McDonough et al. 1995; McKee & Squire 1993). Although the outcome of this process is often used to support the analogy between infants and amnesics, recent empirical work in at least two new domains — deferred imitation and response-to-novelty tasks — indicates that no such analogy exists.

Deferred imitation tasks

Adult amnesics have recently been shown to fail on two other nonverbal tasks that are typically used with infants — deferred imitation and response-to-novelty tasks (McDonough et al. 1995; McKee & Squire 1993). McDonough et al. (1995), for example, found that human adults with amnesia did not exhibit retention in a deferred imitation task when tested after a 24-hour delay. In their study, an experimenter demonstrated a series of three-step actions with objects. Healthy adults, patients with frontal-lobe damage, and patients with amnesia were then given the opportunity to reproduce those actions 24 hours later. Although healthy adults and patients with frontal lobe damage reproduced more of the actions during the test than they had prior to the demonstration (i.e., during baseline), patients with amnesia did not.

Although imitation, like DNMS, has traditionally been viewed as a relatively late developmental milestone (McCall et al. 1977; Piaget 1962; Uzgiris 1981), more recent research has shown that at some point during the first year of life, infants are able to exhibit imitation even when tested for the first time after a delay (i.e., deferred imitation). In the first experiment of this kind,

Meltzoff (1988) demonstrated deferred imitation by 9-month-old infants who were tested after a 24-hour delay. Consistent with Schacter and Moscovitch's (1984) original view, Meltzoff's (1988) finding is often cited as new evidence in support of a transition in memory processing at around 9 months (Mandler 1990; Nelson 1995, 1997). The subsequent finding that infants as young as 6 months can imitate a wide range of novel behaviors after a delay (Barr et al. 1996; Barr & Vieira 1999; Collie & Hayne 1999; Hayne et al. 2000a; Heimann & Nilheim 1999), however, clearly demonstrates that infants less than 9 months of age can solve a memory task that human adults with amnesia fail.

Response-to-novelty tasks

Although Schacter and Moscovitch (1984) originally argued that response-to-novelty tasks tap the early (implicit) memory system, some investigators have argued more recently that this task taps explicit memory. First, given the procedural similarity between the response-to-novelty tasks and DNMS tasks described earlier, it has become increasingly difficult to argue that one task taps explicit memory while the other does not (Bachevalier, Brickson & Hagger 1993; Diamond 1995). McKee and Squire (1993), for example, found that human adults with amnesia show extremely rapid forgetting when tested on response-to-novelty tasks. In their study, amnesic patients and healthy controls were tested using a visual paired-comparison procedure. Although the novelty preference of the two groups did not differ immediately after familiarization, the novelty preference of the amnesic group was significantly lower than that of the control group when subjects were tested after a 2-min delay.

Even during the first few days of life, however, human infants exhibit robust recognition memory in a response-to-novelty task like that used by McKee and Squire (1993) to discriminate the memory performance of amnesics from that of healthy controls (Field et al. 1984; Pascalis & DeSchonen 1994; Pascalis et al. 1995). In a study that was actually motivated by the McKee and Squire finding, Pascalis and DeSchonen (1994) familiarized 3- to 4-day-old infants with a picture of a woman's face using an infant-controlled habituation procedure. Independent groups of infants were then given a paired-comparison test with the familiar picture and a picture of a previously unseen woman either 2 min or 24 hours later. After both delays, infants looked proportionally longer at the novel picture. Thus, even newborn infants exhibit retention under conditions that human amnesics do not.

Do infants have conscious awareness?

Explicit memory is often distinguished from implicit memory in that explicit memory is thought to require conscious recollection, whereas implicit memory is not. That the memory performance of amnesics is selectively impaired in certain memory tasks is indisputable; however, current evidence disputes the claim that amnesics' memory performance parallels the memory performance of developing infants on equivalent tasks. Our review of the empirical literature on infant memory has shown that very young infants succeed in tasks that amnesics often fail. Given this, are we willing to conclude that infants, unlike amnesics, experience conscious recollection of their past? On a more fundamental level, are we willing to conclude that the same processes that mediate adults' performance also mediate infants' performance on the same tasks?

Some researchers have argued that inferences can be made regarding the conscious and unconscious processes that underlie infants' success or failure on a particular memory task. Mandler (1990), for example, claimed that because verbally competent subjects solve deferred imitation by recall — which she thinks requires conscious recollection, then deferred imitation by nonverbal infants must require conscious awareness as well. Although Bauer (1996) recognized the interpretative difficulty that an exclusive reliance on nonverbal behavior imposed, she also used that behavior as a surrogate measure of consciousness:

> "Recall is, by definition, a conscious product. When an adult provides a verbal report of a past experience, there is ample evidence that the remembered material has been made accessible to the conscious mind. Because the participants of research on memory for experiences early in life are preverbal or barely verbal, we are unable to query them to ensure their awareness that their behaviors result from some previous experience. There is ambiguity, then, as to whether the basis on which we infer memory, namely, a change in nonverbal behavior, results from conscious recollection or unconscious influence....What is needed...is a nonverbal task analogous to verbal recall: The mnemonic behavior must be derived from a task that engages the same cognitive processes as those involved in verbal recall by older children and adults...an excellent candidate is elicited imitation of specific action sequences" (pp. 30–31).

Bauer's conclusion is shared by others in the field. According to McDonough, for example:

> "successful deferred imitation relies on brain structures essential for declarative memory, the capacity for intentionally calling to mind specific facts and events" (quoted in Bower 1995, p. 86).

This conclusion, however, has been vigorously challenged. Thompson (1990a), Fagan (1990), and Werker (1990), to name a few, have pointed out that nothing in the behavior of preverbal infants performing a deferred imitation task provides direct evidence of conscious awareness — or intentionality, for that matter, nor can there be. The conclusion that infants use conscious recollection in tasks of deferred imitation is only *inferred* from the assumption that there is a one-to-one mapping of a particular task onto a particular memory system — an assumption that Jacoby (1991) characterized as "more than a little shaky." Tulving (1990) noted that:

> "memory should have something to do with remembering and remembering *is* a conscious experience. To remember an event means to be consciously aware now of something that happened on an earlier occasion" (p. 1).

He warned, however, that because conscious experience and performance on an explicit memory test are not necessarily related, *conscious recollection cannot be inferred from such behavior.* Finally, Jacoby and Witherspoon (1982) demonstrated that remembering without awareness can accompany adults' memory for a specific prior episode. As in studies with rats and monkeys, whether preverbal infants ever experience conscious recollection of their prior experiences is impossible to determine, regardless of what experimental tasks are used to test their memory.

Although we will never know if and how infants re-experience their own personal past, we can gain some critical understanding of the principles that describe their memory processing by comparing the effect of various experimental manipulations on their performance on priming (implicit) and recognition (explicit) memory tasks. This analysis is the focus of Chapter 7.

Conclusions

The assumption that the Jacksonian principle extends to the normal development and dissolution of memory systems is intuitively appealing, but evidence on the development of memory in human infants and its dissolution in amnesics has not supported this assumption. This result is hardly surprising given that the demise of memory function in adults with severe brain damage does not even parallel the loss of memory function in healthy, aging adults (Campbell et al. 1984). In fact, brain-damaged adults do not even provide a suitable model for understanding many developmental disorders (Karmiloff-Smith 1998).

The empirical evidence reviewed in this chapter provides no basis for the analogy between the development of memory in infants and the dissolution of memory in amnesic adults. First, across experimental tasks, even very young infants exhibit retention in tasks that adult amnesics do not (see Table 6.1). Second, age-related changes in infants' performance within a given task give no hint of the stage-like transition in memory performance that would be expected if a fundamentally different memory system, such as the one that is subsequently lost in amnesia, were to emerge *de novo* at some point during development (see Figure 6.2 and Figure 6.6). Third, the memory of preverbal infants differs in a number of other ways from the memory of adult amnesics. Not only have infants yet to develop language, for example, but also they have yet to develop the vast networks of associations that adult amnesics acquired over a lifetime. Finally, the poor memory that is exhibited by developing organisms is not a pathological condition, whereas the poor memory that is exhibited by brain-damaged amnesics clearly is (Campbell et al. 1984). Given the preceding considerations, the fact that some scientists still take the decline in memory performance during amnesia as evidence of how memory normally develops is surprising.

Table 6.1 . The Success of Adults and Human Infants < 9 Months of Age on the DNMS, Deferred Imitation, and Novelty-Preference Tasks

Group	Memory Task		
	DNMS	Deferred Imitation	Novelty Preference
Adult Amnesics	No	No	No
Infants < 9 months	Yes	Yes	Yes

CHAPTER 7

Memory Dissociations In Infants

The ontogenetic hierarchy in which implicit memory develops before explicit memory was originally inferred from the excellent memory performance of amnesic adults on priming tests and their poor memory performance on recall/recognition tests. Similar functional memory dissociations have been produced in normal adults by means of different test instructions. This chapter reviews evidence that very young infants exhibit memory dissociations exactly like those exhibited by normal adults on priming and recognition tests, and they do so in response to manipulations of all of the same independent variables.

Recall that infants and amnesics were commonly assumed to possess only implicit memory. To determine when explicit memory develops, therefore, some researchers attempted to find tasks that amnesics fail, but normal adults can solve. Once such a task was found, they then asked at what age preverbal infants could first solve them. Studies in which researchers took this approach were discussed in Chapter 6. A second approach to the development of explicit memory, however, is to ask at what age infants exhibit the same functional memory dissociations as adults. Studies that have addressed this question are the focus of Chapter 7.

Memory dissociations in adults

Teuber (1955) was the first to propose the idea of a double dissociation in memory performance. Tulving (1983) described the *rule of experimental dissociation* as follows:

> "Dissociation is said to have occurred if it is found that the manipulated variable affects subjects' performance in one of two tasks, but not in the other, or affects the performance in different directions in the two tasks. Thus,

dissociation refers to the absence of a positive association between dependent variables of two different tasks" (p. 73).

He suggested applying an analogous logic to studies of developmental or pathological dissociations by comparing the performance of groups differing in either age or pathology on two different memory tasks.

Warrington and Weiskrantz (1970), for example, reported a memory dissociation between two patient groups that differed in pathology. Brain-damaged amnesics and a control group of patients without brain damage were administered free-recall and recognition tests and two priming tests — word-fragment completion involving degraded letters and stem-completion tests. Amnesics' retention on the first two tests was impaired, but their performance on the priming tests was not. Today, these tests are referred to as *explicit* and *implicit memory tests*, respectively. Since then, many researchers using a variety of explicit and implicit tests (see Chapter 2) have obtained similar results, namely, impaired memory performance on explicit tests but spared memory on implicit tests (Jacoby & Witherspoon 1982; Moscovitch 1982; Shimamura 1986; Shimamura & Squire 1984). Crowder (1988) interpreted these findings as an indication that amnesics are capable of initially encoding information but have difficulty in subsequently gaining awareness of it. Mandler (1989) similarly interpreted them as reflecting the inability of amnesic patients "to use access routes to information that is not available automatically" (p. 96). Others, however, interpreted the dissociations as reflecting the fact that implicit and explicit tests tapped functionally different memory systems, and memory dissociations on implicit and explicit tests have now become a common diagnostic for the existence of two memory systems.

Memory dissociations like those found in studies with amnesics were subsequently documented in studies with normal adults. In these studies, adults were instructed to respond on an implicit test with the first word that came to mind, making no reference to a prior episode, or to respond on an explicit test with an item from a previously studied list or on the basis of a specific prior episode (Graf et al. 1982; Graf & Schacter 1985; Schacter et al. 1989; see Chapter 2). In addition, researchers have found that adults perform differently on implicit and explicit tests as a function of a number of different independent variables (Hintzman 1990; Jacoby & Dallas 1981; for reviews, see Richardson-Klavehn & Bjork 1988; Schacter 1987). In every instance, the manipulated variable produces a functional dissociation that mimics the impact of amnesia on implicit and explicit tests, impairing memory performance on explicit tests but having little or no impact on memory performance on implicit tests.

Memory dissociations in preverbal infants

Tulving's (1983) original suggestion of applying the logic of experimental dissociation to groups differing in age on two different memory tasks has been followed in studies with children on tasks like those used with adults (see Chapter 4). The tasks that were used with children and adults, however, are inappropriate for preverbal infants. To apply the logic of experimental dissociation to infants, therefore, it is necessary to incorporate their instructions directly into the structure of the tasks. In addition, because different independent variables affect adults' memory performance on implicit and explicit tests differently, we have manipulated these same variables to see if they produced corresponding dissociations in infants' memory performance on the two kinds of tasks.

Tasks that produce infant memory dissociations

Two general types of task produce dissociations in infants' memory performance — *delayed recognition tasks* and *reactivation (priming) tasks*. These tasks are not specific to a particular paradigm; rather, both have been used with a variety of infant memory procedures, including response-to-novelty (Cornell 1979), operant conditioning (Hartshorn & Rovee-Collier 1997; Rovee-Collier, Sullivan, Enright, Lucas & Fagen 1980), deferred imitation (Barr 1997; Barr & Vieira 1999), auditory localization (Perris, Myers & Clifton 1990), and reenactment (Sheffield & Hudson 1994). In addition, both tasks are introduced after the initial study or training period (e.g., familiarization, conditioning, modeling) is over. Because the original memory is encoded before the manipulations that differentiate the two tasks are introduced, differences in infants' memory performance on them cannot be attributed to how the response got into their behavioral repertoire in the first place. This condition satisfies the retrieval intentionality criterion (Schacter et al. 1989).

Delayed Recognition Task. In this task, the infant is exposed to a retrieval cue during a long-term retention test that is administered after a specified amount of time has elapsed since training or modeling (see Figure 7.1a). This is a *contemporaneous-cuing* procedure (Spear 1978). During the test, infants are simply shown the study or training cue (a particular mobile, train, or other prop) and indicate if they recognize it by producing the appropriate response (kicking, lever-pressing, or other target action). If they do not recognize it, then they respond at chance (i.e., at the baseline level).

By testing with different types of retrieval cues as memory probes after different delays, it is possible to ascertain what is still accessible in the original memory representation at different points in time (e.g., the details or general features of the training mobile, the immediate and remote context) and what is not. If infants fail to recognize the altered test stimulus, then we conclude that the details that were altered or absent at the time of testing must have been represented in the training memory and are critical for its retrieval. If infants respond to the altered test stimulus, however, then we conclude that the details that were altered or removed were either not represented in the original training memory or were forgotten by the time of testing. This strategy was

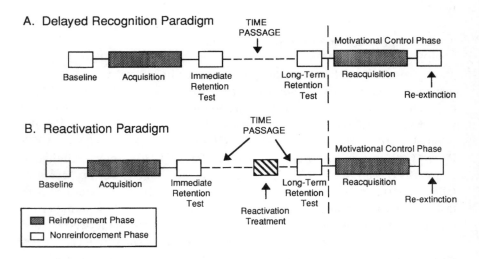

Figure 7.1. (*A*) Schematic of the delayed recognition task showing training and the long-term retention test (i.e., the delayed recognition test). (*B*) Schematic of the reactivation task, showing training, the reactivation treatment, and the long-term retention test. The only difference between these tasks is the brief reactivation (priming) treatment prior to the long-term retention test. The memory probe in (*A*) serves as the reactivation stimulus or memory prime in (*B*); the long-term retention test is usually with the original training stimulus.

previously used by Tulving (1983) in studies of explicit memory with adults and has revealed that infants forget different kinds of memory attributes at different rates (Bhatt & Rovee-Collier 1994, 1996; Boller, Rovee-Collier, Gulya & Prete 1996; Hitchcock & Rovee-Collier 1996; Rovee-Collier & Sullivan 1980).

Reactivation Task. The reactivation task is based on the observation that many memories which have been forgotten (i.e., there is no evidence of retention in performance on a long-term retention test) can subsequently be reactivated. Apparently, these memories still remain *available* in long-term memory even after they are no longer *accessible* to retrieval cues that are presented at the time of the long-term retention test — a distinction originally made by Tulving (Tulving 1972; Tulving & Pearlstone 1966). During a reactivation treatment, infants are briefly exposed to a memory prime at some point before the long-term retention test (see Figure 7.1B). This is a *prior-cuing* procedure (Spear 1978). The prime presumably reactivates the latent memory, increasing its accessibility. Whether the prime was effective (i.e., whether the memory was actually reactivated) is then assessed later on a standard delayed recognition test. If the prime was effective, then infants respond appropriately to the retrieval cue just as they had at the end of training. The memory prime is a fractional component of the original event — as are word stems or word fragments in studies with adults — that is likely to be represented in the training memory. In most studies, the prime is presented at a time when infants cannot recognize it — a practice that mimics the amnesic test condition. (The effect on retention of presenting a prime when infants can still recognize it is discussed in Chapter 9, *Priming and the State of the Memory.*)

Although reactivation was originally used with infant animals (Spear & Parsons 1976), it was subsequently adapted for preverbal infants (Fagen & Rovee-Collier 1983; Rovee-Collier et al. 1980; Sullivan 1982) and has since been used with toddlers who possess some facility with language (Barr 1997; Sheffield & Hudson 1994). Memory primes that have been used with young infants include stimuli as diverse as a previously familiarized photograph (see Figure 7.2a) in response-to-novelty studies (Cornell 1979), the mobile (see Figure 7.2b) or distinctive training context (see Figure 7.2c) in operant conditioning studies (Rovee-Collier & Hayne 1987), and the hand-puppet (see Figure 7.2d) in deferred imitation studies (Barr 1997). As a memory prime for 14- and 18-month-olds, a demonstration of three of six activities in which

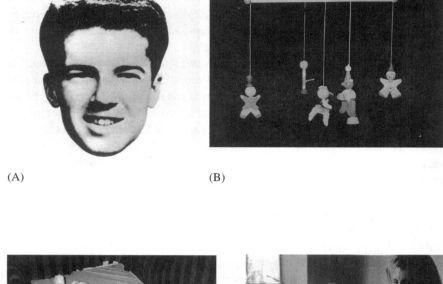

(A)   (B)

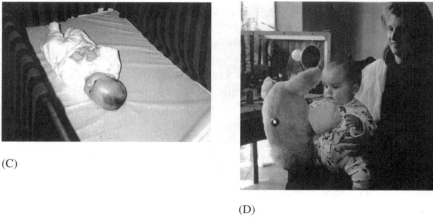

(C)

(D)

Figure 7.2. Stimuli that have served as memory primes for preverbal infants. (*A*) the photograph that 5-month-olds had viewed during the familiarization phase of a response-to-novelty task (photograph courtesy of J.F. Fagan, III.); (*B*) the mobile that had been used during operant conditioning with 2-, 3-, and 6-month-olds; (*C*) the training context that had been present during mobile conditioning with 3-month-olds; (*D*) the hand-puppet on which target actions had been demonstrated to 6-month-olds in the presence of the train (the bell is pinned on the puppet's back instead of inside its mitten).

toddlers had previously engaged reactivated their memory of remaining three activities (Sheffield & Hudson 1994). Effective memory primes for 24-month-olds were a small-scale model of a room in which infants had engaged in the activities, a photograph of each of the activities, and a video of three of the six activities (Agayoff, Sheffield & Hudson 1999).

Figure 7.3 presents data illustrating performance in the delayed recognition and reactivation tasks. Shown at the left is the forgetting function of 3-month-old infants whose initial training was completed at Time 0. The first curve depicts the performance of independent groups on delayed recognition tests that were administered after different posttraining delays. As can be seen, the original memory was gradually forgotten within 6 to 8 days. Thirteen days after training, infants were exposed to a memory prime. The curve at the right is the reforgetting function of the reactivated memory, which was the performance of independent groups on standard recognition tests that were administered at different points in time after reactivation. The figure shows that the

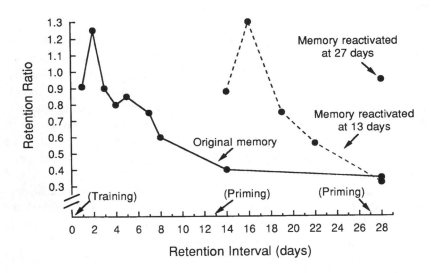

Figure 7.3. The forgetting and reforgetting functions of the original memory and the reactivated memory, respectively, as a function of the number of days after training or priming when retention testing occurred. The memory prime was presented either 13 or 27 days after training was over (*priming*), when forgetting was complete. Each data point represents a different group of 3-month-old infants.

prime reactivated the memory and restored infants' retention to the same level that it was immediately after training. Note also that the reactivated memory was not transient but was reforgotten at approximately the same rate as the original memory.

Examples of Delayed Recognition and Reactivation Tasks. The distinction between the delayed recognition and the reactivation tasks is well-illustrated in a series of experiments with 3-month-olds in which we asked if infants are sensitive to the same primitive perceptual units as adults (Rovee-Collier, Hankins & Bhatt 1992a). These units, called textons (Julesz 1984) or critical features (Treisman & Gelade 1980), are thought to be the building blocks of perception. In the delayed recognition task, 3-month-olds failed to discriminate between a pair of horizontal and vertical bars (two textons) that were in different spatial relations (L versus T) after 24 hours, but they did discriminate +s from both Ls and Ts. Presumably, the latter discrimination occurred because a + contains an additional texton — a line crossing. In the reactivation task, however, 3-month-olds discriminated between pairs of horizontal and vertical black bars in all combinations. The procedural details of these two studies are described below.

The *delayed recognition task* was used in Experiment 1. Here, independent groups of infants were trained in their home cribs for 2 days (9 min per day) with a five-object, pink-block mobile displaying two computer-generated black bars arranged as an L, T, or + on all sides of each block. The mobile was suspended from one of two flexible stands that were clamped to opposing crib rails (in studies with 6-month-olds, infants are situated in a sling seat inside a playpen, and the mobile is suspended from one of two horizontal bars on floor microphone stands that are placed on opposite sides of the playpen.) During training, infants lay supine in their home cribs, and a white satin ribbon was connected without slack from one ankle to the overhead mobile suspension bar (see Figure 6.4b). In this arrangement, each footkick moved the overhead mobile with a rate and intensity proportional to the rate and vigor of kicking (*conjugate reinforcement*: Rovee & Rovee 1969).

Each training session began and ended with a 3-min nonreinforcement period when the ankle ribbon was attached to an empty stand. At the outset of session 1, this 3-min period was the *baseline phase* when the infant's unlearned kick rate was measured; at the end of session 2, this 3-min period was an *immediate retention test* when the infant's final level of learning and retention after zero delay were measured. The 3-min *long-term retention test* was identical to the baseline phase and immediate retention test and occurred 24 hours after training was over. At this time, either the same mobile (i.e., a mobile displaying Ls for infants who were trained with Ls) or a different one (i.e., a mobile displaying Ts or +s for infants who were trained with Ls) was hung over each infant (see Figure 6.4a).

Retention was indexed by two individual measures of relative responding. The primary measure, the *baseline ratio* (response rate during the long-term test divided by the same infant's baseline rate), indicated the extent to which test responding exceeded an infant's pretraining baseline. Thus, if a group kicked significantly above its pretraining baseline (i.e., *M* baseline ratio significantly > 1.00), then this was taken as evidence of retention (if the test mobile was the same as the training mobile) or generalization (if the test mobile was different). If a group did not kick significantly above baseline (i.e., *M* baseline ratio not significantly > 1.00), then this was taken as evidence of no retention or discrimination, respectively. Convergent evidence of no retention/discrimination was provided by the *retention ratio* (response rate during the immediate retention test divided by the same infant's response rate during the long-term test). Thus, if a group kicked significantly less during the long-term test than it had immediately after training (i.e., *M* retention ratio significantly < 1.00), then this was taken as evidence of discrimination (if the test mobile was different from the training mobile) or forgetting (if, for example, the training and test mobiles were the same).

In Experiment 1, the no-change control group exhibited excellent retention on the 24-hour delayed recognition test, as did infants who were trained with Ls and tested with Ts (or vice versa). Infants who were trained with either Ls or Ts and were tested with +s (and vice versa), however, failed to respond above baseline during the 24-hour test, indicating that they discriminated the test stimulus from the training one.

The *reactivation task* was used in Experiment 2. Here, independent groups of infants were tested exactly like the no-change group in Experiment 1 but were allowed 2 weeks to forget the original training memory first. Twenty-four hours before the long-term test (13 days after training), these infants were primed for 3 min with either the original training mobile or a different one (see Figure 7.4). During the reactivation treatment, the end of the ribbon was not attached to the infant's ankle but was drawn and released by the experimenter at the same rate that each infant had kicked during the final 3 min of training. In this way, each infant saw the mobile moving in a way that was phenomenologically equivalent to what that same infant had seen at the end of acquisition. During a standard delayed recognition test with the original training mobile 24 hours after the reactivation treatment (14 days after training), we tested infants' retention to determine whether or not the prime had actually reactivated their forgotten memory. We also tested two control groups that are requisite in studies of reactivation — a reactivation control group and a forgetting control group. The *reactivation control group* was not originally trained but was primed with the training mobile. This group ensured that the reactivation treatment per se did not induce new learning that might be misconstrued as retention during the long-term test. The *forgetting control group* was originally trained but was not primed. This group ensured that forgetting was complete by the time of the long-term retention test.

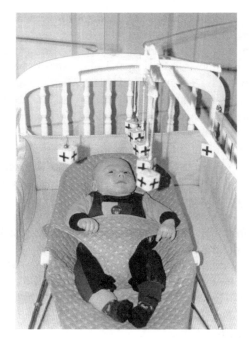

Figure 7.4. The experimental arrangement during the reactivation or priming treatment with 3-month-olds. The ribbon was not connected to the infant's ankle but was held by the experimenter, who pulled it to move the mobile at the same rate that the infant had moved it by kicking during the last few training minutes. The infant seat minimized spontaneous kicking during the reactivation treatment.

The *no-change* group, which was primed with the original training mobile, exhibited excellent retention, but the forgetting control group and the reactivation control group exhibited none. Infants who were trained with Ls and primed with either Ts or +s also exhibited no retention during the long-term test. The fact that Ls were not effective primes for infants trained with Ts and vice versa suggested that infants in Experiment 1 had originally encoded the difference between Ls and Ts but had forgotten this distinction by the time of the 24-hour retention test with the other mobile. This suggestion was subsequently confirmed: Infants who received a delayed recognition test only 1 hour after the end of training discriminated Ls from Ts and vice versa (Adler & Rovee-Collier 1994).

The preceding experiments illustrate an important distinction between reactivation and delayed recognition tasks. Recall that in a delayed recognition task, infants are tested with a stimulus that is either the same as or different from the training one, whereas in a reactivation task, infants are reactivated with a stimulus that is either the same as or different from the training one. In a delayed recognition task, infants may fail to exhibit retention (i.e., they discriminate) if the *test stimulus* differs from the training one; in the reactivation task, however, they fail to exhibit retention because the *reactivation stimulus* differs from the training stimulus — not because the reactivation stimulus differs from the test stimulus. In other words, they exhibit no retention if their forgotten memory was never reactivated in the first place (Hayne & Rovee-Collier 1995; for review, see Rovee-Collier & Hayne 1987).

Comparison between infant and adult memory tasks

The delayed recognition and reactivation tasks that have been used with infants correspond to two of the prototypic tasks that have been used in tests of implicit and explicit memory with adults. The delayed recognition task is analogous to the standard yes/no (e.g., Dorfman, Kihlstrom, Cork & Misiaszek 1995) and old/new recognition tests (e.g., Mitchell & Brown 1988; Musen & Treisman 1990) that have been used in studies of explicit memory with adults. As in the adult studies, the retrieval cue is presented at the time of the retention test instead of before it (see Table 7.1). The reactivation task is analogous to repetition priming tasks that researchers use to study implicit memory with adults (see Graf & Schacter 1985; Nelson 1995). In studies with infants, the reactivation stimulus (i.e., the memory prime) is a fractional component of the original event — as is a word stem or word fragment in repetition priming studies with adults — that is likely to be represented in the infant's training memory and is presented immediately before the retention test. Also, the prime is presented at a time when infants cannot recognize it — a practice that mimics the amnesic test condition. Despite being unable to recognize the prime, infants exhibit item-specific priming, as do adults.

Table 7.1. Tasks That Produce Implicit/Explicit Memory Dissociations in Adults and Corresponding Tasks Used With Infants

Memory System	Adult Task	Infant Task
Implicit	Priming	Reactivation
Explicit	Recognition	Delayed Recognition

In adults, priming is thought to initiate a relatively pure perceptual identification process that occurs automatically, devoid of an active search component (Jacoby 1991; Musen & Treisman 1990). According to Vriezen, Moscovitch and Bellos (1995):

> "the mere presentation and processing of an item is sufficient to leave a trace in the perceptual representation system (Schacter 1990, 1992; Tulving & Schacter 1990). It is the *reactivation* [our italics] of this trace on subsequent presentations that accounts for the repetition priming effect" (p. 944).

These descriptions are equally applicable to infants. The initial perceptual processing of a stimulus makes the future processing of that stimulus more rapid (Cave 1997; Mitchell & Brown 1988; Musen & Treisman 1990). Thus, Reinitz and Alexander (1996) reported that adults' perceptual identification of primed (old) and unprimed (new) pictures was perfectly predicted by a multiplicative model which assumes that prior exposure to a stimulus increases the rate at which visual information is subsequently acquired from the primed stimulus. Cave, Blake and McNamara (1998), however, reported that priming decreased the naming latencies of old objects on a perceptual identification task only when the primes were processed during periods of binocular dominance. Primes that were presented during binocular suppression, which prevents their perceptual attributes from reaching the processing stage at which they are assembled into nameable objects, did not facilitate adults' subsequent naming. On the basis of these data, Cave et al. concluded that successful visual repetition priming requires that the perceptual attributes of the prime be processed at a stage that assembles those attributes into "relatively high-level representations" but is below the stage of conscious awareness. Recall that priming effects are manifested without the need for conscious recollection of specific prior episodes (Graf & Schacter 1985).

The similarity between the reactivation task and the priming tasks used with adults has been noted elsewhere (Mandler 1984; Naito & Komatsu 1990; Nelson 1995). Like primes used in studies of implicit memory with adults, a prime reactivates either a preexisting memory representation (Tulving & Schacter 1990) or a representation established by a single exposure to a stimulus (Graf & Schacter 1985; Musen & Treisman 1992; Naito & Komatsu 1990). Although effects of priming are typically measured in terms of changes in reaction time for adults and as renewed retention on an ensuing delayed recognition task for infants, a closer analysis reveals that these are the same. Amnesics, in fact, exhibit retention by producing the previously studied response to a memory prime (e.g., the stem of a previously studied word) on the ensuing test, and infants exhibit retention by producing the previously acquired response to the memory prime (e.g., a particular mobile or hand-puppet) on the ensuing test.

This parallel is best illustrated by infants' performance in reactivation tasks in which two memories were initially associated, for example, a mobile/ kick response and a music box/arm-pull response (Timmons 1994) or a train/ lever-press response and a puppet/imitation response (Barr & Vieira 1999). In each case, both associates were reactivated by priming with only one member of the associated pair. Which response infants subsequently produced during testing, however, depended on the particular associate (analogous to a word-stem) that was presented as the test cue — even if it was not the particular associate that had reactivated the otherwise inaccessible memory in the first place. Thus, for both adults and infants, retrieval of the inaccessible memory was initiated implicitly before the test. For adults, this process occurs prior to the retention test via the initial verbal instructions to respond with whatever word comes to mind before they are presented with the cue fragment (Schacter et al. 1989); for infants, this process occurs via the initial *visual* instructions produced by exposure to the moving mobile, the moving train, or the moving and ringing puppet — also before the cued-recall test — to respond with whatever response comes to mind — and they do, depending on the particular fragment or associate that is presented immediately before the test. When infants are very young, the initial retrieval process takes time, but when they get older, it occurs instantaneously (Hildreth & Rovee-Collier 1999a; see following section). Even 3-month-olds respond instantaneously, however, if their initial study phase is closer in time to the test, as usually is the case in studies with amnesics or instructed adults.

Although whether or not their retrieval is actually intentional is open to speculation, the delayed recognition and reactivation tasks that have been used with preverbal infants meet the basic assumptions of the *retrieval intentionality criterion* (Schacter et al. 1989, see Chapter 2). Because initial training or study is identical for the delayed recognition and reactivation tasks, differences in infants' memory performance on these tasks cannot be attributed to differences in encoding. Also, because retention testing in the delayed recognition and reactivation tasks is conducted under identical circumstances with identical cues present, differences in infants' memory performance on the two tasks cannot be attributed to differences in the retrieval cues that are present at the time of testing. Additionally, the reactivation task is typically administered after delays so long that infants cannot recognize the target information, just as amnesics cannot recognize the target information at the time they are presented with a memory prime. Because infants are preverbal, however, the instructions in the two tasks are contained in the structure of the environment. These instructions consist of the different experimental manipulations that are introduced between training and testing. In the reactivation (implicit memory) task, the retention test is preceded by exposure to a memory prime, whereas in the delayed recognition (explicit memory) task, it is not.

The parallel between the infant and adult tasks is confirmed by the parallel results that have been obtained with adults and infants; to put it colloquially, "the proof is in the pudding." In reaction time studies with adults, for example, priming decreased correct naming latencies to items of any previously studied size (Biederman & Cooper 1992), and in mobile studies with infants, priming with items of any previously studied size was successful (Gerhardstein, Adler & Rovee-Collier, 2000) — even though on a recognition test, both adults and infants had discriminated the same items if they differed in size from the previously studied size. That is, adults had longer reaction times to items whose size differed from the previously studied size on a cued-recall (recognition) test, and infants did not respond above baseline to items whose size differed from the previously studied size on a cued-recall (delayed recognition) test. Data such as these reveal that the test that reveals the effect of priming is not what distinguishes priming from recognition — the test is the same; rather, the prior-cuing procedure and the particular instructions that precede the test are the distinguishing factors. Twelve other independent variables that also produce parallel memory dissociations for adults and infants on recognition and priming tests are reviewed below.

Infants' response latency to a memory prime

Some researchers have objected to the analogy between reactivation tasks that are used with infants and priming tasks that are used with adults. Their objection has been based on initial evidence that the latency of response to a memory prime by 3-month-olds (Fagen & Rovee-Collier 1983) and 6-month-olds (Boller, Rovee-Collier, Borovsky, O'Connor & Shyi 1990) in a reactivation task is so slow — from 1 to 24 hours, whereas in adults, the response latency to a word fragment or word stem is essentially instantaneous. Hildreth and Rovee-Collier (1999a), however, found that the latency of responding to a reactivation stimulus (i.e., a memory prime) decreases linearly over the first year of life. By 9 months of age, infants respond to a prime within 1 min, and by 12 months of age, they respond instantaneously, like adults.

These data are summarized in Figure 7.5, which also includes the latency data previously collected from 3- and 6-month-olds. As can be seen, the latency of response to a memory prime decreases linearly over the entire first year of life. This result is particularly impressive when one considers that the time between forgetting and priming in all experiments was held constant over age; that is, at all ages, the prime was always presented 1 week after infants had last remembered the task. Because infants take progressively longer to forget the original training memory over the first year of life, the prime was necessarily presented after increasingly longer delays with age. Thus, the prime was presented 13 days after the original event to 3-month-olds, but it was presented 2½ months after the original event to 12-month-olds. Despite this, the latency of priming decreased linearly between 3 and 12 months of age. In contrast, priming has never been studied in normal adults after forgetting is complete (i.e., when subjects cannot recognize the stimulus) but only in amnesics.

The preceding results suggest that a *maturation-based factor* is responsible for the age-related decrease in priming latency. This suggestion is consistent with prior evidence that experimental manipulations that accelerate or retard CNS maturation in mice produce corresponding effects on long-term

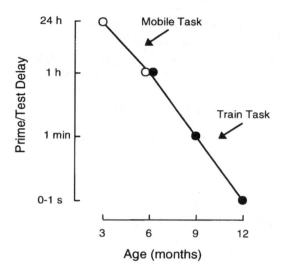

Figure 7.5. The decrease in the latency (log s) of responding to a memory prime over the first year of life. Three-month-olds were trained, primed, and tested in the mobile task (*open circles*), whereas 9- and 12-month-olds were trained, primed, and tested in the train task (*filled circles*); 6-month-olds were studied in both tasks.

memory without affecting original learning (Nagy 1979; Nagy, Misanin, Newman, Olsen & Hinderliter 1972) and that infant guinea pigs, whose central nervous system is already mature at birth, display adult levels of retention (Campbell, Misanin, White & Lytle 1974). Although this evidence reveals that increasing neurological maturity contributes to the age-related improvement in memory performance, the specific neural mechanisms or circuits that are implicated in the decreased response latency to priming are unknown.

Increasing CNS maturation, however, is not the sole means by which infants' response latency to a memory prime can decrease. Even at 3 months of age, infants responded instantaneously to a prime that was presented only 1 day after training but, still, when infants did not recognize the particular test mobile (Gulya, Rovee-Collier, Galluccio & Wilk 1998). These data reveal that the *age of the memory* (i.e., its relative accessibility) can also be a significant factor in the latency of response to a memory prime. In addition, the response latency to a prime can decrease if infants are primed a second time (Hayne, Gross, Hildreth & Rovee-Collier 2000b). When 3-month-olds were exposed

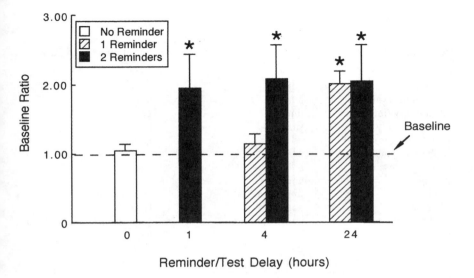

Figure 7.6. The decrease in 3-month-olds' latency of responding after a second memory prime. Independent groups of infants were given one *(striped columns)* or two *(dark columns)* reactivation treatments and then were tested from 1 to 24 hours later (14 days after training). The no-reminder control group *(open column)*, which received no reactivation treatment, exhibited no retention during the 14-day test.

to a single memory prime 13 days after mobile training, they did not exhibit renewed retention until 24 hours later. When they were exposed to two primes — the first on day 7 and the second on day 13, they exhibited renewed retention only 1 hour later (see Figure 7.6). The preceding data reveal that *prior retrieval experience* is also a significant factor in the latency of response to a memory prime. The latter result is reminiscent of Tulving's (1983) description of a reduction in access time to information in semantic memory as a consequence of repeated retrievals in adults. He characterized this reduction as an improvement in retrieval skill with practice.

Independent variables that produce memory dissociations in adults

Table 7.2 lists 13 independent variables that produce dissociations on two tasks — priming and recognition — that are commonly used to distinguish between implicit and explicit memory, respectively, in studies with amnesics

Table 7.2. Independent Variables and Their Effects on Adult Performance in Implicit and Explicit Memory Tasks

Independent Variable	Effect on Implicit Tasks	Effect on Explicit Tasks
age*	none	large
amnesia*	none	large
retention interval	none	large
vulnerability (interference)	limited	great
number of study trials	small	large
study (exposure) time	none	large
number of items studied	none	large
level of processing	none	large
spacing effects	none	large
affect*	important	less important
affect	none	large
serial position	transient or none	persisistent primacy effect
studied size	none	large
memory load	none	large
context dependency	less pronounced	more pronounced

*Subject variable

and normal adults. These same variables produce the same dissociations in the memory performance of very young infants, who are thought to lack explicit memory, on reactivation and delayed recognition tasks. In this section, we present data from adults that illustrate the memory dissociation produced by each independent variable on implicit and explicit tasks and data from infants that illustrate the corresponding memory dissociation produced by the same independent variable on delayed recognition and reactivation tasks. The bulk of the infant data was compiled from mobile studies with infants, but infant data that are available from other paradigms are also presented.

1. Age. As Tulving put it, "The neural pathways that subserve episodic remembering, maturing late in childhood and deteriorating early in old age, are not necessary for priming" (Tulving 1991, p. 16). In fact, tests of explicit memory with 3- to 11-year-olds and young adults (Carroll, Byrne & Kirsner 1985; Greenbaum & Graf 1989; Mitchell 1993; Naito 1990) have found that recall and recognition improve with age, but the amount of priming remains stable across age. Performance also improves with age on imitation tests of explicit memory. The number of logically ordered steps that toddlers success-fully imitated on an immediate cued-recall test increases between 13 and 20 months of age (Bauer 1996), and the level of deferred imitation of a three-step sequence also increases between 6 and 18 months of age (Hayne et al. 2000a; Hayne 1997).

Memory performance in mobile studies similarly improves with increasing age over the first half year of life in the delayed recognition task (the explicit memory task) but not in the memory reactivation task (the implicit memory task). Gekoski, Fagen, and Pearlman (1984) compared the memory performance of premature infants who were born between 31.1 and 39.7 weeks of gestational age on a delayed recognition test with that of full-term 3-month-olds. The mean conceptional age of the preterm and full-term infants at the time of testing did not differ (51.3 and 53.4 weeks, respectively), but their mean chronological age did (156.4 and 81.7 days, respectively). All infants were trained in the mobile task and were tested for recognition of the training mobile 1 week later. During the 1-week test, only full-term infants exhibited significant retention. This difference in retention resulted despite the fact that the preterm infants were of equivalent conceptional age and almost 3 months older in chronological age than the full-term infants. The memory performance of the premature group paralleled that of full-term 2-month-olds, who also fail to exhibit significant recognition after a 1-week delay.

Figure 7.7 shows that the magnitude of infants' retention in a delayed recognition test 1 week after training increases as a function of age despite the fact that the final levels of acquisition were equivalent (Hayne 1990; Hill, Borovsky & Rovee-Collier 1988; Rovee-Collier 1984; Sullivan, Rovee-Collier & Tynes 1979). The same figure also shows that the magnitude of retention following a reactivation treatment that was administered 3 weeks after training is not affected by age (Davis & Rovee-Collier 1983; Hayne 1990; Hill et al. 1988; Rovee-Collier 1984; Rovee-Collier et al. 1980; Vander Linde, Morrongiello & Rovee-Collier 1985).

The age-related increase in infants' memory performance on delayed recognition tasks is not unique to the mobile procedure. Hartshorn et al. (1998b) trained infants between 6 and 18 months of age in the train procedure (Hartshorn & Rovee-Collier 1997; see Chapter 6) and tested their delayed recognition after delays that incremented in 1-week steps until they failed to exhibit significant retention for 2 consecutive weeks. These data were then combined with delayed recognition data previously obtained from infants between 2 and 6 months of age who were identically trained and tested in the mobile procedure. Figure 7.8 summarizes the resulting age changes in retention over the first year-and-a-half of life. This figure presents infants' mean

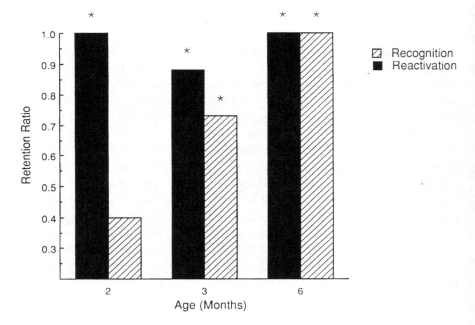

Figure 7.7. Memory performance of 2-, 3-, and 6-month-olds on a delayed recognition test (*striped columns*) 1 week after training and on a reactivation test (*filled columns*) 3 weeks after training. (A retention ratio = 1.00 indicates no forgetting from the immediate to the long-term test.) Asterisks mark groups that displayed retention (*M* baseline ratio significantly > 1.00).

retention ratios after a 0-day retention interval, after the longest retention interval at which infants of a given age performed significantly above baseline, and after the longest retention interval at which infants of a given age were tested (i.e., when they no longer performed significantly above baseline). As can be seen, all infants exhibited equivalent retention after short test delays, but infants remembered after progressively longer delays with age, irrespective of task.

These findings are identical to those originally obtained by Campbell and Campbell (1962) and in subsequent animal studies of memory development with a variety of different species (for reviews, see Campbell & Coulter 1976; Coulter 1979; Nagy 1979). In those studies, animals ranging from preweanlings to adults were required to learn a simple response-reinforcement contin-

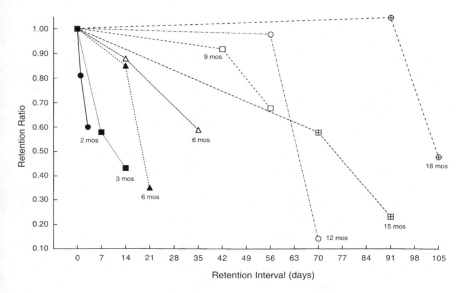

Figure 7.8. Mean retention ratios of independent groups of infants between 2 and 18 months of age who were trained for 2 consecutive days in the mobile task (2 to 6 months, *filled symbols*) or the train task (6 to 18 months, *open symbols*) and received an immediate retention test after the conclusion of acquisition on day 2. Six-month-olds were trained and tested in both tasks. Infants of each age received a delayed recognition test after different retention intervals until, as shown in the last point on each curve, they exhibited no retention (i.e., *M* baseline ratio not significantly > 1.00).

gency that was well within the sensorimotor capacity of all ages studied. With the exception of preweanlings, who occasionally responded at slightly lower rates and reached the learning asymptote more slowly than more mature subjects, animals showed no age differences in acquisition, reached the learning asymptote at the same rate, and exhibited similar levels of retention shortly after learning. Despite this, younger animals consistently forgot more rapidly.

The maximum duration of retention that was exhibited by infants between 2 and 18 months of age in the mobile task (Hartshorn et al. 1998b) and between 6 and 18 months of age in the deferred imitation task (Hayne & Campbell 1997; Herbert & Hayne 2000) was described in Chapter 6 (see Figure 6.6). These functions reveal that long-term memory improves monotonically as a function of age over the first 2 years of life. There is no suggestion that long-term memory is suddenly enhanced at 8 months of age, as was postulated by Kagan (1984; Kagan & Hamburg 1981), or that delayed recognition changes abruptly at 8 or 9 months of age, when the late-maturing memory system was thought to become functionally mature (Nadel & Zola-Morgan 1984; Schacter & Moscovitch 1984), or when the transition from implicit to pre-explicit memory was hypothesized to occur (Nelson 1995, 1997). Nor is there any indication that memory changes qualitatively with the emergence of language in the second year of life (Best 1995; Herbert & Hayne 2000; Nelson 1990).

These age differences in retention (see Figure 7.8 and Figure 6.6) are not due to differences in the baseline levels of activity or the original levels of learning in either the conditioning or imitation tasks — there were no age differences. Analyses revealed that infants' operant levels and degree of original learning did not change with age whether they were studied in the mobile or train task over the period of 2 to 18 months (Hartshorn et al., 1998b) or in the imitation task between 6 and 24 months of age (Herbert & Hayne 2000). These results are particularly striking when one considers the major physical, behavioral, and cognitive changes that occur over the course of the infancy period (see Figure 7.9), including marked changes in motoric and linguistic competence.

The preceding findings demonstrate that immature infants are as capable of encoding memories as more mature infants. We conclude, therefore, that age differences in explicit memory must arise from maturational differences in the neural mechanisms that are responsible for either maintaining access to the

Figure 7.9. Left to right: Infants 2, 3, 6, 9, 12, 15, or 18 months of age. Note the dramatic physical and behavioral differences between younger and older infants over the first year-and-a-half of life.

stored memory over time or retrieving it. We suspect that these neural mechanisms involve the perceptual mechanisms that are associated with selective
attention. Younger infants would have leaner memories, for example, if they
selectively attended to fewer elements in a given situation. As a result, fewer
effective retrieval cues would be available for them to reperceive at the time of
testing (Treisman 1992), and their retention would suffer. We have previously
obtained evidence from 2- and 3-month-olds that supports this possibility
(Rovee-Collier, Earley & Stafford 1989). At 2 months of age, infants do not
appear to process information about the environmental context within which
mobile training occurs, but at 3 months of age, they do. In a related vein,
Gordon (1979) proposed that age differences in retention might reflect differences in the content of what is encoded at different ages. By this account,
infants of different ages acquire different kinds of information in the same
learning situation — perhaps because they have different learning histories or
find different components of the learning situation salient. Evidence of ontogenetic differences in stimulus selection in animals has also been reported by
Spear and Kucharski (1984).

Additional support for the proposition that age differences in selective
attention affect age differences in retention comes from the finding that at 3
months of age, the duration for which infants can recognize a particular
stimulus can be increased or decreased relative to control performance simply
by increasing or decreasing their attention to that stimulus during original
training (Adler, Gerhardstein & Rovee-Collier 1998; see *Level of Processing*,
below).

A dissociation in memory performance on cued-recall and reactivation
tasks was also found for infants of different ages in a study that used a
reenactment procedure (Sheffield & Hudson 1994). In this study, 14- and 18-
month-olds engaged in a different activity at each of six different stations in a
laboratory playroom during a single visit. Each activity consisted of a defined
set of target actions (e.g., get fish food from the cabinet, feed the fish, put the
food back in the cabinet). On the cued-recall test, children returned to the
playroom and produced as many of the target actions at each station as they
could. The 14-month-olds remembered the initial activities for 8 weeks,
whereas the 18-month-olds remembered them for 10 weeks. After forgetting
was complete, new groups at both ages again engaged in the original activities. After their original memory was presumably forgotten, they received a
reactivation treatment in which they watched an experimenter model *half* of

the original activities. When tested for retention of the remaining half of the activities 24 hours later, infants of both ages exhibited the same magnitude of reactivation (i.e., the number of *nonmodeled* activities performed). The delayed recognition/reactivation dissociation found in this study was identical to the dissociation that was obtained in mobile studies with younger infants, despite the fact that the experimental paradigms were very different. Whereas the younger infants had learned to produce the target response (kicking) via a conditioning procedure, infants in the preceding study were initially shown how to find and use the materials required for each activity and then reenacted that target response.

In the response-to-novelty task, infants who were familiarized with the training stimulus in a single session also remembered progressively longer with age on a explicit (recognition) test. Rose (1981) found that 6- and 9-month-olds exhibited an equivalent novelty preference when given a paired-comparison test with four different stimuli immediately after familiarization. After delays ranging from 75 to 150 s, however, 6-month-olds exhibited a novelty preference only for a facial stimulus, but 9-month-olds continued to show a novelty preference for all of the stimuli that they had preferred on the immediate response-to-novelty test. Greco and Daehler (1985) familiarized even older infants — 2-year-olds — with exemplars of basic-level categories and found that they still exhibited a novelty preference after 1 week. (Data from a reactivation task were not collected.)

2. Retention Interval. A basic observation of human memory is that retention on standard recognition, cued-recall, and free-recall tests declines with the passage of time (Wickelgren 1972; Woodworth 1938). In contrast, priming effects are long-lasting in both normal adults and children (Cave 1997; Komatsu & Ohta 1984; Mitchell & Brown 1988; Roediger & Blaxton 1987; Tulving et al. 1982) and amnesics (Cave & Squire 1992; Schacter, Chiu & Ochsner 1993a; Tulving, Hayman & Macdonald 1991). Tulving et al. (1982), for example, primed subjects with words and found that their memory performance on a word-fragment completion test was stable over a period of 1 week, but their performance on a yes/no recognition test declined over the same delay. Similar data were reported by Naito (1990, Experiment 3), who assessed the proportion of correct word-fragment completion and recognition scores for old and new items in Japanese first graders, sixth graders, and college students after delays of 7 min and 6 days. As in Tulving et al., recognition memory scores declined over the retention interval for all ages, but word-fragment completion did not change over the same delay.

Musen and Treisman (1990), using visual patterns with adults, also found a perceptual priming effect that remained stable across delays ranging from a few hours to 1 week, but pattern recognition declined significantly across the same period. In the perceptual priming task, subjects were briefly exposed to a series of visual patterns that they had previously studied or that were novel. After each exposure, they attempted to draw the pattern just seen, and the difference in accuracy between subjects' reproductions of previously studied and novel patterns was taken as the measure of implicit memory. For the measure of explicit memory, subjects were asked to select which pattern of four alternatives they remembered having studied. Using a picture-naming paradigm, Cave and Squire (1992) found that amnesics demonstrated a repetition priming effect that was of normal magnitude 1 week after study, yet amnesics cannot recognize pictures (an explicit task) after even a short delay.

In adults, repetition priming effects can be quite long-lasting. Mitchell and Brown (1988) obtained a robust priming effect on a picture-naming task that remained stable across delays ranging from 1 to 6 weeks, and naming times were not affected by whether or not the picture was recognized. In contrast, performance on an old/new picture recognition task declined over the same period. Cave (1997) replicated their results and found in addition that adults still exhibited significant repetition priming after delays as long as 48 weeks in the same task. Similarly, 9-month-olds still exhibit a significant priming effect almost 6 weeks after reactivation in the operant train procedure, and 12-month-olds still exhibit a significant priming effect at least 8 weeks afterward (Hildreth & Rovee-Collier 1999b).

The same pattern of memory dissociations was obtained in studies of deferred imitation with infants. Bauer, Hertsgaard and Wewerka (1995) reported that the number of correctly ordered pairs of actions produced by 14-month-olds immediately following a verbal prime was approximately equivalent whether children were tested after 1 week or after 1 month, but children's imitation performance on a cued-recall test (i.e., an explicit memory test) decreased as the retention interval increased from 1 week to 1 month. Hayne and her colleagues have likewise reported that retention in a deferred imitation task varies both as a function of the retention interval and age. In all studies, older infants remembered longer (Barr & Hayne, 2000; Herbert & Hayne 2000)

A similar memory dissociation was found for 14- and 18-month-olds who were trained to perform six distinct activities in a single session in a multiple-activities paradigm. The magnitude of retention in the delayed recognition task progressively declined as the retention interval between training and testing increased to 8 and 10 weeks, respectively (Hudson 1994), but the magnitude of retention following a reactivation treatment was the same whether the delay between training and priming was 8 weeks or 10 weeks (Sheffield & Hudson 1994).

In mobile studies with infants ranging in age from 2 through 6 months, performance on delayed recognition tests is also affected by the retention interval, but performance on priming tests is not. Figure 7.10, for example, shows that the memory performance of 3-month-olds on a delayed recognition test declined steadily with increases in the training-test delay (Hayne 1990; Rovee-Collier 1984; Sullivan et al. 1979), but the magnitude of their retention 24 hours after a reactivation treatment was the same whether the interval

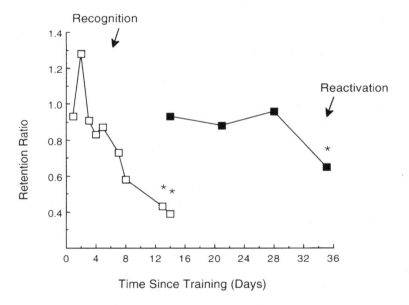

Figure 7.10. Magnitude of delayed recognition or reactivation as a function of the retention interval for independent groups of 3-month-olds (a retention ratio = 1.00 indicates no forgetting from the immediate to the long-term test). Asterisks mark groups that displayed no retention (*M* baseline ratio not significantly > 1.00).

between training and priming was 2, 3, or 4 weeks (Hayne 1990; Rovee-Collier et al. 1980). The memory was either recovered or it was not. Of the nine infants primed 34 days after training and tested 1 day afterward, for example, four infants exhibited perfect retention, and five infants exhibited none. Similarly, the magnitude of reactivation on priming tests is unaffected by the delay between priming and testing (see Figure 7.6). Three-month-olds exhibited the same magnitude of reactivation whether they were tested 1 hour, 4 hours, or 24 hours after priming (Hayne et al. 2000b).

    3. Vulnerability. There is a rich tradition of research documenting that adults' performance on explicit memory tasks is vulnerable to interference (Barnes & Underwood 1959; Postman & Underwood 1973), but evidence that adults' performance on implicit memory tasks is not vulnerable to interference is more recent (Graf & Schacter 1987; Sloman, Hayman, Ohta, Law & Tulving 1988; Tulving 1983). Priming in word-fragment (Sloman et al. 1988), word-completion (Graf & Schacter 1987), and lexical-decision (Bentin & Moscovitch 1988) tasks, for example, is unaffected by the same interference manipulations that impair memory on recognition, cued-recall, and modified free-recall tests.

    A similar dissociation has been observed for infants' memory performance on delayed recognition and reactivation tasks as well. When 3-month-olds were trained with one mobile in session 1 and with a different mobile in session 2, they failed to recognize the session-1 mobile during a 24-hour delayed recognition test — a classic example of retroactive interference (Fagen, Morrongiello, Rovee-Collier & Gekoski 1984). This retroactive interference effect occurred even when infants were trained with a single mobile for a total of 30 min in two sessions and then, immediately after the end of training, they were merely allowed to view — for only 3 min — a different mobile being moved by the experimenter. As before, infants failed to recognize the training mobile during a delayed recognition test 24 hours later (Bhatt 1997; Rossi-George & Rovee-Collier 1999; Rovee-Collier, Borza, Adler & Boller 1993a). At 6 months of age, infants shown the novel mobile for only 2 min after delays as long as 13 days after training were unable to recognize the training mobile on a delayed recognition test 24 hours later. In contrast, infants with no interpolated exposure exhibited near-perfect retention on the long-term test (Muzzio & Rovee-Collier 1996).

    Retroactive interference in infants' delayed recognition performance is not limited to an interpolated exposure to another mobile. A similar result was obtained when infants were trained with the same mobile in different contexts (distinctively colored-and-patterned crib or playpen liners) in each of two sessions and were then tested for recognition of the mobile in the session-1 context. At both 3 months (Rovee-Collier & DuFault 1991) and 6 months (Amabile & Rovee-Collier 1991), training in a different context in session 2 impaired infants' ability to recognize the mobile in the original context during the 24-hour delayed recognition test. Retroactive interference also occurred when both 3-month-olds (Rossi-George & Rovee-Collier 1999) and 6-month-olds (Boller & Rovee-Collier 1992) were trained in the same context for 2 days and then were simply allowed to view a novel context immediately after training. Infants could no longer recognize the training mobile in the original context 24 hours later; instead, they could recognize it only in the new context.

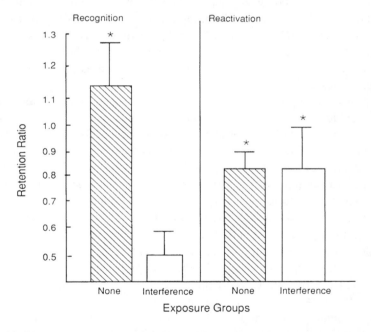

Figure 7.11. Magnitude of delayed recognition (*left panel*) 1 day after training and magnitude of reactivation (*right panel*) 3 weeks after training at 6 months of age. After reactivation in the original context, groups of 6-month-olds were exposed to a novel context between training or priming and testing (*Interference*) or were not exposed to an interpolated context (*None*) and were tested in the original training context 1 day later. (A retention ratio = 1.00 indicates no forgetting from the immediate to the long-term retention test). Asterisks mark groups that displayed retention (*M* baseline ratio significantly > 1.00).

In contrast to a memory's vulnerability to interference on a delayed recognition test, a reactivated memory is relatively impervious to interference by new information that is interpolated between the reactivation treatment and testing. Using the same novel-context exposure conditions that had previously interfered with 6-month-olds' ability to recognize the mobile in the training context (see Figure 7.11, *left panel*), we were unable to modify a reactivated memory for contextual information at 6 months of age (Boller & Rovee-Collier 1994). Whether infants were exposed to the novel context immediately after a successful reactivation treatment or after delays that extended to 24 hours, infants continued to recognize the mobile in the original context and never recognized it in the exposed one (see Figure 7.11, *right panel*).

4. Number of Study Trials. In studies with adults, recognition improves as the number of study trials or stimulus presentations increases, but the number of study trials has little or no effect on priming. Musen and Treisman (1990), for example, gave adults visual patterns to study for 3 s each, after which a pattern was removed, and subjects were allowed to rehearse it for 7 s before the next pattern appeared. After this initial study period, some subjects were reexposed to the sequence of patterns four times (each pattern was re-exposed for only 1 s), while others received only the initial study trial. Explicit memory was measured in a fixed-choice recognition test in which subjects indicated which one of the four test stimuli they had previously studied. Implicit memory was measured in a perception test in which studied patterns and distractor patterns were presented singly, followed by a mask, and subjects were instructed to draw what they had just seen. The priming effect was measured by comparing performance on the old and the new patterns. Subjects in both the repeated- and the single-trial conditions were tested immediately after the first session and 8 days later. In addition, some subjects in the repeated-trials condition were tested in a second session 1 to 3 hours after their first. Musen and Treisman found that the number of study trials had a small-to-nonexistent effect on priming whether subjects were tested later on the same day or after an 8-day delay. In contrast, the decline in recognition accuracy was almost three times greater in the single-trial group than in the repeated-trials group after the 8-day delay.

Bentin and Moscovitch (1988) exposed adults to a set of unfamiliar faces for either one trial or five trials during a study session with lags (number of items interpolated between stimulus repetitions) of 0, 4, or 15 in each learning condition. After one trial per set, stimulus repetition facilitated recognition at lag 0 and lag 4 but not at lag 15; after five trials, however, repetition facilitated recognition, as measured in both reaction time and accuracy, after all lags (Experiment 3). In addition, although the repetition effect in a recognition (explicit memory) task was bigger in the five- than in the one-trial learning condition, in a structural (implicit memory) face/nonface discrimination task, it was independent of the number of study trials (Experiment 4).

In deferred imitation studies with infants, the benefit of additional study trials has also been demonstrated. Bauer et al. (1995) gave 14-month-olds either one or three trials and measured their ability to reproduce a series of ordered events either 1 week or, for the three-trial group only, 1 month later. Infants who received only a single trial exhibited excellent cued-recall after 1 week but poor cued-recall after 1 month; infants who received three trials, however, performed as well after 1 month as infants who received only one trial performed after 1 week. Likewise, Barr et al. (1996) found that 6-month-olds could imitate target actions on a hand-puppet 24 hours after watching six but not three demonstrations of the actions.

In mobile studies with 3-month-olds, the number of training trials also affects memory performance on delayed recognition tests but not on reactivation tests. Figure 7.12 shows that increasing the number of study trials from one to three significantly extended the delayed recognition of 3-month-olds (Ohr, Fagen, Rovee-Collier, Vander Linde & Hayne 1989) but had no effect on the magnitude of their retention after a reactivation treatment (Greco, Hayne & Rovee-Collier 1990; Rovee-Collier et al. 1980). Here, each additional trial prolonged recognition by an additional week, but both two and three successive training trials produced exactly the same magnitude of retention 1 day following a reactivation treatment that was administered 3 weeks after the end of training.

This result was not age-specific: At 2 months of age, infants trained for 18 min exhibited excellent retention 1 week later, but infants trained for 6 or 12 min exhibited none (Rovee-Collier 1984; Vander Linde et al. 1985). Similarly, at 6 months of age, two training trials also produced poorer 24-hour delayed recognition than three (Merriman & Rovee-Collier 1995), but two training trials produced the same magnitude of retention 1 day after a reactivation treatment (Borovsky & Rovee-Collier 1990) as three (Gulya, Sweeney & Rovee-Collier 1999) or four (Timmons 1994) training trials. In our experience, however, an operant task that was acquired in only a single training trial cannot be reactivated between 2 and 6 months of age, although actions that

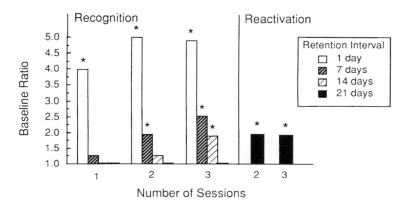

Figure 7.12. The effect of number of training sessions at 3 months on the magnitude of delayed recognition (*left panel*) after different delays and the magnitude of reactivation (*right panel*) 3 weeks after training. Asterisks mark groups that exhibited retention (*M* baseline ratio significantly > 1.00).

were modeled in a single trial can be reactivated at 6 months of age if they were associated with an operant task that had been acquired in two sessions (Barr & Vieira 1999) or if infants were older (i.e., 18 months; Barr 1997).

Finally, the retention advantage of a greater number of trials on a delayed recognition test occurred even when the total amount of training time was held constant. Vander Linde et al. (1985) trained 2-month-olds in the mobile task for either a single 18-min trial or three 6-min trials that were spaced by 24 hours. Three weeks later, infants whose training time was distributed into three trials exhibited near-perfect retention on a delayed recognition test, whereas infants who were trained for a single session exhibited none.

The magnitude of priming is also unaffected by the number of prior reactivations (Greco et al. 1990; Hayne 1990; Hayne et al. 2000b; Rovee-Collier et al. 1980). Hayne (1990), for example, found that the magnitude of retention 21 days after training (1 day after a reactivation treatment) was identical whether 3-month-olds received one, two, or three reactivations (see Figure 7.13), and Hayne et al. (2000b) found the same result 14 days after training (1 day after a reactivation treatment) whether 3-month-olds had received one or two reactivations (see Figure 7.6). The same magnitude of retention was also obtained 21 and 34 days after training (again, 1 day after a reactivation treatment) whether 3-month-olds received two reactivations or three (Hitchcock & Rovee-Collier 1996).

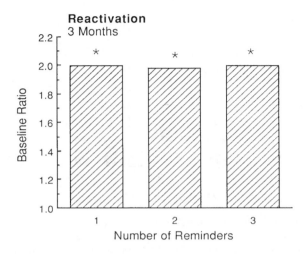

Figure 7.13. The magnitude of reactivation 3 weeks after training for 3-month-old infants who had received one, two, or three reactivations. In each case, retention was tested 1 day after the final reactivation treatment.

5. Spacing Effects. In studies with adults, superior performance on tests of recall and recognition when study trials are distributed instead of massed is a common result (for reviews, see Cohen 1985; Crowder 1976). In contrast, spacing effects on implicit memory tests are inconsistent and relatively infrequent (e.g., Jacoby & Dallas 1981; Perruchet 1989). Although Greene (1990) found a spacing effect on a perceptual identification test under intentional-learning instructions, for example, the effect disappeared when learning was incidental or when spacing was manipulated between study lists. Jacoby (1978; Cuddy & Jacoby 1982) attributed the retention advantage of spaced study to the greater processing that is required for successful retrieval on successive repetitions. Assuming that each presentation of an item or trial initiated the retrieval of its prior presentation, he proposed that retrieval was so trivial when trials were massed that little processing was required; conversely, when the interval between successive trials was greater, retrieval was more difficult, and more processing was involved.

Bjork and his colleagues (Anderson, Bjork & Bjork 1994; Bjork 1975; Schmidt & Bjork 1992) similarly attributed the retention advantage of spaced study to the greater retrieval difficulty that is associated with a greater amount of time since the last retrieval. In a classic study (Landauer & Bjork 1978), adults learned a number of names or name-picture associations during a single study session in which each item was presented once. They then received three or four cued-recall tests, but the intervals between succeeding tests were filled with different numbers of names. Retention was poorest when test items were massed (no intervening names), better when four or five items intervened between successive tests, and best when the number of items (hence the time) between successive tests progressively increased. They concluded that retention was facilitated because the expanding series of intertrial intervals permitted adults to practice retrieval under increasingly difficult conditions. Subsequently, Rea and Modigliani (1985) found that children's ability to recall multiplication facts and spelling lists was significantly enhanced when they used an expanding series of practice tests.

Both 2-month-olds (Vander Linde et al. 1985) and 3-month-olds (Rovee-Collier, Evancio & Earley 1995) also exhibited significantly better delayed recognition a week later when the interval between training sessions was increased from 1 to 2 days. When the intersession interval was increased to 4 days for the 3-month-olds, however, the infants exhibited no retention whatsoever. This result was interpreted in terms of the "time window" construct (Rovee-Collier 1995), which holds that there is a limited period of time following an initial event (i.e., session 1) within which subsequent information (i.e., session 2) can be integrated with the memory representation of the initial event; if the new information is encountered after the time window has shut, then it is not integrated with the initial event. In the Rovee-Collier et al. (1995) study, the time window for integrating the effects of successive training sessions apparently shut after 3 days (see Figure 7.14). When 3-month-olds were trained and tested in a reactivation paradigm, however, the magnitude of retention 1 day after priming was the same whether the sessions were spaced by 1 or 2 days; for infants whose second session was 4 days after their first (outside the time window), however, the reactivation treatment was ineffective (Rovee-Collier et al. 1995).

In another study (Rovee-Collier, Greco-Vigorito & Hayne 1993b), 3-month-olds were trained for three sessions and then were shown a novel moving object either immediately after training was over (when the time window opened) or 4 days later (at the end of the time window, which closes after 4 days with three training sessions). Infants who were exposed to the object at the beginning of the time window recognized it for only 4 days, but

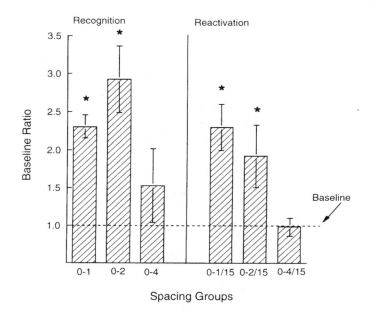

Figure 7.14. The effect of spacing between successive training sessions (session 1 = day 0; session 2 = day 1, 2, or 4) on the magnitude of delayed recognition (*left panel*) 8 days after session 1 and the magnitude of reactivation (*right panel*) 15 days after session 1 at 3 months of age. Asterisks mark groups that displayed retention (*M* baseline ratio significantly > 1.00). The magnitude of recognition of *group 0–2* is significantly greater than that of *group 0–1*, but the magnitude of reactivation of the two asterisked groups does not differ. The second training session on day 4 was not integrated with the first training session on day 0; that is, day 4 fell *outside of the time window*.

infants who were exposed to the object at the end of the time window recognized it for 10 additional days. Although the delay between training and exposure to the novel object affected infants' magnitude of delayed recognition after a retention interval of 1 day, it had no effect on their magnitude of reactivation after a retention interval of 3 weeks (see Figure 7.15; Greco et al. 1990; Rovee-Collier et al. 1993b).

In studies with 3-month-olds (Greco et al. 1990; Hayne, Rovee-Collier & Perris 1987; Ohr et al. 1989), infants trained for three sessions on successive days (days 0–1–2) had exhibited significant retention after 2 weeks but not after 3 weeks. Hartshorn, Wilk, Muller and Rovee-Collier (1998c) replicated this finding. In addition, they trained other groups for three sessions but

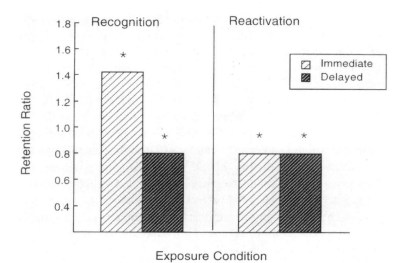

Figure 7.15. The effect of the timing of a brief posttraining exposure to a novel object on the magnitude of delayed recognition of that object (*left panel*) 1 day after the exposure and on the magnitude of reactivation (*right panel*) 3 weeks after training at 3 months of age. (A retention ratio = 1.00 indicates no forgetting.) Asterisks indicate that all groups displayed retention (*M* baseline ratio significantly > 1.00).

programmed their intersession intervals in either an expanding series (days 0–2–8) or a constant series (Days 0–4–8). As in Landauer and Bjork (1978), the mean interval between successive retrievals (i.e., sessions) was the same for both groups (*M* = 4 days). During a delayed recognition test 3 weeks after the final session, the expanding-series group exhibited excellent retention, but the constant-series group exhibited none.

Using the response-to-novelty task, Cornell (1980) familiarized 5-month-olds with two photographs of the same face, presented side-by-side, for four trials. Each familiarization trial lasted until infants had looked at the face for a total of 5 s. In the massed condition, successive trials were separated by 3 s, and in the distributed condition, they were separated by 60 s. Infants in both spacing conditions received a paired-comparison recognition test either 5 s, 1 min, 5 min, or 1 hour after the final familiarization trial. Infants who were tested 5 s after familiarization exhibited a significant novelty preference in both conditions, but after longer delays, only infants in the distributed condition exhibited a significant novelty preference.

6. *Exposure or Study Time.* The *total time law* is a widely-accepted principle in human memory. This law states that the degree to which an item is recalled is a direct function of its total study time, irrespective of the manner in which that time was distributed (Cohen 1985; Cooper & Pantle 1967; for review, see Crowder 1976). In addition, the amount of perceptual processing that can be completed at the time of encoding is constrained by the length of time a stimulus is physically available to the perceiver. As stimulus exposure time increases, the perceiver should be able to extract more perceptual information from the stimulus. In general, studies with adults find that neither study time nor stimulus exposure time affects measures of implicit memory, but both affect measures of explicit memory. Greene (1986), for example, found that the duration of rehearsal had no effect on memory performance in a word-stem completion task but significantly improved memory performance on a recall task. Similarly, von Hippel and Hawkins (1994, Experiment 1) measured retention in three implicit tasks (word-fragment completion, perceptual identification, and general knowledge) and found that increasing stimulus exposure time had no effect on implicit conceptual memory performance when the encoding task focused on perceptual features of the stimulus. Other researchers have also reported that increasing stimulus exposure time has no effect on performance in either a perceptual identification task (Jacoby & Dallas 1981) or a word-fragment completion task (Neill, Beck, Bottalico & Molloy 1990) but improves performance in explicit memory tasks (Debner & Jacoby 1994; Jacoby & Dallas 1981; Neill et al. 1990), including the free recall of word lists (Roberts 1972b).

Using nonverbal stimulus materials, Schacter et al. (1991a) exposed adults to either single or multiple presentations of visual objects and measured their memory performance in an object decision task — presumably, a test of implicit memory. With an exposure duration of 5 s, a single exposure was as effective as multiple exposures in facilitating priming. With an exposure duration of 1 s, however, multiple exposures led to significant priming, but a single exposure did not. When Musen (1991) increased the duration of a single exposure of a novel visual figure from 1 s to 10 s, however, she found that performance on a priming task was not affected, but recognition performance was significantly enhanced.

Using a deferred imitation task and a cued-recall test with 6-month-olds, Barr et al. (1996) similarly found no evidence of imitation after a 24-hour delay in a cued-recall test when infants were exposed to the demonstrator for only 30 s. When the exposure period was increased to 60 s, however, infants' 24-hour deferred imitation was excellent.

In mobile studies with 3-month-olds, increasing the study time similarly enhances performance on a delayed recognition test. Figure 7.16, for example, shows that infants receiving a single session lasting 6 or 9 min failed to recognize the original mobile 1 week later; however, infants displayed significant recognition for 1 week if given a 12-min session and for 2 weeks if given an 18-min session (Ohr et al. 1989).

In studies with 3-month-olds, infants were exposed to a novel mobile for either 180 s or 10 s immediately after training. On a delayed recognition test 24 hours later, the 180-s exposure interfered with recognition of the original mobile and led infants to treat the exposed mobile as if they had actually been trained with it; the 10-s exposure, however, produced these effects on a delayed recognition test after 1 hour but not after 24 hours (Bhatt 1997). No reactivation (priming) data are available from any of the infant studies of exposure duration; however, those who claim that very young infants possess only an implicit memory system would probably concede that exposure

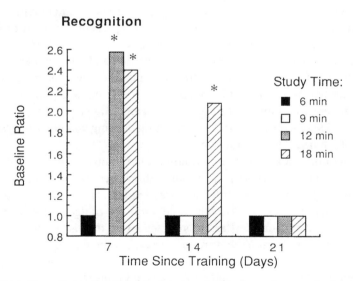

Figure 7.16. The effect of study time (session duration) on the magnitude of delayed recognition of independent groups of 3-month-olds tested 7, 14, or 21 days later. Asterisks mark groups that displayed retention (*M* baseline ratio significantly > 1.00).

duration has no effect on a priming (implicit memory) test. It is the strong effect of exposure duration on infants' performance on a delayed recognition (explicit memory) test for which they cannot account.

7. *Number of Studied Items.* Mandler (1985) characterized non-automatic memories as capacity demanding and distinguished them from automatic memories with no capacity demand. Although he eschewed the explicit-implicit distinction, similar differences in capacity demand have been found to affect performance in explicit and implicit memory tasks, respectively. Thus, for example, increasing the number of studied items produces a dissociation in both adult and infant memory performance on recognition and priming tasks. In studies with adults, increasing the number of studied items decreases performance on explicit memory tasks but does not affect performance on implicit memory tasks.

It is well documented that adding new items to a study list impairs subsequent retention in free-recall, cued-recall, and recognition tasks (Atkinson & Joula 1973; Ratcliff & Murdock 1976; see Crowder 1976, for review). Reinitz and Demb (1994), for example, had college students study a list of compound words and then tested them with old words, recombined words, compound words in which either the first or second parts were new, and completely new words on either an old/new recognition test or on a perceptual identification test (each word presented for 40 ms, followed by a 300-ms mask). On the recognition test, the number of false recognitions increased with the number of studied components. On the perceptual identification task, however, priming occurred only for old words; identification of the other test items was poor irrespective of the number of previously studied components. Mitchell and Brown (1988) similarly found that the magnitude of repetition priming was not affected by the number of studied items or list size.

In a mobile study with 2- and 3-month-old infants, the number of studied items was defined in terms of the number of different types of blocks on the training mobile — all five mobile blocks were identical, or each was different (Rovee-Collier et al. 1989). At both 2 and 3 months of age, performance on a 24-hour delayed recognition test was better when the list was shorter (i.e., when all objects on the mobile were the same), but the magnitude of retention following a reactivation treatment administered 3 weeks after training was unaffected by the number of studied items (see Figure 7.17).

A similar effect on delayed recognition was found when infants were trained with mobiles containing different numbers of feature combinations.

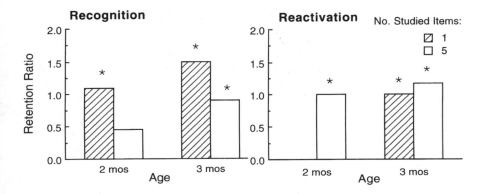

Figure 7.17. The effect of the number of different objects (*studied items*) on the training mobile on the magnitude of delayed recognition 1 day after training (*left panel*) and the magnitude of reactivation (*right panel*) 3 weeks after training at 2 and 3 months of age. (A retention ratio = 1.00 indicates no forgetting.) Asterisks mark groups that displayed retention (*M* baseline ratio significantly > 1.00).

Three-month-olds were trained with a six-block mobile containing either two sets of feature combinations (i.e., three blocks per set) or three sets of feature combinations (i.e., two blocks per set). For infants in the two-set group, three mobile blocks displayed *red As on a black background*, and three displayed *green 2s on a yellow background*; for infants in the three-set group, two blocks each displayed the preceding feature combinations, and two displayed *brown Xs on a blue background.* During the 24-hour delayed recognition test, one of the features was switched or recombined between the sets. Infants trained with two sets of features, for example, were tested with a figure-color recombination (*green* As on a black background and *red* 2s on a yellow background), a figure recombination (red *2s* on a black background and green *As* on a yellow background), or a background color recombination (red As on a *yellow* background and green 2s on a *black* background). If infants discriminated that the features had been recombined, then this was taken as evidence that they had learned which training features belonged together. Otherwise, this was taken as evidence that they recognized the features but did not remember which features went with which others.

In fact, infants who were trained with two sets of features discriminated the recombinations (Bhatt & Rovee-Collier 1994, 1996), but infants who were trained with three sets of features did not (see Figure 7.18, *left panel*), although they did discriminate mobiles on which one of the test features was novel (Bhatt & Rovee-Collier 1997). Even though they had not discriminated a feature recombination during the delayed recognition test, however, only the original mobile reactivated the forgotten memory 2 weeks later; a mobile displaying feature recombinations did not (see Figure 7.18, *right panel*). This is yet another instance of an infant memory dissociation on recognition and reactivation tests.

Finally, Gulya et al. (1998) trained 6-month-olds to kick using a serial list composed of three different mobiles. Infants successively viewed each mobile for 2 min per session for three sessions. Infants subsequently recognized the

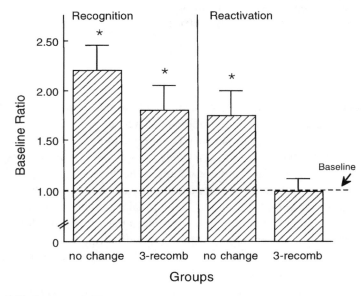

Figure 7.18. Left panel: The 24-hour delayed recognition performance of 3-month-olds who were tested with a mobile displaying three sets of features either in their original combinations (*no change*) or in new combinations (*3-recomb*). *Right panel:* The magnitude of reactivation following priming with a mobile displaying three sets of features either in their original combinations (*no change*) or in new combinations (*3-recomb*). Asterisks mark groups that displayed retention (*M* baseline ratio significantly > 1.00).

test mobile from serial position 1 but not the mobiles from serial positions 2 and 3 during a 24-hour delayed recognition test — a classic primacy effect (see Figure 7.19, *left panel*). When the number of mobiles on the study list was increased from three to five, however, the primacy effect disappeared during the 24-hour test. Instead, infants recognized mobiles from all serial positions but failed to recognize a mobile that had not been on the study list (see Figure 7.19, *right panel*). Here, the impairing effect of increasing the number of studied items on infants' memory for serial order was manifested as a paradoxical increase in test responding. This increase, however, reflected the fact that infants still recognized all of the items on the study list but, as evidenced by elimination of the primacy effect, no longer remembered their original serial order. A similar result was obtained with adults by Murdock (1962), who found that increasing the number of words on the study list impaired adults' memory for order but not item information.

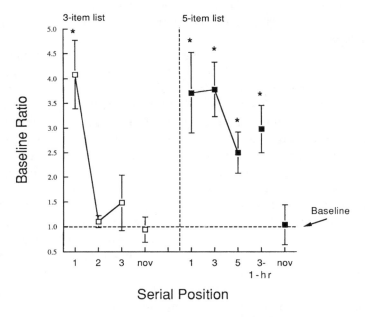

Figure 7.19. The 24-hour delayed recognition performance of independent groups of 6-month-olds who were tested with mobiles from the first, middle, and last serial positions of a three-mobile list (*left panel*) and a five-mobile list (*right panel*). Infants trained with both lists failed to recognize (i.e., discriminated) a novel test mobile. Asterisks mark groups that displayed retention (*M* baseline ratio significantly > 1.00).

8. Level of Processing. Level of processing (LOP) is an encoding variable that affects performance on implicit and explicit memory tasks differently. In their original exposition, Craik and Lockhart (1972) suggested that the duration of a memory was determined by the level or depth at which the perceptual input for that memory was processed. Thus, the shallower processing of phonemic and orthographic features (e.g., searching for specific letters in a word) should lead to a shorter duration of retention, while the deeper processing required by the generation of a verbal associate or a semantic orienting task (e.g., rating the pleasantness of words on a study list) should lead to a longer duration of retention. Since that time, a number of other hypotheses and theories have been advanced. Craik and Tulving (1975), for example, attributed retention differences to the degree of stimulus elaboration instead of to differences in processing depth during encoding, retaining the term "depth" to refer to "degree of semantic involvement." Others introduced terms such as meaningfulness, differentiation, integration, distinctiveness, and so forth (for review, see Tulving 1983) in attempts to explain encoding difficulty in terms of a single factor.

In memory studies with adults, manipulations of LOP have been found to produce strong effects on explicit tests but none on implicit tests (Besson, Fischler, Boaz & Raney 1992; Graf et al. 1982, 1984; Moscovitch 1994; Roediger, Weldon, Stadler & Riegler 1992). One of the earliest demonstrations of this dissociation was reported by Jacoby and Dallas (1981). They asked college students to answer three yes/no questions about each word on a long list and then assessed their retention on either a perceptual identification task (an implicit memory task) or a recognition task (an explicit memory task). The questions pertained to the letters in the word, a rhyme question (both, shallow encoding conditions), or the meaning of the word (a deep encoding condition). Initially, each question was presented on a screen for 1 s and then was replaced by the target word, which remained on the screen until the student answered the question. During the recognition test, words were presented for 2 s each, and students responded "yes" to those that had been presented in the first phase and "no" to those that were new. During the perceptual identification test, words were simply flashed on the screen and students reported each word immediately. Jacoby and Dallas found that the semantic question had longer reaction times than the other two questions, and "no" responses took longer than "yes" responses. On the recognition memory test, the probability of a hit (a correct word identification) was significantly higher for semantic questions and questions requiring a "yes" response; on the perceptual identification test, however, neither question type nor whether the question required a "yes" or "no" answer affected the probability of a hit. Although there was no effect of LOP, presentation of a word in the first phase did produce a significant priming effect in the second phase: Perceptual identification was significantly enhanced when test items were old; moreover, the amount of priming was the same whether recognition memory was very poor or near-perfect.

Examples of the dissociation produced by LOP manipulations have also been reported in the developmental literature. Carroll et al. (1985) presented a list composed of pictures to 5-, 7-, and 10-year-olds and a group of adults, instructing participants either to search for pictures marked with a cross (the shallow encoding condition) or to judge the weight of the objects that were pictured (the deep encoding condition). At each age, performance was measured on both a recognition test (explicit memory task) and a naming test (implicit memory task). As expected, recognition improved with age. In addition, however, picture recognition was better in the deep than in the shallow encoding condition, but the priming measure was unaffected by either age or encoding condition. Lindberg (1980, Experiment 1) found that explicit memory performance (free recall) significantly increased from kindergarten to adulthood following elaborative encoding but not after physical encoding. Naito (1990) replicated this result and extended the analysis to implicit memory performance. She found no effect of encoding condition (orthographic or elaborative encoding) on performance in the implicit word-completion test for 6-, 8-, and 11-year-olds and college students. Memory performance on the explicit free-recall test, however, was significantly better with elaborative encoding at all but the youngest age (see Chapter 4).

Adler et al. (1998) obtained a robust effect of LOP on 3-month-old infants' memory performance in a delayed recognition task. Infants' attention during encoding was enhanced by training them with a pop-out display composed of a single target (L or +) amidst six distractors (+s or Ls, respectively). This display is thought to enhance attention to the target *at the expense* of attention to the distractors (see Figure 7.20).

In Experiment 1, infants who were tested with a mobile composed entirely of targets or distractors recognized both the original target and the original distractors during a 24-hour delayed recognition test, confirming that both were encoded during training. In Experiment 2, infants who were trained

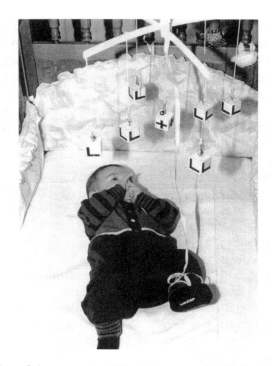

Figure 7.20. One of the pop-out mobiles that was used with 3-month-olds to enhance attention during training. The single target (+) amidst six distractors (Ls) stood out from the display and captured infants' attention. As a result, infants tested with a mobile displaying seven +s remembered it longer than infants whose training mobile displayed seven +s in the first place (see Figure 6.4a).

with the single L target amidst six + distractors recognized a test mobile displaying seven Ls after delays more than twice as long as infants who were originally trained with a mobile composed of seven Ls; conversely, the delay after which infants trained with the pop-out mobile recognized a test mobile displaying seven +s was less than half as long as that of controls who were originally trained with a mobile composed of seven +s (Adler & Rovee-Collier 1994). Finally, Experiment 3 demonstrated that the retention advantage gained by enhancing infants' attention with a pop-out mobile was not specific to the particular character that had been used as the target during encoding. Experiment 2 was replicated even when the characters that served as target and distractors were reversed. These results were consistent with the adult findings that increasing attention to an item during encoding increases its depth of processing and thereby protracts its retention on an explicit memory task (see Figure 7.21).

Training and priming 3-month-olds with a pop-out mobile, however, did not differentially affect the magnitude of their retention following a reactivation treatment. Rather, the magnitude of reactivation was the same as when they were trained and primed with a homogeneous mobile--results consistent with the effect of LOP on implicit memory tasks used with adults.

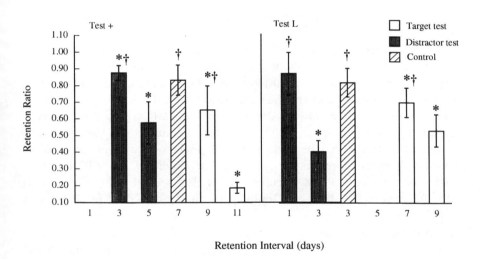

Figure 7.21. The LOP effect at 3 months of age shown as the protracted recognition over days of +s (*left panel*) and Ls (*right panel*) when they were the target (*white columns*) on the pop-out training mobile. Also shown is the maximum duration of retention of control groups (*striped columns*) who were trained with a homogeneous + or L mobile, respectively, and the diminished recognition over days of +s and Ls when they were the distractors (*dark columns*) on the L or + pop-out training mobile, respectively. The corresponding control group for the distractors was trained with a homogeneous mobile displaying the same character as the distractor. (A retention ratio = 1.00 indicates no forgetting). Asterisks mark groups that displayed retention (*M* baseline ratio significantly > 1.00).

9. *Affect*. Most of the research on the role of affect in retention has focused either on the congruence of the mood during encoding and retrieval or on the congruence between the nature of the mood at the time of retrieval and the nature of what is retrieved (e.g., Bower 1981; Eich, Macaulay & Ryan 1994; for review, see Blaney 1986). Recently, researchers have begun to explore the contribution of affect to memory performance on implicit and explicit tests (Denny & Hunt 1992; Hertel & Hardin 1990; Macaulay, Ryan & Eich 1993; Watkins, Mathews, Williamson & Fuller 1992). Research with both normal adults and adult patient populations has demonstrated that performance on explicit tests is sensitive to affect, but performance on implicit tests is not (Tulving 1983).

Using a between-subjects measure, Hertel and Hardin (1990) queried nondepressed (scores < 6 on the Beck Depression Inventory; Beck, Ward, Mendelson, Mock & Erbaugh 1961) and naturally depressed (BDI scores > 6 and < 9) college students about the uncommon meanings of homophones, gave them depressive- or neutral-mood inductions, and then tested both their spelling (an implicit task) and their recognition of old and new homophones. Neither induced nor naturally-occurring depression affected spelling, but both impaired recognition of the old homophones. Watkins et al. (1992) assessed memory for affectively valenced words with adults who were clinically diagnosed with major depression or dysthymia (BDI scores > 19; *M* BDI score = 27.53) or were normal (BDI scores < 8, *M* BDI score = 3.71). Relative to nondepressed adults, depressed adults' performance on a cued-recall test was impaired, but the two groups performed equivalently on a word-completion test. Similarly, Denny and Hunt (1992) found that the free recall of affectively valenced words was impaired in a clinically depressed patient population relative to nondepressed adults, but the two groups performed equivalently on a word-fragment completion test.

In mobile studies with 3-month-olds, Fagen and his colleagues have repeatedly found that infants' delayed recognition is highly sensitive to affect, but their memory performance in a reactivation task is not (for review, see Fagen & Prigot 1993). In these studies, infants were typically trained for two sessions with a 10-object mobile and then were shifted to a nonpreferred 2-object mobile during a final session. In response to the shift, approximately 50% of the infants usually cried. During delayed recognition tests either 1 day or 1 week later, noncriers exhibited excellent retention irrespective of whether they were tested with the 10-object or 2-object mobile, while criers recognized the test mobiles after a 1-day retention interval but not after a 1-week delay (see Figure 7.22, *left panel*; Fagen, Ohr, Singer & Klein 1989). Despite the impaired performance of criers on the 1-week delayed recognition test, when a reactivation treatment was administered 3 weeks after the conclusion of training, all infants exhibited the same magnitude of reactivation 1 day later whether they had cried after a mobile shift or not (see Figure 7.22, *right panel*; Fagen, Ohr, Fleckenstein & Ribner 1985).

Singer and Fagen (1992) repeated this procedure but used a measure of infants' facial expressions of affect (*AFFEX*; Izard, Dougherty & Hembree 1980) in addition to crying. Following the shift to the 2-object mobile, criers exhibited decreasing amounts of interest expressions and increasing amounts of anger and sadness expressions. During the 1-day recognition test, criers again displayed significantly more anger expressions than noncriers, but during the 7-day recognition test, they displayed none. In addition to provid-

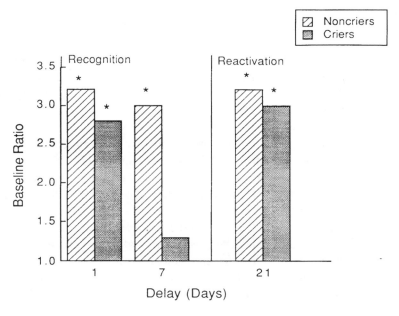

Figure 7.22. The effect of crying on the magnitude of delayed recognition 1 day or 7 days after training (*left panel*) and the magnitude of reactivation (*right panel*) 3 weeks after training at 3 months of age. Asterisks mark groups that displayed retention (*M* baseline ratio significantly > 1.00).

ing a convergent measure of affect, these data confirmed that the poor performance of criers during the 1-week test was not simply a result of their refusal to participate in the task but an instance of true forgetting (Fagen & Prigot 1993).

Finally, the interval between training with the preferred (preshift) mobile and training with the nonpreferred (postshift) mobile is an important determinant of the degree of impairment in infants' delayed recognition performance (Fagen et al. 1989). When a delay of 0, 2, 5, or 15 min was interpolated between infants' exposure to the pre- and post-shift mobiles, criers again failed to recognize the test mobile 1 week later; when the interpolated delay was increased to 30 min, however, their performance on the delayed recognition test was excellent. The performance of noncriers on the 1-week test, by comparison, was excellent after all pre- to post-shift delays.

The preceding studies with infants were based on between-subjects measures, as in the Hertel and Hardin (1990) study with adults. For both age groups, affect differentially affected the magnitude of recognition but not the magnitude of reactivation (priming). Within-subjects measures of preference yield the same result but in a slightly different form. In studies with adults, implicit preference is associated with familiarity: Individuals prefer items that were on the original study list even though they cannot recognize them. Engen and Ross (1973), for example, asked college students to indicate whether different odors were familiar or unfamiliar and whether they liked, disliked, or were indifferent to each odor. On this implicit test, students were more likely to like the odors that they had said were familiar and to either dislike or be indifferent to the odors that they had said were unfamiliar. Of the familiar odors, for example, 46% were rated *like*, whereas of the unfamiliar odors, only 11% were. After delays of 1, 7, or 30 days, they gave students a forced-choice (explicit) recognition test in which odors from the original study list were pitted against new odors. Students' accuracy of recognition was unrelated to whether they had initially classified the odors as familiar. Using a slightly different procedure, Kunst-Wilson and Zajonc (1980) similarly found that adults preferred visual stimuli that they had previously seen relative to new ones, even though the stimuli were exposed for durations too brief to be recognized.

Using a between-subjects design, Wilk, Klein and Rovee-Collier (2000) obtained a similar result. They trained 3-month-olds with a particular mobile and gave them a delayed recognition test in which the original mobile and a novel one were simultaneously presented either 1 day or 4 days later. During testing, they measured both kicking and looking. Typically, 3-month-olds exhibit no retention if tested exclusively with a novel mobile 1 day after training, but they exhibit near-perfect retention if tested exclusively with the training mobile after the same delay (Hayne, Greco, Earley, Griesler & Rovee-Collier 1986). As the interval between training and testing increases, however, 3-month-olds increasingly respond to a novel test mobile, and by 4 days after training, they kick as robustly to a novel mobile as to the training one (Rovee-Collier & Sullivan 1980). The latter data are taken as evidence that infants gradually forget the specific details of their training mobile until, after 4 days, they cannot discriminate between them. In the Wilk et al. study, as expected, infants exhibited significant recognition 4 days after training. Despite prior evidence that they cannot discriminate between these test mobiles after 4 days on the kicking measure, however, infants also looked proportionally longer at the original mobile than at the new one after both test delays. Thus, as in the Kunst-Wilson and Zajonc (1980) study with adults, although infants do not discriminate the new mobile from the old one after 4 days on the kicking measure, they do discriminate them on the looking measure, implicitly preferring to look at the familiar mobile.

   10. Serial Position. The serial position of items on a study list has long been known to produce strong and persistent primacy and/or recency effects on immediate tests of free recall, cued recall, and recognition memory (e.g., Bousfield, Whitmarsh & Esterson 1958; Gershberg & Shimamura 1994; Murdock 1962; Wright et al. 1985). A handful of researchers have found recency effects on implicit tests of both word-stem completion (McKenzie & Humphries 1991; Rybash & Osborne 1991) and word-fragment completion (Sloman et al. 1988), but Brooks (1994) observed that the instructions and procedures in these reports were either suspect or reported in insufficient detail.

   Two laboratories have recently used the same study instructions and test stimuli but different instructions for the implicit and explicit tests. Gershberg and Shimamura (1994) obtained inconsistent evidence for primacy and recency effects across three experiments. Implicit word-stem completion tests, for example, yielded a primacy effect in two experiments and a recency effect in one, and these effects were highly transient when they did occur. Different explicit tests (word-stem cued recall, free recall) also yielded inconsistent primacy and/or recency effects across experiments. Using word-stem completion and word-stem cued-recall tests with normal adults, Brooks (1994) found primacy effects on an explicit test in two experiments and, when the last items studied were the first ones tested, a recency effect in the second of these. In neither experiment, however, did serial position affect performance on the implicit test. Taken together, the data indicated that the serial order of the items on the study list had no effect on performance in implicit tests but produced a primacy effect in explicit tests. Finally, in two experiments with Korsakoff and nonKorsakoff amnesic patients, both patient groups performed more poorly than controls on tests requiring the recall, recognition, and sequencing of words and facts (Shimamura, Janowsky & Squire 1990).

Delayed recognition tests with both 3- and 6-month-olds also reveal a strong and persisting primacy effect (Gulya et al. 1998; Merriman, Rovee-Collier & Wilk 1997). Independent groups of infants were trained with a list composed of three different mobiles for 2 min each for 3 successive days and were given a recognition test 24 hours later with either a mobile from one of the three serial positions or a completely novel mobile. Infants of both ages responded only to the test mobile in serial position 1–a strong primacy effect (see Figure 7.23, *left panel*). In a follow-up study (see *Number of Studied Items*), when the number of mobiles on the original list was increased from three to five, the primacy effect was eliminated, and infants recognized all of the mobiles on the 24-hour delayed recognition test. Even so, they still discriminated a novel test mobile that had not been on the study list (Gulya et al. 1999).

Gulya et al. (1998) conjectured that infants who had been trained with the three-mobile list in the initial study had failed to recognize the test mobiles from serial positions 2 and 3 because those mobiles were *out of order* when they had been presented singly to independent groups of infants at the time of testing. (Recall that infants had always seen the mobile from serial position 1 first at the outset of each daily training session.) In addition, they observed that a single mobile is not a retrieval cue for serial order, which entails relational information and hence requires two cues (i.e., this-before-that or this-after-that). Therefore, they primed 3- and 6-month-old infants who had been trained on a three-mobile list with the mobile from the preceding serial position immediately before the 24-hour test. This priming task was procedurally identical to word-stem and word-fragment completion tasks used in priming studies with adults except that the materials were not verbal. Although they had failed to recognize the mobile from serial position 2 on the delayed

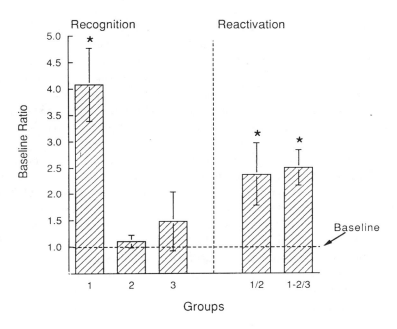

Figure 7.23. The effect of the serial position of mobiles on a three-mobile list on the magnitude of delayed recognition (*left panel*) and the magnitude of reactivation (*right panel*) 24 hours after training at 3 months of age. The delayed recognition function (*left panel*) shows a classic primacy effect which was eliminated when mobiles in serial positions 2 and 3 were primed with mobiles from the preceding serial position(s) immediately before the test (*right panel*). Asterisks mark groups that displayed retention (*M* baseline ratio significantly > 1.00).

recognition test, this time infants of both ages responded to the test mobile from serial position 2 on the 24-hour test when they were initially primed with the mobile from serial position 1–the familiar explicit-implicit dissociation (see Figure 7.23, *right panel*). If infants were primed with the mobile from serial position 3, however, they still did not recognize it. In addition, even though infants of both ages had failed to recognize the mobile from serial position 3 after 24 hours, when they were successively primed immediately before the test with the mobiles from serial positions 1 and 2 for 1 min each, they did respond to the mobile from serial position 3–again, the familiar explicit-implicit dissociation. When primed for 2 min with the mobile from serial position 1, however, they failed to respond to the test mobile from serial position 3. These data demonstrated that only valid order cues were effective memory primes at both 3 and 6 months of age, whereas invalid order cues were not. This result confirmed that even though infants of both ages had previously failed to recognize the same mobiles, they responded selectively to a valid order prime on the basis of their prior training experience.

Using a response-to-novelty task, Cornell and Bergstrom (1983) familiarized independent groups of 7-month-olds during multiple study periods with a serial list composed of three photographs of adult female faces that were spaced by 1 s. Infants received a paired-comparison test with a preexposed and a novel face after delays of 5 s, 1 min, or 5 min. As in recognition studies with adults (Crowder 1976; Wright et al. 1985), Cornell and Bergstrom obtained a classic U-shaped serial position effect with both primacy and recency effects after the shortest delay (5 s) and a persisting primacy effect after the longest delay (5 min). This result resembles that of Merriman et al. (1997) and Gulya et al. (1998), who also found only a primacy effect after a long delay (24 hours) when 3- and 6-month-olds were trained and tested on a three-item list in the mobile procedure.

11. Studied Size. Ungerleider and Mishkin (1982) conjectured that the memory system represents objects in two separable representations — one that is size-sensitive and one that is size-invariant — which function in different situations. In studies with normal adults and amnesic patients, changes in the studied size of an object at the time of testing impair performance on recognition memory tasks (Biederman & Cooper 1992; Jolicoeur 1987; Milliken & Jolicoeur 1992; Schacter, Cooper & Treadwell 1993b) and object decision (Cooper, Schacter, Ballesteros & Moore 1992; Schacter et al. 1991a) tasks, but these same study-to-test size changes do not affect priming on either object naming tasks (Biederman & Cooper 1991, 1992) or object decision tasks (Schacter, Cooper, Tharan & Rubens 1991b; Schacter et al. 1993b), whether the objects are novel or familiar.

Biederman and Cooper (1992), for example, presented adults with a set of line drawings of common objects and asked them to identify the objects. Following their first exposure, adults who performed a recognition task (same/different judgment) were slower to recognize previously viewed objects at a new size than previously viewed objects that were the same size as in the first exposure. When asked simply to name the objects on their second exposure, however, the amount by which their naming latency was facilitated by the prior exposure was the same whether the objects' size was changed between exposures or not. The facilitative effect of the prior presentation of an item on memory performance is taken as an indication of priming (Tulving & Schacter 1990). Biederman and Cooper interpreted these findings as indicating that separate memory systems, one sensitive to size (*size-sensitive*) and the other not (*size-invariant*), were accessed by the two different tasks. These systems, they suggested, corresponded to explicit and implicit memory, respectively (Musen & Treisman 1990; Schacter 1987; Tulving & Schacter 1990).

Cooper et al. (1992) obtained similar results using an object decision task. Adults judged the direction each object faced on its first exposure and, following a delay, received either a recognition task (old/new judgment) or a possible/impossible object (perceptual) decision task. The size of the objects was manipulated between the first and second exposures. Like Biederman and Cooper (1992), Cooper et al. (1992) found that adults' latency to recognize old objects at a new size was substantially slower than their latency to recognize old objects at their original size. Performance on the object decision task, however, was not sensitive to size. Adults showed equal priming whether the possible objects were presented at the studied size or at a different one (impossible objects showed no priming). Also like Biederman and Cooper, Cooper et al. (1992) attributed this dissociation to two, functionally different memory systems — an episodic system in the case of the recognition task, and a semantic system in the case of the object decision task. A similar dichotomy in memory performance on recognition and priming tasks has been found for other stimulus dimensions as well, including color, pattern, contrast, illumination, reflection, and translation (Biederman & Cooper 1991; Cave, Bost & Cobb 1996; Cooper et al. 1992; Srinivas 1996).

Cave et al. (1998) found that binocular rivalry suppressed repetition priming in a picture-naming task. This was not due to a general reduction in attention during suppression — focal attention is not necessary to elicit priming (Stankiewicz, Cooper & Hummel 1994), and divided attention has little or no effect on repetition priming (Mulligan 1997; Mulligan & Hartman 1996). Rather, the binocular suppression disrupted neural events at an early stage of visual processing, erasing the target (as well as the prime), which is normally visible, from consciousness for several seconds at a time. This, in turn, prevented the local features of the object representation from being (re)assembled into meaningful global figures or objects during a late, high-level processing stage, although they were registered. In other words, priming must transpire at a stage of visual processing that is subsequent to the early stage, where binocular suppression occurs, and during which relatively abstract object representations are registered (Cave et al. 1996; Tulving & Schacter 1990). Because priming occurs for visual stimuli that never enter conscious awareness (Kihlstrom, Schacter, Cork, Hurt & Behr 1990; Kunst-Wilson & Zajonc 1980; Mandler, Nakamura & Van Zandt 1987), this stage of processing must be intermediate between the stage that mediates suppression and the stage that supports conscious visual awareness.

The same dissociation — impaired recognition but preserved priming — has been obtained with 3-month-olds in delayed recognition and reactivation tests, respectively, following transformations in studied size. In an initial study, infants who were trained with a mobile composed of seven pink blocks with a computer-generated black L on each side exhibited excellent retention in a 24-hour delayed recognition test with the same characters (the control group); when tested with Ls that were either reduced or increased in size by 25%, however, infants' performance on the delayed recognition test was significantly impaired (Adler & Rovee-Collier 1994). In a follow-up study, Gerhardstein et al. (2000) asked whether 3-month-old infants show a memory dissociation on delayed recognition and reactivation tests analogous to the dissociation exhibited by adults on size-sensitive (explicit) and size-invariant (implicit) memory tests. They found that the 24-hour delayed recognition performance of 3-month-olds who were trained with a mobile displaying +s of a particular size was significantly impaired when they were tested with +s that were either reduced or increased in size by 33% (see Figure 7.24, *left panel*). In contrast, their magnitude of retention following a reactivation treatment with mobiles displaying identically size-transformed +s was unaffected by whether the +s used to prime the memory were larger or smaller than the +s they saw during training (see Figure 7.24, *right panel*). In each case, controls who were trained and either tested 24 hours later or primed 2 weeks later with a mobile displaying characters of the same size exhibited excellent retention.

The finding that 3-month-olds, like normal adults, show preserved priming across size transformations and, also like normal adults, are sensitive to size transformations on same/different recognition tests suggests that the same memory systems mediate their memory performance.

12. Memory Load. The term *memory load* has been used with reference to both the length of the retention interval (i.e., longer test delays creating a greater memory load; Quinn & Eimas 1996) and the amount of information that must be retained (Mandler 1985). Both usages were considered earlier (see

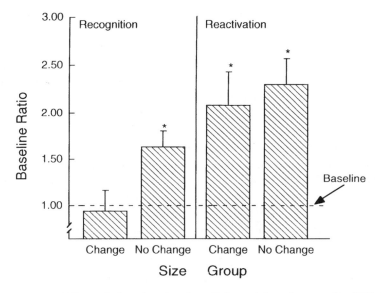

Figure 7.24. The effect of changing the size of the training character by 33% on the magnitude of delayed recognition 24 hours after training (*left panel*) and the magnitude of reactivation (*right panel*) 3 weeks after training at 3 months of age. The performance of no-change control groups who were trained and either tested or primed with the original character is also shown. Asterisks mark groups that displayed retention (*M* baseline ratio significantly > 1.00).

Retention Interval and *Number of Studied Items*). Recall that in both instances, increasing the memory load impaired memory performance on recognition tests but not on priming tests. A third factor that affects the memory load is the nature of the to-be-remembered information. For infants as for adults, for example, relational information creates a greater memory load than absolute information. Adler and Rovee-Collier (1994) reported that 3-month-old infants could discriminate horizontal and vertical line segments (two textons) in different spatial relations (L versus T) during a 1-hour delayed recognition test but not during a 24-hour test. However, they could discriminate +s, which contain a line crossing (a third texton), from both Ls and Ts during a 7-day test. In addition, infants recognized Ls and Ts for only 3 days, but they recognized +s for 7 days. These data illustrate the predicted memory dissociation: Absolute information (texton number) was remembered longer than relational information (spatial arrangement) on delayed recognition tests. Infants' magnitude of reactivation, however, was equivalent when exactly the same stimuli were used as memory primes with 3-month-olds (Rovee-Collier et al. 1992a) and 6-month-olds (Bhatt, Rovee-Collier & Weiner 1994).

In the following studies, increasing the memory load also selectively impaired infants' retention of relational information on a delayed recognition task but not on a reactivation task. In a sequel to the feature combinations study described earlier (Bhatt & Rovee-Collier 1997; see *Number of Studied Items*), 3-month-olds differentially forgot the correlations between different training features (*relational information*) as the retention interval increased from 1 day to 3 days, but they still recognized the individual features (*absolute information*) and discriminated them from novel features on a delayed recognition test after a 4-day retention interval (Bhatt & Rovee-Collier 1996). When the number of feature sets on the training mobile was increased from two to three, infants recognized the feature relations on the two-set mobile but not on the three-set mobile during a 24-hour delayed recognition test. In a reactivation task, however, the three-set mobile was an effective memory prime 2 weeks later if it displayed the original feature combinations but not if it displayed feature recombinations (Bhatt & Rovee-Collier 1997).

Finally, recall that 6-month-olds who were trained with a three-mobile list had recognized only the mobile from serial position 1 — a classic primacy effect — during a 24-hour delayed recognition test (see Figure 7.19, *left panel*). When the length of the list was increased from three mobiles to five mobiles, however, the primacy effect on the delayed recognition test disappeared (Figure 7.19, *right panel*; Gulya et al. 1999). In other words, increasing the memory load impaired infants' retention of order (relational) information but not their retention of item-identity (absolute) information. Murdock (1962) had similarly found that the primacy effect disappeared when the number of words that were presented to adults on a study list was increased.

13. Context. The role of context in retention has been of interest to psychologists for more than 2 decades, yet the term has been used in many different ways (for review, see Clark & Carlson 1981). Broadly speaking, the context refers to global aspects of the experimental environment, including both external (the room, the experimenter, and the apparatus) and internal (the inner state of the subject, including the pharmacological context, the mood or affective state, or the point in the circadian cycle) conditions. However, the context can also refer to the visual stimuli that surround or precede a target object or the items that accompany the target item on each study trial, also called the *local context*. In the latter situations, the context facilitates the interpretation of the target stimulus. As a rule, retention is better when the encoding and retrieval contexts are the same than when they differ (Cohen 1985; Spear 1978).

Tulving (1983) claimed that episodic memories included spatiotemporal details, whereas semantic memories did not. Mandler (1985) rejected a multiple-memory-systems approach but similarly considered non-automatic (i.e., explicit) memories to be context-dependent and automatic (i.e., implicit) memories to be context free. Neely (1989; Neely & Durgunoglu 1985), however, concluded that the evidence for these distinctions was ambiguous. Although a change in context between study and test has been shown to impair adults' memory performance on recognition and recall tests (Thomson & Tulving 1970; Underwood & Humphreys 1979), the effect of a context change on memory performance on implicit tests is less clear. Richardson-Klavehn and Bjork (1988), for example, observed that small but persistent context effects appeared over a wide range of perceptual identification (implicit memory or priming) studies, even though the effects within a particular study were often not significant.

Jacoby (1983) asked college students to read a list of words and then gave them a perceptual identification test containing different proportions of words from the previously read list. Their perceptual identification was facilitated by the proportional overlap between the study and the test list. Likewise, Graf and Schacter (1985) found a larger priming effect on a word-fragment completion task when college students and amnesic patients were primed with a word from a word pair on a prior study list (same context condition) than with other words (different context condition), but this difference emerged only when the study task required elaborative processing. More recently, however, Allen and Jacoby (1990) determined that the priming effect on a perceptual identification test was equivalent whether test words had been generated during study (i.e., were easily recognized) or had only been read (i.e., were poorly recognized). Changes in the modality of presentation (Roediger & Blaxton 1987), the visual display of the target stimuli (Jacoby & Dallas 1981), the environmental setting of encoding and retrieval (Graf 1988; Smith, Heath & Vela 1990), the perceived sense or meaning of a word (Lewandowsky, Kirsner & Bainbridge 1989), and mood (Macaulay et al. 1993) have also been reported to disrupt memory performance on implicit tests.

For many years, studies of context effects with young infants were relatively sparse, probably because the brain structures responsible for representing information about the environmental context in adults were thought to be functionally immature in infants younger than 8 or 9 months of age. Research with both infant rats (Richardson, Riccio & McKenney 1988) and human infants, however, subsequently challenged this belief. For 3-month-old human infants, changing the context at the time of testing has no impact on retention after a retention interval of 1 day (Butler & Rovee-Collier 1989; Hayne, Rovee-Collier & Borza 1991) but impairs retention after longer delays (Butler & Rovee-Collier 1989; Rovee-Collier, Griesler & Earley 1985a). At 6 months, a context change impairs retention after both 1 day and 3 days but has no effect on retention after longer delays (Borovsky & Rovee-Collier 1990). Training in one room and testing in another one has the same impairing effect as training in the presence of a distinctive cloth panel and testing in the presence of another one (Hartshorn & Rovee-Collier 1997).

In addition, memory reactivation is impaired by a context change at both 3 months (Butler & Rovee-Collier 1989; Hayne et al. 1991) and 6 months (Borovsky & Rovee-Collier 1990; Hartshorn & Rovee-Collier 1997; Shields & Rovee-Collier 1992). Two-month-olds have not been tested in an altered context, but attempts have been made to enhance their long-term retention by both training and testing them in a highly distinctive context (Rovee-Collier et al. 1989). Although this manipulation facilitates retention in Korsakoff patients (Winocur & Kinsbourne 1978) and 3-month-olds (Butler & Rovee-Collier 1989; Hayne & Rovee-Collier 1995), it does not facilitate retention in 2-month-olds.

In an initial study, 3-month-olds recognized the original mobile 1 week after training in the original context but not in a different one, and the training context alone — without the mobile — could reactivate the memory 2 weeks after training, but a novel context could not (Rovee-Collier et al. 1985a). Hayne and Findlay (1995) replicated the context-alone reactivation result after delays of 3 and 4 weeks. If the original context, by itself, is an effective retrieval cue, then it must have been represented in infants' memory. Butler and Rovee-Collier (1989) subsequently tested 3-month-olds after delays ranging from 1 to 5 days with all combinations of cues and contexts that were the same or different from training to testing. This study yielded three important results. First, infants did not treat the cue and context as a stimulus configuration. Had they done so, then changing either the cue or the context would have impaired retention, but a context change did not impair retention during the 1-day test. Second, the focal cue, an otherwise effective memory prime, was rendered ineffective in a novel context. This result has been replicated many times with both 3- and 6-month-olds. And third, a highly distinctive training and test context facilitated discrimination of a novel test mobile from the training mobile after delays when generalization to a novel mobile was seen in its absence. This result reflects the disambiguating function of context when the memory of the original cue is fuzzy (Bouton & Bolles 1985).

Butler and Rovee-Collier (1989) proposed a hierarchical, attention-gating model of memory retrieval, adapted from Reeves and Sperling's (1986) model of retrieval from visual short-term memory, to account for the role of context in memory retrieval. According to their model, the memory representation of an event is organized hierarchically, with contextual information occupying a relatively high node. Thus, attention to potential retrieval cues is first filtered or screened at the level of the context, and perceptual identification (an automatic or parallel process) of appropriate retrieval cues in the context permits attention to flow to the next level (the focal cue). A mismatch between the contextual information present during testing and that represented in memory (i.e., a failure of perceptual identification), however, prevents the attention gate from opening and blocks the flow of attention to the cue. As a result, the retrieval process is terminated, and infants fail to recognize the cue during the test. Like Reeves and Sperling, Butler and Rovee-Collier also assumed that the attention gate might be partially opened under some circumstances, for example, if a partial match is made or if a sufficient number or kind of critical retrieval cues are detected. The latter assumption was supported by findings that infants exhibit recognition if the test context contains certain critical features that were present during initial encoding (Earley, Bhatt & Rovee-Collier 1995; Rovee-Collier, Schechter, Shyi & Shields 1992b).

Context effects have now been studied in the mobile and train tasks with infants over the entire first year of life (Hartshorn, Rovee-Collier, Gerhardstein, Bhatt, Klein et al. 1998a). These data revealed that a context change impairs retention only at the end of the forgetting function at all ages except 6 months (Borovsky & Rovee-Collier 1990), when it impairs recognition for only a few days after training only. In deferred imitation studies with 12- to 18-month-olds, infants similarly generalize across widely varying training-test contexts after delays from 3 min to 4 weeks (Hanna & Meltzoff 1993; Hayne et al. 2000a; Klein & Meltzoff 1999). At 6 months, however, a context change impairs 24-hour deferred imitation (Hayne et al. 2000a), just as it impairs 24-hour delayed recognition in mobile studies at this age (Borovsky & Rovee-Collier 1990; Shields & Rovee-Collier 1992).

The deleterious effect of a context change on delayed recognition can be overridden by explicitly training infants in a different context in each session (Amabile & Rovee-Collier 1991; Rovee-Collier & DuFault 1991) — a condition that has long been known to override the debilitating effect of a context change on recall by adults (Pan 1926). The same effect has been obtained at 6 months of age by merely exposing infants briefly to a different context within a day of training (Boller & Rovee-Collier 1992; Boller et al. 1996) and, at 3 months of age, by repeatedly reactivating the original memory (Hitchcock & Rovee-Collier 1996). In the latter study, after forgetting was complete, infants were initially primed with the original mobile in the original context, but their last (either their second or third) reactivation treatment occurred in a different context. During these subsequent reactivation treatments, their training memory was successfully primed in the different context. Even during a third reactivation treatment, however, the original memory could not be reactivated by a different focal cue (the mobile) in the original context *unless* that reactivation treatment occurred after a very long delay (i.e., 5 weeks after training). Apparently, memory attributes become inaccessible over successive retrievals, and those that represent contextual information are lost before those that represent the focal cue (see also Riccio, Ackil & Burch-Vernon 1992).

Conclusions

The functional dissociations in infants' memory performance in delayed recognition and reactivation tasks exactly mirror the functional dissociations that commonly distinguish two different memory systems in adults. Although the infant data might be dismissed as merely reflecting dissociations within a single (implicit) memory system, it is illogical to use evidence of the same dissociations to argue for the existence of two different memory systems in adults and only a single memory system in infancy. McDonough (cited in Bower 1995, p. 86), for example, described infants' memory performance in the delayed recognition task with mobiles as "only procedural" (see also Bauer 1996; Bauer & Hertsgaard 1993; Mandler 1984, 1990) because the response that infants use to indicate recognition is initially learned via an operant conditioning procedure. Similarly, Bauer (1996) dismissed evidence from mobile studies of delayed recognition and memory reactivation as revealing anything about infants' ability

> "...to construct and maintain accessible...memories ...because the behaviors from which they are derived do not meet the criteria for recall....Because the participants of research on memory for experiences early in life are preverbal or barely verbal, we are unable to query them to ensure their awareness that their behaviors result from some previous experience. There is ambiguity, then, as to whether the basis on which we infer memory, namely a change in nonverbal behavior, results from conscious recollection or nonconscious influence" (p. 30).

Both Bauer and McDonough take the position that deferred imitation is an explicit memory task. Their approach to the study of memory development in infants is to find a task that amnesics cannot solve, but normal adults can — and use conscious recollection to do so (see Chapter 1). Because preverbal infants can also solve a deferred imitation task, these investigators infer that they must use conscious recollection to solve it as well. Deferred imitation per se, however, is neither an explicit nor an implicit task; rather, the type of memory task (either recognition/cued-recall or priming) in which it is used is what determines the form of memory it yields. To date, however, only two studies of deferred imitation have used a reactivation or priming (implicit memory) task (Barr 1997; Barr & Vieira 1999); all others have used only cued-recall (explicit memory) tasks.

In retrospect, the mobile and deferred imitation procedures are more similar than they are different, as the form of the retention function obtained with each procedure shows. Demonstrating target actions on a particular object(s) is simply a way of introducing infants to the target information and providing them with a nonverbal means of indicating whether they recognize the specific test cue. Likewise, putting critical stimulus information on the sides of the mobile blocks and reinforcing a distinctive response (a footkick) in their presence is simply a way of introducing infants to the target information and providing them with a nonverbal means of indicating whether they recognize the specific test cue.

Because operant training in mobile studies (or exposure to the demonstration in deferred imitation studies) occurs *prior* to the introduction of the manipulations that differentiate reactivation from delayed recognition tasks, any subsequent performance differences in these tasks cannot be attributed to how the response got into the infant's behavioral repertoire in the first place.

Consider, for example, that even verbally proficient children and adults initially had to learn the verbal labels for the objects and patterns with which they are subsequently tested in implicit and explicit memory tasks. Yet, thought is rarely given to the specific manner in which these verbal labels were actually acquired in the first place. Why? Because that information is *unimportant* in accounting for adults' functional dissociations in implicit and explicit memory tasks. As this chapter documents, that same information is equally unimportant in accounting for infants' functional dissociations in implicit and explicit memory tasks.

We conclude that the functional memory dissociations that are exhibited by preverbal infants, normal children and adults, and amnesics on priming and recognition tasks are the same whether the target response was initially acquired by operant conditioning, modeling (deferred imitation), familiarization (response-to-novelty), or verbal instructions ("study this list of nonsense syllables"). Without exception, evidence from infant memory dissociations reveals that the development of explicit and implicit memory is not hierarchical during the infancy period, hence is not described by the Jacksonian principle. In terms of multiple memory systems, these data reveal that the memory systems that support implicit and explicit memory are both present from early in infancy.

CHAPTER 8

Structural and Processing Accounts of Memory Dissociations

In this chapter, we consider some of the major theoretical accounts that have been advanced to explain the functional memory dissociations that are exhibited by brain-damaged and normal (instructed) adults. Whereas accounts based on multiple memory systems emphasize the cognitive architecture and neural structures that underlie different kinds of memory performance, processing accounts focus on the cognitive operations that are required to perform different kinds of memory tasks. Our position is that a satisfactory account must also explain the memory dissociations that are exhibited by very young infants. Therefore, we briefly review the major theoretical accounts and consider their implications for the development of implicit and explicit memory.

Throughout the preceding chapters, we have seen that tasks have been designated as either explicit or implicit on the basis of whether or not amnesics can succeed on them, and the common usage of those terms was extended to refer to the underlying brain systems that were presumed to be responsible for that performance. In response to this situation, Gardiner and Java (1993) complained that the science of memory had become obfuscated by "terminological confusion and excess." They were referring to the fact that the same terms — implicit and explicit — were used to signify different memory tasks, different memory systems or processes, and different states of awareness. Their concern was that such labeling presupposed an "identity between the task and the system or process, between the system or process and the state of awareness, [and] between the state of awareness and the task" (Gardiner & Java 1993, p. 163).

Making matters worse, a variety of different labels have been given to similar memory systems, and increasing numbers of new memory systems and subsystems have begun to flood the taxonomy of memory classification. Many of these new systems have resulted from the stochastic and functional independence that has been found within tasks of implicit memory (see Chapter 2).

Within just a few years of the introduction of implicit and explicit memory, for example, Roediger (1990a) had counted as many as 25 memory systems (for a cursory list, see Table 8.1), and that number has continued to grow. Noting the proliferating number of memory systems, Roediger, Rajaram and Srinivas (1990, p. 585) mused, "Although parsimony is not a pristine scientific virtue and must be abandoned when the data demand it, we wonder if that point has been reached yet."

Perhaps the most fundamental question left to answer is whether multiple memory systems even exist (e.g., Anderson & Ross 1980; Baddeley 1984; Craik 1983; Hintzman 1984; Jacoby 1984; Johnson 1992; McKoon, Ratcliff & Dell 1986; Roediger 1990a; Roediger & Blaxton 1987). Because the multiple-memory-system view has become so widely accepted in the fields of developmental psychology, cognitive psychology, and behavioral neuroscience, we

Table 8.1. Proposed Memory Systems

Memory Systems	Associated Theorist(s)
imagery/verbal	Paivio 1971
episodic/semantic	Tulving 1972, 1983; Kinsbourne & Wood 1982
memory in the wide sense/memory in the narrow sense	McDougall 1923; Piaget & Inhelder 1973
specific/general memory	Nelson & Brown 1979; Nelson 1984
sensorimotor/representational (conceptual)	Mandler 1988, 1990
habit/memory	Hirsh 1974; Bachvalier & Mishkin 1984
stimulus-response/representational\organized	Ruggiero & Flagg 1976
reference/working	Honig 1978
horizontal/vertical	Wickelgren 1979
associative/abstract/representational	Oakley 1981, 1983
knowing how/knowing that	Cohen & Squire 1980; Cohen 1984
procedural/declarative	Squire 1987
early-developing/late-developing	Schacter & Moscovitch 1984
procedural/semantic/episodic	Tulving 1987
semantic/cognitive mediational	Warrington & Weiskrantz 1982
event memory/knowledge systems/ associative memory priming	Weiskrantz 1987
taxon/locale	Jacobs & Nadel 1985; Nadel 1992
declarative/nondeclarative	Squire 1992a
procedural/perceptual representation system/ semantic/episodic/short-term (working)	Tulving 1993
implicit/pre-explicit/explicit	Nelson 1995, 1997

sometimes forget that not all memory researchers share this view. An alternative to the multiple-memory-system view is that memory is the result of a unitary process and that experimental dissociations between particular tasks merely reflect the processing operations that are required by different memory tasks at the time of study and testing (e.g., Jacoby 1983; Johnson 1983; Mandler 1980; Roediger & Blaxton 1987). Some of the major multiple-memory-systems and processing accounts are briefly reviewed below. Each account is accompanied by a brief analysis of the role of conscious awareness, its implications for implicit/explicit memory and memory development, and its relation to memory data from human infants.

Multiple-memory-systems accounts

Criteria for proposing different memory systems

One of the critical issues associated with the proliferation of memory systems concerns the rules for inferring them (Johnson & Hasher 1987; Roediger et al. 1990; Sherry & Schacter 1987; Tulving & Bower 1974; Weiskrantz 1990), but some attempts at establishing these rules have been less successful than others. In some of the earlier studies of memory, for example, researchers commonly varied the types of materials that were presented to subjects. Paivio (1971), for example, reported that college students who saw either a list of pictures or a list of the names of the same pictures remembered the pictures better. Moreover, they remembered pictures of concrete objects better than pictures of abstract ones. Data such as these led him to propose that there are two different representational systems — the imagery system and the verbal system. This distinction found some support in neuropsychological evidence that verbal and nonverbal functions are lateralized in the cerebral hemispheres (e.g., Gazzaniga 1972).

Tulving and Bower (1974) reacted to Pavio's proposition by questioning if every dissociation that resulted from using a different set of experimental materials would justify the creation of another memory system:

> "It is not clear how one gets from this evidence to two memory systems or two memory stores. It seems to us that the evidence for a 'visual imagery' store is no better than that for a 'tactual store,' 'olfactory store,' 'proprioceptive store,' 'color store,' and the like. The question is whether we should postulate

a distinct memory system for every discriminable stimulus variable and for every variation of events along values of that variable that produces differences in memory for those events. If we did, we would soon have more memory systems or memory stores than we could name. If we did not, it is necessary to spell out the rules for such postulation when it is deemed appropriate or necessary. In this connection, it is also interesting to note that it has not yet been made clear by anyone how the task of explaining memory phenomena is materially aided by the hypothesized existence of different memory stores and systems..." (Tulving & Bower 1974, p. 273).

In fact, the same question could be raised today (e.g., Roediger et al. 1990).

A number of different criteria for inferring new memory systems from performance on explicit and implicit tests have been proposed by different researchers (for review, see Roediger et al. 1990). These criteria include stochastic independence (Tulving et al. 1982), functional independence (Tulving 1985), different underlying neural structures (Squire 1986; Zola-Morgan & Squire 1990b), functional incompatibility of operations (Sherry & Schacter 1987), and multiple tests (Tulving 1987). The criteria of stochastic and functional independence were previously considered in Chapter 2; the remaining criteria are considered below.

Different Underlying Neural Structures. One of the most successful arguments for postulating different memory systems rests on the assumption that different neural processes underlie performance on implicit and explicit tasks. Most of the data in support of this view have come from studies of brain-damaged humans and from monkeys with experimentally induced lesions (see Chapter 3). On the basis of these data, it is currently assumed that the cerebellum mediates performance on classical conditioning tasks, the medial temporal-diencephalic and frontal lobe structures mediate event memory, the temporal and parietal neocortex mediate knowledge systems and representations, and the cerebellum and/or basal ganglia mediate(s) perceptual-motor skills (Weiskrantz 1990, p. 106).

Although developmental dissociations in memory performance that are ascribed to maturation of the brain are also often used to support the multiple-memory-system view, these developmental dissociations do not actually occur — as least, not in primates (see Chapters 5 and 6). In one particularly unsuccessful attempt to draw a one-to-one relation between maturation of the brain and infants' memory performance, Nelson (1995, 1997) reviewed neurological evidence that related different parts of the nervous system to performance on different kinds of memory tasks during early development. Using the terms *implicit* and *explicit* to refer to underlying memory systems, he conjectured that the components of the explicit memory system are not functional before the end of the first year of life. However, his analysis contained a number of errors pertaining to the nature of the tasks per se. For example, his analogy between infants' footkicking in the mobile task and the spinal reflex of the decerebrate cat totally disregarded the critical distinction between simple classical conditioning, which is reflexive, and operant conditioning, which is not. The spinal reflex of the decerebrate cat is an unconditional reflex that is *elicited* by an electrotactile stimulus, and the characteristics of the classically conditioned response reflect the parameters of the eliciting stimulus (e.g., shock intensity or duration).

In contrast, an operant footkick is *emitted* only when, according to Skinner (1953), the conditions are ripe. Thus the subject may or may not respond in the presence of a particular stimulus. Nelson's analysis also failed to distinguish between the process of *learning* and the process of *memory* for what was previously learned. This distinction was described by Watson (1984) as *memory in learning* and *memory of learning*, respectively. Indeed, most cognitive psychologists have failed to recognize that learning and memory entail different processes. Forming an association between two events during the course of learning requires only short-term (active) memory, and the interval between successive events cannot exceed a few milliseconds to seconds (except in the case of taste aversion learning) or the association will not be acquired. The process of retrieving what was previously learned from long-term memory into active memory, however, can occur after retention intervals ranging from a few minutes to several months or longer. Thompson (1990a, p. 512) made an identical point many years ago when Mandler (1990) failed to distinguish between the acquisition process during conditioning and the memory of what was conditioned.

Shimamura (1990) cautioned that a single memory dissociation on implicit and explicit tasks, as found in amnesics, does not mean that each measure of memory depends exclusively on a particular underlying neural process or structure. Rather, it means only that the measure on which memory performance is *not* impaired does *not* depend on the process or structure in question. As an example, he described a scenario in which many different neural components or modules interact with each other to produce performance on a task presumed to measure one form of memory or another. In this scenario, some — but not all — of the components that are critical for memory performance on one task (e.g., recall) are also implicated in a second task (e.g., recognition), but not in a third one (e.g., word-stem completion). In this example, disrupting one component by lesioning would impair memory performance on the two tasks for which it was a critical link but would not impair it on the third task. Importantly, however, this dissociation would reveal nothing about how many or what other neural components the two affected tasks might share; rather, it would only reveal that the lesioned component did not contribute to memory performance on the third task.

Functional Incompatibility of Operations. Another criterion for postulating more than one memory system grew out of a consideration of the evolution of multiple memory systems. Sherry and Schacter (1987) argued that unique, specialized memory systems evolved to handle new environmental demands that existing memory systems could not. They suggested that different specialized memory systems for song, imprinting, and spatial location in birds, for example, may have evolved to subserve the different functional demands associated with mating, maternal care, species recognition, food caching, and navigation. Presumably, each specialized memory system was uniquely constrained by temporal factors associated with the encoding (e.g., critical periods) or retrieval (e.g., seasonal migration) of information admitted into it. Thus, remembering the prior location of a food cache, a nest, or a predator would require the storage and retrieval of details of a particular episode. When and where a given food source is accessible, such as when worms can be found in the farmer's field or when a truck arrives at the garbage tip (McFarland 1977), however, could change weekly, monthly, or seasonally. Thus, that memory system would have to be sufficiently flexible that details about time or place could be updated. From an evolutionary perspective, then, particular memory systems can be found in species whose adaptations reflect the same functional demands.

Many psychologists, however, have assumed that the appearance of different memory systems during ontogeny reflects their order of appearance during phylogeny and have given little or no consideration to the particular specializations that different species evolved in the course of adapting to different niches. Analyses of the hierarchical development of multiple memory systems that are based on the simple notion that ontogeny recapitulates phylogeny make two fundamental errors. First, new memory systems, such as the system that is implicated in seed-caching by nutcrackers, are species-specific and reflect an organism's specialized adaptation to its niche.

Human infants, who occupy a very different niche (or series of niches), do not require these same memory systems. Second, ontogeny is linear, but phylogeny is not. Evidence gathered over the last half-century now shows that phylogeny is tree-like and branching rather than ladder-like and linear. In short, there is no simple relation between the appearance of a capacity in phylogeny and its appearance in ontogeny.

Multiple Tasks. Tulving (1987) argued that the inference of multiple memory systems requires that the same dissociation be exhibited on several tasks, each of which presumably taps the same underlying memory systems. Thus, if a particular independent variable affects performance on the battery of tasks thought to tap one memory system differently from the way it affects performance on the battery of tasks thought to tap a different system, then it is safe to conclude that the tasks within each battery share something not shared with the tasks in the other battery. Although some would use such findings to argue that what is shared by these tasks are common memory systems, it is just as reasonable to argue that what is shared are common processing operations.

In fact, most studies with adults that have revealed memory dissociations on one task but not on another have used only two tasks, each presumably tapping a different underlying memory system. The same criticism — the use of only two tasks to illustrate an experimental dissociation in memory performance — can be levied against most of the infant studies cited in Chapter 7. Unlike the adult studies in which the materials and temporal parameters of study and test vary from report to report, however, all of the mobile studies with infants used exactly the same two tasks, the same task parameters, and infants from the same population. Thus, instead of manipulating a *single independent variable* and producing the same dissociation across *multiple* implicit and explicit tasks as in adult studies, the infant studies manipulated *multiple independent variables* and produced the same dissociation on a *single* implicit and explicit task. In doing so, however, the infant studies have amassed a large amount of convergent evidence of functional memory dissociations.

Although we have focused on the explicit/implicit distinction in this book, a number of multiple memory systems have been proposed over the years that meet one or more of the criteria outlined above. Below, we consider in more detail the two major classifications of multiple memory systems that have been proposed, *episodic and semantic memory* and *declarative and procedural (nondeclarative) memory*, and their implications for memory development.

Episodic and semantic memory

Tulving (1972) was the first to distinguish episodic and semantic memory as two, functionally distinct memory systems and to differentiate them in terms of the content of the memories they stored. The episodic system stored autobiographical information about personally experienced events (*episodes*) that were specified by spatiotemporal details. The semantic system, in contrast, stored the individual's general (*organized*) knowledge. Although retrieval from the episodic system altered its content (e.g., by supplementing or modifying it), retrieval from the semantic system did not. Tulving did not explicitly specify the relation of episodic and semantic memory to the traditional distinction between long-term and short-term memory, but by describing episodic memory as what psychologists studied in laboratory tasks, he implied that episodic memories were of shorter duration than semantic ones.

Episodic/semantic distinction and development

Tulving proposed that episodic and semantic memory develop sequentially during ontogeny, with the semantic memory system developing first. The same developmental sequence is suggested in Schacter and Moscovitch's (1984) sequence of early-maturing and late-maturing memory systems, which correspond closely to the semantic and episodic memory systems, respectively. Other theorists, however, viewed this developmental sequence as incorrect, arguing that general knowledge (semantic memory) develops *out of* an individual's highly specific experiences or episodic memories (e.g., Anglin 1977; Cermak 1984; Kintsch 1974; Nelson & Brown 1978). The flavor of their argument is captured in the following quote:

> "Are not autobiographic, very long-term memories typical episodic memories? What happened on your fifth birthday is surely part of your knowledge of the world, of your long-term memory — but it is not semantic. Rather, it is episodic; it reflects an event that actually occurred, it is also a part of real world knowledge, and it may be reconstructed using inferential processes" (Nelson & Brown 1978, p. 234).

In fact, the question of whether development proceeds from the specific to the general or from the general to the specific has long occupied developmental psychologists. Some early researchers viewed development as a process of increasing generalization. This view is reflected in Watson's (1930) account of the development of fears and conditioned reflexes and in Bridges' (1932) account of the development of emotions. Others, however, viewed development as a process of increasing differentiation. This view is reflected in Gibson's (1969) account of perceptual development and in Olson and Strauss' (1984) account of the development of infant memory:

> "The period from 3–7 months is characterized by elaboration of the infant's basic information processing skills….By the end of this period, the infant has in place the skills for a series of major achievements in cognitive and social development that will begin in the second half of the first year….Although the younger infant can only readily show memory for bold patterns and sharp contrasts between test alternatives, the infant of 6–7 months shows a broad range of encoding skills that include recognition of details of patterns and subtle aspects of stimuli" (Olson & Strauss 1984, p. 35).

The latter view, however, does not characterize the development of infant memory. A large number of studies using different paradigms have now documented that infants' early memories are initially highly specific and become increasingly generalized with age (Hartshorn et al. 1998a; Hayne et al. 1997), as originally argued by Nelson and Brown (1978). In mobile studies, for example, even 2-month-olds can detect if their test mobile differs ever so slightly from the highly detailed, five-object mobile with which they were trained 24 hours earlier. If more than a single object on the test mobile differs from what appeared on the training mobile, then they cannot recognize it; otherwise, their 24-hour recognition is excellent (Hayne et al. 1986). Similarly, if 3-month-olds are trained with a block mobile displaying As on all sides in a single color (red, green, black, or blue) and are tested 24 hours later with an identical mobile that displays As (the same form) in a different color, they cannot recognize it. Nor can they recognize a test mobile that displays 2s (a different form) in the original training color (Hayne et al. 1987). In other words, even 3-month-olds can discriminate a difference in just a single attribute after a 24-hour delay.

In other studies, Gerhardstein et al. (2000) found that 3-month-olds could not recognize a test mobile 24 hours later if the characters it displayed (Ls or +s) were 33% smaller or larger than the characters on their training mobiles (see Chapter 7, *Studied Size*), and Adler and Rovee-Collier (1994) found that 3-month-olds could not recognize a test mobile 24 hours later if it displayed characters that were 25% smaller. Finally, recall that after 3-month-olds were trained with a six-block mobile displaying two different sets of feature combinations (red As on black blocks and green 2s on yellow blocks), they discriminated different recombinations of these features (figure color, figure form, block color) on their test mobiles, even though all of the features that were present at the time of encoding were still present when they were tested 1 day later (Bhatt & Rovee-Collier 1994). After a 4-day retention interval, infants generalized to test recombinations of all attributes; even then, however, they still discriminated if the test mobile contained a single feature that had not been on the training mobile (Bhatt & Rovee-Collier 1996). Taken together, the preceding data provide compelling evidence that infant's early memories are highly specific.

By 9 months of age, however, infants generalize to physically different stimuli, but they do so after short retention intervals only (see Figure 8.1). After longer retention intervals, older infants — like younger ones — continue to discriminate a test stimulus that differs from the stimulus that was present during training (Hartshorn et al. 1998a). Their pattern of generalization/ discrimination as a function of the length of the retention interval indicates that their generalization after short test delays does not result from perceptual confusion (i.e., an inability to perceptually distinguish between the training and the test stimuli). If it did, infants would be unable to discriminate between the same cues after longer retention intervals. The fact that older infants begin to generalize to novel stimuli after short delays only suggests that their generalized responding is strategic — as if they were *testing the waters* in order to determine if the discriminably different new objects are functionally equivalent to the objects that they had previously encountered in the same context.

This analysis is supported by evidence that the same pattern — increasing generalization with age — has been observed in studies of deferred imitation with infants (Barr & Hayne, 2000). Six-month-olds do not imitate previously modeled actions 24 hours later if the test object is novel (Hayne et al. 1997 2000a). By 12 to 14 months of age, however, infants generalize to a test object that differs from the object seen during the demonstration in color only. They do so only after a short delay (i.e., 10 min; Barnat, Klein & Meltzoff 1996; Hayne et al. 1997), however, and not after a longer one (i.e., 1 day; Hayne & Campbell 1997; Hayne et al. 1997). By 18 months, they generalize to a cue that differs in color only after a longer delay (i.e., 1 day), and by 21 months, they generalize to a cue that differs *both* in color and form after 1 day (Hayne et al. 1997). This pattern of development continues throughout the infancy period (Herbert & Hayne 2000).

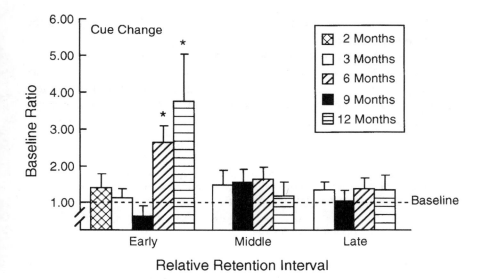

Figure 8.1. Mean baseline ratios of independent groups of infants between 2 and 12 months of age who were trained for two sessions and tested with a different cue in the original context after common relative retention intervals that corresponded to the shortest (*Early*) or longest (*Late*) test delays or to the midpoint (*Middle*) of the forgetting function for each age group. An asterisk indicates that a group exhibited significant retention (i.e., *M* baseline ratio significantly > 1.00). Vertical bars indicate + 1 *SE*.

Nelson and Brown (1978) complained that Tulving (1972) originally used the term *episodic* to refer both to a *type of memory* and to a class of *laboratory tasks* (i.e., tasks in which isolated lists of verbal materials were deliberately learned). Adults used deliberate mnemonic strategies and were quite good in solving these tasks, but children — lacking efficient mnemonic strategies — were not. As a result, theorists generally assumed that children had poor episodic memories. In the quote at the outset of this section, however, Nelson and Brown had argued that real world episodic memories (i.e., not memories measured in artificial laboratory tasks), being autobiographical, are the only kind of memories that young children have before the semantic component has evolved. They concluded that the characterization of young children's episodic memory as poor resulted from a failure to distinguish the underlying type of memory from the particular class of laboratory tasks that were used to measure it.

Nelson and Brown (1978) also complained that Tulving's choice of the term *semantic* to refer to words and word meanings reflected the fact that researchers always used verbal materials in studies with adults — a practice that was extended to studies with children, although pictures or objects were substituted for words in studies with very young children. But, they argued, children's *nonverbal* memories for actions, spatial locations, cognitive maps, scripts, and so forth, were neither clearly semantic nor clearly episodic:

> "How such an organized semantic language-based system emerges is at least one important and central developmental question. But if all real world knowledge — language based or not, categorically structured or not — is termed "semantic memory," the question cannot even be asked using an episodic-semantic distinction" (p. 240).

Criticisms of the episodic/semantic distinction

In a critical analysis of episodic and semantic memory, McKoon et al. (1986) concluded that the empirical and neuropsychological evidence supporting the distinction between them was weak. In response, Tulving (1986) argued that the distinction was useful for classifying memory phenomena and that future neurological evidence would justify the distinction. To this, Ratcliff and McKoon (1986) replied that neurophysiological evidence alone would never be able to provide an understanding of the mind and that Tulving and Bower's (1974, pp. 296–297) original conclusion was still valid:

> "It is only in the context of a particular process model that inferences can be meaningfully drawn from the experimental data. This restriction holds up regardless of what method is used. When we noted, in discussing various methods, that the logic was not entirely clear, the difficulty usually lay in the absence of a set of statements or assumptions about the principles governing the utilization of the stored information at the time of retrieval. The process models that would help make sense out of the data on ...[memory systems] need not be complex or highly sophisticated or "correct." But they must enter the picture in some form. Even a bad process model is better than none at all. It would help make clear the logic of the method of specifying...[memory systems], aid communication, and facilitate cross-comparison of data obtained with different methods. Moreover, it can be improved, revised, or replaced with a better one. A nonexistent model cannot" (Tulving & Bower 1974, quoted in Ratcliff & McKoon 1986, p. 313).

Modifications of episodic and semantic memory

The finding that functional dissociations were found within both explicit and implicit tests revealed that a single memory system could not underlie memory performance on each type of test. As a result, theorists were motivated to expand their original dichotomies. Thus, for example, Squire (1987) expanded the procedural/declarative dichotomy (Squire 1986) to include priming, simple classical conditioning, and skill learning as subcategories of procedural memory and episodic (working) and semantic (reference) memory as subcategories of declarative memory. Likewise, Tulving (1985) added procedural memory to the semantic/episodic dichotomy, viewing episodic memory as roughly corresponding to *explicit memory* and procedural and semantic memory as roughly corresponding to *implicit memory* (Tulving 1987). He characterized the three-system arrangement as *monohierarchical*, with episodic memory being a specialized subsystem that evolved out of semantic memory, and semantic memory being a specialized subsystem that evolved out of procedural memory. By this account, the procedural memory system appeared first in phylogeny and ontogeny, and succeeding memory systems appeared later:

> "Semantic memory develops earlier in childhood than episodic memory: Children are capable of learning facts of the world before they can remember their own past experiences" (Tulving 1993, p. 68).

As we saw in preceding chapters, however, this was a statement of faith, not fact.

Subsequently, Tulving (1993) added working (primary, or short-term) memory and the perceptual representation system (Tulving & Schacter 1990) to the preceding three, making a total of five human memory systems. His major writings, however, have continued to focus on the episodic/semantic distinction.

The *structural descriptions system*, a part of the perceptual representation system (PRS) that has particular relevance for interpretations of infant memory, was introduced as a subsystem of the perceptual representation system to account for memory performance that is based solely on perceptual properties (Schacter 1990). The structural descriptions system is dedicated to the representation of information about the form and structure of visual objects, including a description of an object's plane of orientation about a central axis (Cooper, Schacter & Moore 1991) but not its size (Schacter et al. 1993b). This system also includes no semantic information about objects, for example, information concerning either the functions that an object can perform or its associative properties.

The dominant paradigm for evaluating memory performance mediated by this system in adults is the object decision task, in which subjects make perceptual decisions about the test stimuli, such as whether or not a particular drawing could possibly exist as a three-dimensional object or not (Schacter & Cooper 1993; Schacter et al. 1990, 1991a). The relevant research findings have demonstrated the familiar memory dissociation: Priming is preserved for both novel objects (e.g., Schacter et al. 1993b) and familiar ones (Cave & Squire 1992), but recognition memory is impaired (Biederman & Cooper 1992; Schacter et al. 1993b).

The structural descriptions system has been described as one of the first memory systems to appear in ontogeny and is thought to mediate memory processing in early infancy (Schacter 1990) — a view consistent with the widespread notion that the primary content of infants' early memories is strictly perceptual (Olson & Strauss 1984). According to Schacter (1990), the structural descriptions system does not represent information about object function, object size, or associative information. Yet, infants as young as 3 to 6 months exhibit memories of this kind of information. The evidence pertaining to the role of object function and associations between memories in very young infants is described below; evidence pertaining to the effect of object size (Adler & Rovee-Collier 1994; Gerhardstein et al., 2000) was previously described in Chapter 7 (see *Studied Size*).

Evidence for memories of object function in young infants. If infants only possess the structural descriptions system, then they should not be able to form memories of object function. However, they can. A mobile that infants had learned to move by kicking is an effective reminder in a reactivation task if it is moving but not if it is stationary (Fagen, Yengo, Rovee-Collier & Enright 1981; Greco et al. 1990). In a delayed recognition task, however, the same mobile readily cues retrieval whether it is moving or not. This difference may reflect the fact that fewer or different cues are needed to retrieve memories that are more accessible (Spear 1978). Functional information is not requisite for reminding, however, if the cue that is used as a reminder was also originally nonfunctional. The original training context or setting did not move, for example, yet it is an effective reminder for the training memory when presented alone, without the original training mobile (Hayne & Findlay 1995;

Rovee-Collier et al. 1985a).

Additional evidence that object function is represented in infant memory comes from studies involving a passive-exposure procedure. In this procedure, infants are merely exposed to (i.e., do not interact with) a novel object functioning in the same way their prior training mobile had functioned. The exposure is brief — only 3 min for 3-month-olds and only 2 min for 6-month-olds — and occurs only once, after a posttraining delay that can be as long as days or weeks. Subsequently, infants receive a delayed recognition test in which either the original mobile or the exposed one is presented as the retrieval cue. In a number of studies, we have found that infants' memories are readily modified so that they include the exposed object in addition to (memory expansion) or in place of (memory impairment) the original mobile (Boller, Grabelle & Rovee-Collier 1995; Boller et al. 1996; Muzzio & Rovee-Collier 1996; Rossi-George & Rovee-Collier 1999; Rovee-Collier et al. 1994; Rovee-Collier et al. 1993a; for review, see Rovee-Collier & Boller 1995), despite the fact that infants otherwise do not generalize to a novel test mobile after a 24-hour delay. Moreover, this modification occurs even when the novel exposed object is highly physically dissimilar to the prior training mobile, as long as it is *functionally* equivalent to the training mobile (Greco et al. 1990). If the novel object is exposed in exactly the same manner and after the same delay but in the absence of equivalent functional information, then infants' memory of the prior training mobile is not modified, and infants continue to recognize it instead of responding to the novel mobile 24 hours later (Boller et al. 1995; Greco et al. 1990).

Evidence for memories of associations in young infants. If infants only possess the structural descriptions system, then they should not be able to form memories of associations between objects, but they can. In the traditional learning literature, this phenomenon is called *sensory preconditioning*, referring to the fact that an association is established by the mere simultaneous occurrence of two sensory events, without the necessity of a distinctive response (Brogden 1939). When 6-month-olds merely saw the two puppets side-by-side for an hour per day for 1 week, for example, then they associated them. This association was not revealed, however, until they subsequently saw the target actions modeled on one puppet. When tested 1 day later, they imitated the target actions on the other puppet (Marrott, Barr & Rovee-Collier, 2000). In contrast, infants who were exposed to the two puppets for the same average amount of time but at different times of day (i.e., unpaired) did not imitate what they had seen modeled on one puppet when they were tested with the other, even though both puppets were equally familiar. These data reveal that infants subsequently transferred the memory of the modeled actions to the second puppet only if they had previously formed an association between it and the puppet on which the actions were modeled and remembered it.

Boller (1997) obtained a similar result when she repeatedly exposed 6-month-olds to two distinctively colored and patterned cloth panels side-by-side for 1 hour per day for 1 week and then subsequently trained them to kick to move a mobile in the presence of one of the panels. When she tested them with the mobile in the presence of the other context 1 day after training, they recognized it. When she preexposed infants to the two panels for an equal amount of time prior to training but at different times of day, however, they subsequently did not recognize the mobile when tested with it in the presence of the other panel, again revealing that infants transferred the training memory they had acquired in the presence of one panel to the other panel by virtue of the memory of the association between the two panels that they had previously formed. If infants were equally familiar with the two panels but had no opportunity to form an association between them, then the memory that infants had subsequently acquired in the presence of one panel did not transfer to the other.

In both of the preceding studies, infants learned that two discriminably different objects were associated in the course of repeatedly seeing those objects appear together, irrespective of the experimental paradigm within which their memory of that association was tested. In both studies, the memory of the association that infants had picked up by merely looking was revealed only when they were subsequently given an opportunity to demonstrate that knowledge through their direct actions.

Evidence for associations between memories in young infants. Finally, if infants only possess the structural descriptions system, then they should not be able to form associations between independent memories. However, they can do this as well. Timmons (1994) obtained evidence that infants form associations between independent memories by 6 months of age. In an initial study, she trained 6-month-olds either to move a mobile suspended over the playpen or to turn on a music box affixed to the front of the playpen by either arm-pulling or footkicking — an analog of the traditional paired-associate task used in studies of verbal learning and memory. Infants were trained in a distinctive context for 2 days on one cue-response pair and, 3 days later, learned the other cue-response pair in the same context. Three days after learning the second pair, infants were tested with each of the cues in a delayed recognition paradigm. During testing, infants produced only the particular response (kicking or arm-pulling) that had originally been associated with a given test cue (mobile or music box), regardless of which response they had learned last. This result confirmed that infants' memory of each cue-response pair had been stored independently and that test responding was highly specific to the retrieval cue that was presented.

In a second experiment, Timmons trained infants as before, but this time she waited until both of the training memories had been forgotten (i.e., 3 weeks) and then exposed infants to either the mobile or to the music box as a memory prime in a reactivation paradigm. On the following day, she administered a long-term retention test to all infants using only the mobile as the retrieval cue. As expected, infants who were both primed and tested with the mobile exhibited the mobile-appropriate response to the mobile retrieval cue — the typical finding in memory reactivation studies. Surprisingly, however, infants who were primed with the music box also exhibited the mobile-appropriate response (and no other) to the mobile test cue (see Figure 8.2).

Recall that the mobile memory was not directly primed with the mobile and that it was forgotten at the time the music-box memory was primed. Timmons assumed, therefore, that the music-box prime had activated the memory node representing the music box paired-associate and that this activation had spread to the memory node representing the mobile paired-associate, thereby enabling infants to perform the mobile-appropriate response to the mobile cue during the subsequent test. Thus, even though the memory of each task was independent and highly specific, the two memories were associatively linked — possibly via the common context in which both tasks had originally been acquired — in a common mnemonic network. As a result, priming one memory brought to mind the memory of the other.

A similar phenomenon was reported by Barr and Vieira (1999), who taught 6-month-old infants to associate the operant train procedure with an imitation procedure. Drawing from Timmons' (1994) finding that one memory can be associated with another if the two memories were acquired in a common context, they asked if 6-month-olds' memory of the puppet task would be associated with a memory of the train task if they acquired the two memories in the same context. Because 6-month-olds remember the puppet task for only 1 day but remember the train task for 2 weeks (see Figure 8.3),

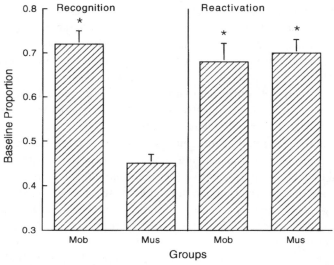

Figure 8.2. Associative priming exhibited by 6-month-olds who originally learned to perform different responses to a mobile and to a music box. *Left panel:* On a delayed recognition test 3 days after training was over, infants who were tested with the mobile produced the mobile response, but infants who were tested with the music box did not. *Right panel:* Priming with either the mobile or the music box 3 weeks after training reactivated the mobile response and facilitated responding to the mobile 24 hours later. The magnitude of reactivation was the same whether reactivation was direct (*Mob*) or indirect (*Mus*). Asterisks indicate significant retention (*M* baseline proportion significantly > .50). Vertical bars indicate + 1 *SE*.

they hypothesized that the longer-lived train memory might "carry" the associated memory of the short-lived puppet task along with it and protract it longer than otherwise possible. If so, then retrieving the train memory 1 or 2 weeks later might also retrieve infants' memory of the puppet task, with the result that infants would imitate the adult's actions on the puppet after the longer delay.

To test this, Barr and Vieira trained 6-month-olds in the train task. Immediately after training was over, the mother — her infant on her lap — turned her chair sideways so that the train was still in view to the infant's side. The experimenter then knelt in front of the infant and demonstrated a series of three actions on a hand puppet (removing a mitten from the puppet's hand, shaking it to ring a bell hidden inside, and replacing the mitten). During the

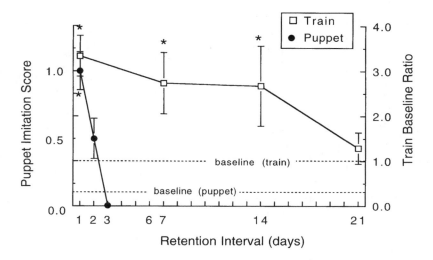

Figure 8.3. The duration of retention of 6-month-olds' independent memories of the operant train task (*open squares, right axis*) and the puppet imitation task (*black circles, left axis*). Asterisks indicate significant retention; vertical bars indicate ±1 *SE*.

initial imitation test that followed immediately after the demonstration and either 1 or 2 weeks later, infants were allowed 120 s from when they first touched the puppet to imitate the experimenter's actions. The hypothesis was confirmed: Infants imitated the target actions after both delays — but only if they were tested first with the train, not if they were tested first with the puppet (see Figure 8.4). In other words, retrieving the train memory was necessary in order to activate infants' memory of the puppet task as well. Infants in a baseline control group did not see the actions modeled originally, and they did not spontaneously produce them during the test. We have recently found that the puppet task can be associated with the memory of the train task even when 2 weeks have elapsed between learning the train task and initially viewing the puppet task. The association is formed if the target actions on the puppet task are modeled *in the presence of the nonmoving train*. These data clearly demonstrate that a short-lived memory (the puppet demonstration) that is associated with a longer-lived memory (the train task) can become longer-lasting as well.

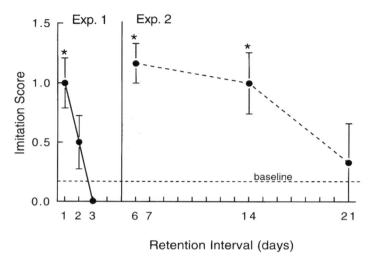

Figure 8.4. The duration of retention of 6-month-olds' independent memory of the puppet task (*left panel, Exp. 1*) and their memory of the puppet task after it had been associated with the train task (*right panel, Exp. 2*). Asterisks indicate significant retention; vertical bars indicate ±1 *SE*.

The first deferred imitation study to use a reactivation procedure was conducted with 18-month-olds, who typically can imitate modeled actions that were previously demonstrated on the puppet after a retention interval of 4 weeks but not longer (Barr 1997). Two weeks after they had forgotten the task (6 weeks after the demonstration), infants who saw the puppet moving and ringing for 30 s (the memory prime) once again imitated the target actions 1 day later. Subsequently, Barr and Vieira (1999) used the reactivation procedure with 6-month-olds to recover their forgotten associated memories of the train and puppet tasks. As in Timmons (1994), they found that reactivating one memory indirectly reactivated the memory that was associated with it. After establishing the train task-puppet task association (see above), they allowed 6-month-olds to forget both tasks. After a retention interval of 20 days, they modeled the target actions on the puppet for 30 s as a reactivation treatment, and immediately before the train test 1 day later, infants were primed with the moving and ringing puppet (see Figure 7.2c). When tested with the train, which they had not seen for 3 weeks, infants again recognized it (see Figure 8.5, *right panel*). Conversely, a 2-min exposure to the moving train reactivated infants' forgotten memory of the puppet task. One day later, infants exhibited significant imitation if they were first primed for 2 min with the train, either moving or nonmoving (see Figure 8.5, *left panel*). These infants had seen the puppet demonstration only once and only briefly 3 weeks earlier. The reactivation control group was not originally exposed to either task but received the train reactivation treatment on day 20 and was primed with the moving train immediately before the puppet test on day 21. This group exhibited no retention when tested with the puppet.

A number of theorists have proposed that memories are represented in a network and are connected to each other by links (e.g., Nelson & Kosslyn 1975). According to spreading-activation models (Collins & Loftus 1975; Collins & Quillian 1969), the presentation of a retrieval cue activates a memory

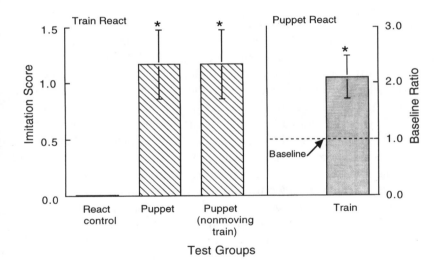

Figure 8.5. Memory performance of 6-month-olds 3 weeks after training/modeling. One day before the test, infants were exposed for 2 min to the train (*left panel*) or for 30 s to the puppet (*right panel*) and were tested with the other stimulus. Immediately before the puppet test, groups were primed for 2 min with either the moving train (*puppet, middle striped column*) or nonmoving train (*right striped column*) to retrieve the puppet memory. The reactivation control group was reactivated, primed, and tested like the puppet group but was not originally trained on either task. Immediately before the train test, infants were again primed for 2 min with the moving and ringing puppet (see Figure 7.2c). Asterisks indicate that the memory was reactivated (i.e., significant retention). Vertical bars indicate ±1 *SE*.

at a particular node in the network; as this excitation subsequently spreads to other nodes that are linked to the original one, they are activated as well. As a result, memories associated with the nodes that have been indirectly activated in this fashion also become more accessible. Although some of the original network models have fallen from favor, others continue to provide useful accounts for the facilitative effect of one retrieval on another. We have found it useful to attribute the priming phenomenon that was observed by Timmons and by Barr and Vieira to spreading activation. By this account, when the node corresponding to either the music box (Timmons 1994) or the train (Barr & Vieira 1999) was activated, the activation spread to the node that corresponds to the mobile or puppet demonstration, respectively, via the association that was formed between the memories of the two tasks in each study and linked them in a common mnemonic network. As a result, priming one memory activated the other as well.

Sheffield and Hudson (1994) observed a similar associative phenomenon in a memory study with 14- to 18-month-old toddlers. Using a reenactment paradigm, they allowed toddlers to actively engage in six different structured activities at different stations in the laboratory. After toddlers' memory of their visit had been forgotten, they were returned to the laboratory, and three of the activities were modeled by the experimenter while the children merely watched. Twenty-four hours later, the children were asked to produce the three activities that they had not seen modeled and the three that they had.

As expected, children of the same age who had not been originally trained but who had viewed the modeling exhibited deferred imitation of the three actions they had seen modeled the day before, and children who were not exposed to the reactivation treatment (the partial modeling) remembered none. However, children who had been originally trained and had also seen three activities modeled were not only able to produce the three modeled activities but also were able to enact the three activities that had not been modeled during the reactivation treatment, despite the fact that they had not engaged in them for 10 weeks. Again, as in Timmons (1994), directly reactivating some activities led to the indirect reactivation of others in the memory network — again, probably mediated by the common context in which the activities had initially been performed. Clearly, associative memory is not unique to the mobile task; it can also be demonstrated in very different memory tasks that involve no prior conditioning of the target response.

These results have major implications for everyday memory processing by persons of all ages. If memories in an associative network need not be directly accessed in order to be retrieved, then in the normal course of interacting with their environment, infants and older individuals are likely to encounter cues that not only directly retrieve the memories in which they are represented but that also mediate the retrieval of other memories that are represented in the same mnemonic network. In our personal experience, this is exactly what happens — remembering one event reminds us of another.

In summary, the preceding evidence demonstrates that information about an object's meaning or function is incorporated into infants' memories by 3 months of age and that memories of associations as well as associations between independent memories are formed by at least 6 months of age. None of these memory phenomena can be accounted for by the structural descriptions system.

Declarative and procedural (nondeclarative) memory

These memory systems were proposed by Squire (1986, 1987) and, like Tulving's (1972, 1983) memory systems, are distinguished by their content and its accessibility to conscious recollection. The declarative memory system stores information about facts and personally experienced events that can be consciously recollected as a proposition or image, whereas the procedural memory system (subsequently called the *nondeclarative memory system*; Squire 1992a) stores acquired information that is embedded in procedures or skills and cannot be consciously recollected (i.e., implicit memory). The different types of information in the two systems have been distinguished as *knowing that* and *knowing how*, respectively (Cohen & Squire 1980). In Squire's formulation, however, episodic memory and semantic memory are *subdivisions* of the declarative system, and *both are accessible to consciousness*. Episodic memory represents autobiographical information, whereas semantic memory represents world knowledge. Likewise, episodic memory represents information that is temporally dated, whereas semantic memory represents information that is not.

Whereas Tulving's systems were distinguished in an attempt to create a taxonomy of memory, that is, for purposes of classification, Squire's systems were created for the purpose of developing a "biologically useful" level of analysis of brain function, that is, an account of "how the brain itself actually stores information" (Squire 1987, p. 160). The declarative/procedural formulation grew out of research with amnesic patients and was necessitated by evidence that the original episodic/semantic dichotomy did not distinguish the different neurological organization of episodic and semantic memories. A case in point is the phenomenon of source amnesia:

> "...some amnesic patients...can remember recently acquired items of information, without remembering when or where they acquired the information. Importantly, source amnesia is a separate deficit, unrelated to memory impairment itself. It does not appear in all amnesic patients, but the ones who show it do so consistently. Moreover, the patients without source amnesia can have just as severe a memory impairment as patients with source amnesia. If the term episodic memory is reserved for acts of remembering that are specifically autobiographical, then episodic memory might refer usefully to that aspect of memory function that is lost in source amnesia and that ordinarily permits a sense of personal connection to one's past. In normal subjects, recall and recognition are ordinarily accompanied by recollection of the learning episode. However, in some amnesic patients the quality of personal familiarity and connectedness to a recent episode can be lost despite successful recall and recognition of material learned in the episode. Preliminary evidence suggests that frontal lobe pathology may contribute to this phenomenon" (Squire 1987, p. 173).

Declarative/procedural memory and the explicit/implicit distinction

Explicit memories contain information that is consciously accessible, whereas implicit memories contain information that is not. Thus, the declarative system stores explicit memories, whereas the procedural memory system stores implicit memories. Although functional dissociations in memory performance on explicit and implicit tasks are predicted by the declarative/procedural formulation, the tasks defined as explicit and implicit are different from the tasks defined as explicit and implicit in Tulving's (1983) dichotomy because the declarative system encompasses both episodic and semantic memories, whereas Tulving distinguished these as separate memory systems. Thus, Tulving predicted memory dissociations between episodic and semantic memories based on the absence of conscious awareness of information retrieved from semantic memory; Squire (1987) did not. However, both predicted a functional dissociation in memory performance between tasks requiring procedural information and those that did not. Although Tulving (1987) introduced a procedural memory system (memory for procedures) that was distinguished from the semantic memory system (generic or factual knowledge), only information in the episodic memory system was accessible to conscious recollection.

Because Squire's formulation assumes that different brain mechanisms subserve the declarative and procedural (or nondeclarative) memory systems, damage to the brain mechanisms associated with one system or subsystem affects its content but does not affect the content of another system. Moreover, because the memories stored in each system and subsystem are *different representations,* brain damage completely obliterates access to a particular representation. A different kind of memory test does not simply access the same representation via a different route; rather, it accesses an entirely different representation.

Declarative/procedural memory and development

Squire (1987) suggested that declarative memory may have evolved relatively late in phylogeny and attained its maximum level of development in mammals. Similarly, he suggested that declarative memory develops later than procedural memory. This suggestion was based on Bachevalier and Mishkin's (1984) evidence from infant monkeys that the *memory system* develops later than the *habit system* (see Chapter 5) and is consistent with other suggestions that two memory systems that support comparable functions develop sequentially (Schacter & Moscovitch 1984; Tulving 1983). As we have argued in previous chapteres, a developmental dissociation between these two memory systems is an article of faith rather than an empirical fact. For this reason, the questions raised earlier about the developmental relationship between semantic memory to episodic memory are also pertinent here.

Processing accounts

Although functional dissociations have been taken as evidence for multiple memory systems (Squire 1987; Tulving 1985), they have also been interpreted as reflecting different information-processing demands of implicit and explicit tests within a single memory system (Dritschel, Williams, Baddeley & Nimmo-Smith 1992; McKoon, Ratcliff & Dell 1986; Roediger 1984; Shallice 1988). Just as the number of proposed memory systems has swelled to accommodate the variety of diverse memory dissociations, so have the number of processing

Table 8.2. *Examples of Different Processing Accounts of Experimental Dissociations on Implicit and Explicit Memory Tests with Normal and Amnesic Populations*

Processing Account	Associated Theorist(s)
data-driven and conceptually-driven processing	Jacoby 1983; Roediger & Blaxton 1987
activation and elaboration	Mandler 1980
incidental and intentional processing	Jacoby 1984, 1991
automatic and controlled processing	Mandler 1980, 1985
conscious and non-conscious processing	Mandler 1989
processing dimensions	Olton 1989
multiple-entry modular model (MEM)	Johnson 1983
coherence model	Hirst 1989

accounts (see Table 8.2). These accounts emphasize different cognitive operations within a unitary memory system instead of the different memory content of different memory systems. The two major processing accounts that have been proposed, *transfer-appropriate processing* and *the multiple-entry modular model*, are considered below.

Transfer-appropriate processing

A widely known processing account, transfer-appropriate processing, was advanced by Roediger and his colleagues (e.g., Roediger 1984; Roediger & Blaxton 1987; Roediger, Weldon & Challis 1989b; Srinivas & Roediger 1990), who argued that in many studies that documented a memory dissociation on implicit and explicit tasks, the type of memory task was confounded with the type of processing it required. According to the transfer-appropriate processing account, evidence of memory would be found only when the mental operations required at the time of testing matched those required at the time of encoding; any discrepancy would result in a retrieval failure. The possible processing operations were described as *data-driven* (i.e., driven by the perceptual or surface features of the stimulus) and *conceptually-driven* (i.e., driven by the deeper meaning of the stimulus). Because most perceptual priming tests involve data-driven processing, for example, memory would be demonstrated on priming tests only to the extent that the study task required data-driven processing; conversely, because most recall and recognition tests involve conceptually-driven processing, memory would be demonstrated on those tests to the extent that the study task required conceptually-driven processing. In general, however, manipulations that require conceptually-driven processing have little or no effect on implicit tests, and manipulations that require data-driven processing have little or no effect on explicit tests.

Although *data-driven* and *conceptually-driven* are usually assumed to correspond to *bottom-up* and *top-down*, respectively, Roediger conceded that the term *data-driven* is a misnomer:

> "...higher level (top-down) processes must be used in recognizing such displays [*a black-and-white fragmented picture of a Dalmatian*]. In all likelihood, repetition of these procedures produces the long-term perceptual priming effect, not lower-level (data-driven) processes. In verbal tests, the processes are likely lexical or involve the visual word system (Nelson, Keelean & Negrao 1989; Tulving & Schacter 1990; Weldon 1991); in nonverbal tests, priming may result from processes in a 'geon assembly layer' (Biederman & Cooper 1991) or a structural descriptions system (Schacter 1990). The point is that the processes that are primed are not as low level as is implied by the term *data-driven*" (Roediger & Srinivas 1993, p. 25).

Transfer-appropriate processing and conscious awareness

Conscious recollection is not implicated in the performance of sensorimotor skills, which are carried out automatically. In fact, pausing to reflect on how to carry out a skilled act may even impair its performance. Although he differs from memory-systems advocates in terms of what makes a given task implicit or explicit, Roediger (1990b) has adopted the view that conscious awareness is associated with memory performance on explicit tests and that implicit tests tap an unaware form of retention.

Transfer-appropriate processing and implicit/explicit memory

The transfer-appropriate processing account of functional dissociations on explicit and implicit tests rests on four basic assumptions: (1) Memory performance will benefit to the extent that the operations required at encoding and retrieval match. (2) Explicit and implicit tests typically require different operations at encoding and retrieval. (3) Explicit tests typically require conceptually-driven processes that require accessing the encoded meaning of concepts or items that were processed by semantic or elaborative manipulations, and so forth. (4) Implicit tests typically require data-driven processes that require accessing the perceptual record of past experiences.

By this account, tasks that tap the same memory system would not be expected to yield the same dissociations in response to every independent variable; rather, the prediction of a dissociation would depend on the processing requirements during encoding and testing in each instance. Although transfer-appropriate processing can account for functional dissociations on implicit and explicit tests by normal adults, it fares less well in accounting for the memory dissociations of clinical populations who have experienced neural insult, such as amnesics and Korsakoff patients (Roediger et al. 1989a).

A number of researchers have argued that implicit memories are less flexible than explicit memories in transferring or generalizing to similar tasks (Cohen & Eichenbaum 1993; Dienes & Berry 1997; Squire 1992b, 1994). Willingham (1997, 1998b), however, argued that this distinction was based on studies in which the structural features of the stimuli were changed at the time of testing. He presented evidence from other studies that implicit and explicit memories transfer equally well if the processes engaged in during encoding and retrieval match and that both forms of memory transfer equally poorly if the processes during encoding and retrieval differ. By this argument, processing differences in flexibility can be understood in terms of the transfer-appropriate processing account (Roediger & Blaxton 1987).

Transfer-appropriate processing and infant memory

Evidence of functional dissociations on implicit and explicit tasks with infants is difficult to explain within a transfer-appropriate processing approach. In the evidence reviewed in Chapter 7, infants studied the material in exactly the same way and were tested on it in exactly the same way in both the delayed recognition and reactivation procedures. This commonality resembles the requirements of a transfer-appropriate processing account. In the reactivation task, however, infants were also exposed to a retrieval cue, or prime, in advance of the test (a *prior-cuing procedure;* Spear 1978). Because the memory was forgotten at the time the prime was presented and remained so for periods ranging from minutes to hours after priming, depending on the infant's age or number of prior reactivations, the reactivation process per se was not directly measured; that is, it was nonapparent. Presumably, the processing that was initiated by the prime, which reactivated the previously inactive memory, was strictly perceptual. If that processing differed from the processing during study, then the transfer-appropriate processing account might be applicable; however, given that the effect of priming was measured during a recognition test and we cannot stipulate the kind of processing in which infants initially engaged, this aspect of the processing analysis is strained.

Although nothing in the infant's behavior allows us to say whether memory retrieval on a delayed recognition test is conscious or intentional, the fact that infants do not recognize the reactivation stimulus at the time it is presented as a memory prime allows us to conclude with confidence that memory retrieval during reactivation does not result from a deliberate or intentional search process and thus cannot be accompanied by conscious awareness. For this reason, we attribute the retrieval that results from reactivation or priming to an all-or-none *automatic, perceptual-identification process.* If the prime is able to reactivate the memory, then we can assume that its structural or perceptual characteristics were represented in the infant's memory at the time of encoding — an assumption consistent with the transfer-appropriate processing account.

The fact that manipulations such as interference or no interference, shallow or deep level of processing, longer or shorter study time, and so forth affect the magnitude of delayed recognition differently than they affect the magnitude of reactivation, however, acceptance of the transfer-appropriate processing account would force us to conclude that the operations required to process these variables at the time of encoding and testing also differ. Yet, processing differences between the delayed recognition and reactivation tasks occur *only* at the time of retrieval. Thus, the onus for matching the input is placed squarely on the conditions that prevail at the time of retrieval. In studies with adults, differentiating the operations at the time of encoding is easier because they can be instructed to attend to different aspects of the study materials (i.e., engage in different types of processing), and at the time of testing, the experimenter can provide material that either matched or not what subjects were instructed to study.

Treisman (1992) referred to encoding and retrieval as *perceiving* and *re-perceiving*, respectively. If an object had not originally been perceived, of course, it could not be re-perceived. We have found it particularly useful to focus on the type of processing in which infants and adults engage at the time of retrieval. There are two fundamental kinds of visual processing — serial and parallel processing (Treisman & Gelade 1980). Parallel processing is automatic, preattentive, and rapid and occurs early in the visual system, whereas serial processing is deliberate, requires focused attention in an element-by-element search, and occurs late in the visual system. In adults, visual pop-out results from parallel processing: A single target that is embedded amidst an array of homogeneous distractors is detected effortlessly and rapidly. The diagnostic for parallel processing is subjects' insensitivity to the number of distractors in which the target is embedded. In serial searches, the amount of time required to detect a target (i.e., the RT slope) increases linearly with the number of stimuli in the array that must be inspected, whereas in parallel searches, the amount of time required to detect a target remains constant (i.e., the RT slope is flat) over increasing numbers of stimuli in the array.

In infants, visual pop-out has been reported in 3-month-olds (Rovee-Collier et al. 1992a) and 6-month-olds (Bhatt et al. 1994) in both delayed recognition and reactivation tasks and is similarly insensitive to the number of distractors. Rovee-Collier, Bhatt and Chazin (1996) trained 6-month-olds to kick to produce movement in a block mobile that displayed +s on all sides. Twenty days later, after they had forgotten the task, infants were exposed to a mobile that contained a single + block amidst a number of blocks that displayed Ls or a single L block amidst +s during a reactivation treatment (see Figure 8.6). The number of distractors ranged from 4 to 12. Twenty-four hours later, all infants were tested with the training mobile (i.e., a mobile displaying all +s).

Typically, reactivation fails if the prime contains more than a single novel object (Rovee-Collier et al. 1985b). If the pop-out display captured infants' attention via a parallel process, however, then only the familiarity or novelty of the single, attended target should affect reactivation. Therefore, we predicted that if the unique *novel* target popped out and captured attention, the reactivation treatment would be unsuccessful, despite the overwhelming number of training objects in which it was embedded; if the unique *training* object popped out and captured attention, however, then the forgotten memory would be reactivated despite the overwhelming number of novel objects in which it was embedded.

In fact, during the 24-hour test, these predictions were borne out. Infants whose reactivation mobile displayed a single novel target exhibited no retention, behaving as if they had received no reactivation treatment at all. In contrast, infants whose reactivation mobile displayed a single training target exhibited excellent retention. More importantly for the parallel-processing

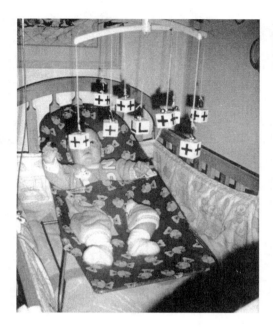

Figure 8.6. A pop-out mobile that was used during reactivation with 6-month-olds. This pop-out mobile contained a single target (L) amidst eight distractors (+s). All infants were trained and tested with a mobile containing nine blocks. For infants in the *novel* pop-out reactivation condition, all blocks on the training and test mobile displayed +s; for infants in the *familiar* pop-out reactivation condition, all blocks on the training and test mobile displayed Ls.

argument, the magnitude of pop-out was the same irrespective of the number of distractors on the reactivation mobile (see Figure 8.7). Only when the reactivation mobile contained 13 objects were the predictions reversed — and for an uninteresting reason: Because the single object was centered in the display, the largest number of objects on the reactivation mobile obscured it.

In the delayed recognition task at 6 months of age, Bhatt et al. (1994) found evidence that a top-down serial process can override the automatic parallel process. Whereas 3-month-olds exhibited significant 24-hour retention on a delayed recognition test if the test mobile displayed the training character as the target (pop-out) stimulus but not if it displayed a novel one, 6-month-olds exhibited significant 24-hour retention whether the single target was the training character or it was novel and the six distractors were training

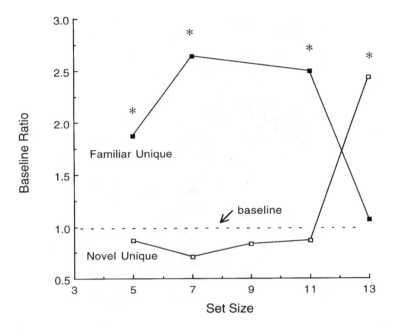

Figure 8.7. Mean baseline ratios as a function of the number of blocks on the reactivation mobile (*set size*). A unique novel (*open square*) or familiar (*filled square*) block was embedded amidst either familiar or novel distractor blocks, respectively, on the reactivation mobile. Whether the reactivation mobile was an effective memory prime was assessed 24 hours later. An asterisk indicates that the memory was reactivated (*M* baseline ratio significantly > 1.00). In both the novel and familiar reactivation conditions, test performance over set sizes from 5 to 11 blocks did not differ.

characters. Because the single familiar target popped out, the single novel one must have popped out as well. In the latter instance, however, infants must have engaged in an attention-demanding serial (element-by-element) search or they would not have located the predictive cue(s) that enabled them to exhibit retention. Thus, although there are age-related changes in perceptual processing, we argue that these are changes in processing speed — not in the fundamental processes (or systems) that underlie memory performance. Here, between 3 and 6 months, infants processed the test stimulus more rapidly, just as they process the prime more rapidly at 6 than at 3 months of age (Hildreth & Rovee-Collier 1999a).

Musen and Treisman (1990) related parallel and serial processing to implicit and explicit memory, respectively. Whereas Tulving and Schacter (1990) viewed parallel processing as an operation of the perceptual representation system, Roediger and Blaxton (1987) interpreted it in terms of transfer-appropriate processing.

Multiple-entry modular memory system (MEM)

The multiple-entry modular model (MEM) describes a unitary memory framework within which different cognitive processes are associated with independent processing subsystems that interact with each other to a greater or lesser degree to give rise to a memory (Johnson 1983). The term *multiple-entry* refers to the fact that any given event can create multiple entries (or traces) in all subsystems. Originally, Johnson envisioned three subsystems — the sensory system, the perceptual system, and the reflection system. The sensory and perceptual subsystems were specialized to detect and preserve information about stimuli and relationships among them, whereas the reflection system was specialized for preserving self-generated thought processes. Subsequently, Johnson (1991b) combined the sensory and perceptual subsystems into a single perceptual system with two subsystems (P-1, P-2) and expanded the reflection system to include two subsystems (R-1, R-2). The P-1 subsystem corresponded to the original sensory system and recorded information pertaining both to modality-specific (e.g., vision, smell, touch) and amodal (e.g., intensity, frequency, solidity, rate of change) properties of stimuli, whereas the P-2 subsystem recorded information about the phenomenal products of perception, such as the identity of objects and events. The components of the reflective subsystem could also function alone or interact. These subsystems and the supervisory and control processes are illustrated in Figure 8.8 (*top panel*).

In addition, each of the four memory subsystems (P-1, P-2, R-1, R-2) was endowed with a unique set of component processes that allow people to sustain, organize, and revive information. As defined by Johnson and Chalfonte (1994, pp. 315–316), the P-1 processes are *extracting* (invariants from perceptual arrays), *tracking* (moving stimuli), *locating* (stimuli), and *resolving* (a perceptual array into primitive perceptual units). These processes are involved in the acquisition of various perceptual-motor skills. The P-2 processes are *structuring* (or abstracting a pattern of organization across a temporally or spatially extended stimulus), *placing* (objects or events in spatial relation to one an-

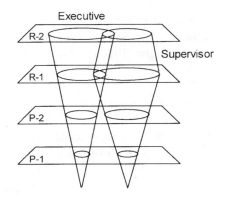

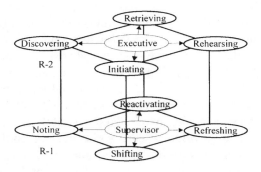

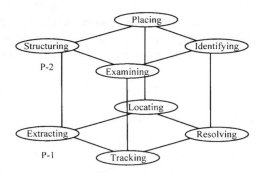

Figure 8.8. A multiple-entry modular memory system (MEM). *Top panel:* Two reflective subsystems (R-1, R-2) and two perceptual subsystems (P-1, P-2). Reflective and perceptual subsystems can interact through a control (the *supervisor*) and monitoring (the *executive*)

process of R-1 and R-2, respectively. These processes are the means by which the perception and reflection subsystems interact. They are depicted as cones passing through the planes that represent the different subsystems. The size of the ellipses at the intersections of the cones and planes indicates the extent to which each of these processes is involved in the activities of each subsystem. Thus, the executive process has greater access to the reflection system than to the perception system and greater access to P-2 than to P-1. *Middle panel:* The component processes of R-1 and R-2. *Bottom panel:* The component processes of P-1 and P-2. ©*1991, Plenum Publishing Corporation; adopted with permission. From M.K. Johnson, Reflection, reality monitoring, and the self. In R. Kunzendorf (Ed.), Mental imagery: Proceedings of the Eleventh Annual Conference of the American Association for the Study of Mental Imagery (pp. 3–16). New York: Plenum.*

other), *examining* (or perceptually investigating one or many aspects of a stimulus array), and *identifying* (objects and events by combining perceptual primitives to yield a sense of what something may be or is). P-2 processes interact to give rise to the phenomenal world of objects and events that make up a meaningful environment (see Figure 8.8, *bottom panel*).

In general, R-1 processes are nonstrategic; they include *noting* (identifying relations among activated information), *shifting* (changing activation from one aspect of a stimulus to another), *refreshing* (prolonging or extending the persistence of ongoing activation), and *reactivating* (activating currently inactive information). In contrast, R-2 processes are strategic; they include *discovering, initiating* (changing one's perspective by strategically seeking ways to activate inactivated aspects of information), *rehearsing* (producing and recycling self-generated codes for activated information, usually with the intent to keep information accessible in a reportable format), and *retrieving* (searching for and self-presenting cues that are not currently active). Whereas refreshing and rehearsing are processes that operate on active information, reactivating and retrieving are processes that operate on inactive information (see Figure 8.8, *middle panel*). Although they share common agendas, the source of information used for refreshing and reactivating (R-1 processes) has been characterized by Johnson and Chalfonte (1994, p. 318) as often being "a fortuitous combination of agendas and cues" such as noting "agendas and cues that were previously active together;" in contrast, the information used for rehearsing and retrieving (R-2 processes) is intentionally self-generated.

Finally, R-1 and R-2 processes have different *agendas* (i.e., goals, intentions, purposes), collectively called *supervisor* and *executive* processes, respectively. These agendas are the means by which reflective and perceptual processes interact (see Figure 8.8, *top panel*) and can be as simple as a task demand ("identify the pronouns") or as complex as a script that specifies the combination of component processes and the order in which they must be engaged. Whereas supervisor processes (R-1) are more holistic and global, executive processes (R-2) are more deliberate and analytic (Johnson & Hirst 1993).

MEM and conscious awareness

In MEM, conscious awareness is neither a defining characteristic of a particular memory subsystem or process nor a causal agent for different types of memory (Tulving 1985). Rather, it is an emergent process:

> "In MEM, the phenomenal experience of consciousness emerges from [various combinations of] component cognitive activities — that is, cognitive activities involved in perceiving and reflecting confer consciousness rather than the other way around. If you disrupt some of these activities, you disrupt consciousness, but it is not possible to disrupt consciousness without inhibiting or disrupting at least some aspects of these activities" (Johnson & Hirst 1993, p. 258).

Earlier, Johnson and Raye (1981) argued that conscious recollection (i.e., experiencing a sense of pastness in remembering) is the consequence of a reality-monitoring process in which a person decides whether a memory originated in an actual experience (the perception system) or in imagination (the reflection system) on the basis of its attributes. Presumably, the memory of an actually experienced event is more vivid, highly detailed, contains spatiotemporal details, and generally consists of more sensory or perceptual attributes than a memory of an imagined event, which arises in the reflection system. In addition, it is consistent with related memories. On the other hand, an inability to discriminate between the attributes of actually perceived and self-generated events (i.e., a break-down of reality-monitoring) can lead to confabulation, when the individual treats an entry in the reflection system as if it originated in the perception system (Johnson 1991a).

MEM and multiple memory systems

Whereas multiple memory systems are characterized by the *common content* of the information about an event that each system encodes and stores (e.g., episodic information, semantic information, procedural information, perceptual representations, declarative information, nondeclarative information, etc.), MEM cuts across memory content and instead distinguishes the *common processes* that are required to perform various cognitive activities. Thus, episodic and semantic memories are the products of interactions of the same (or some of the same) component processes distributed across different subsystems. Likewise, whereas multiple memory systems, in some views, do not interact (Schacter & Sherry 1987; Squire 1986, 1987), the component processes of MEM interact within and between its subsystems, depending on the requirements of the task at hand. For this reason, these component processes are viewed as part of a single memory system.

Recall that in Tulving's (1972, 1983) scheme, episodic memories are distinguished from semantic memories by two critical features — they are accompanied by a conscious awareness of having previously experienced an event and their time and/or place of occurrence can be specified. In MEM, however, there are not separate stores for autobiographical and generic memories. Rather, a memory is *judged* by the rememberer to be autobiographical or not. This is accomplished by a reality-monitoring process (see preceding section) in which its attributes are evaluated for the degree of perceptual and emotional detail. In MEM, spatiotemporal attributes do not have a privileged status but are simply among the memory attributes that are evaluated. Likewise, in MEM, conscious awareness is not a defining characteristic of episodic memory but is conferred on the memory only if it is judged to be autobiographical (see preceding section).

Finally, MEM side-steps the proliferation problem that results from the creation of a new memory system to account for each new functional dissociation that is found within tasks previously thought to tap an existing system (e.g., Tulving 1993; Tulving & Schacter 1990). The different combinations of existing subprocesses, programmed in different functional orders, can accommodate the processing of content as diverse as riding a bicycle, solving a crossword puzzle, recognizing a face, or remembering directions to a party. Likewise, disruptions in specific subprocesses can account for specific patterns of deficit, whereas disruption of an entire memory system would presumably result in a deficit for all of the memories stored in that system-episodic, procedural, or whatever.

MEM and transfer-appropriate processing

MEM is consistent with the predictions of transfer-appropriate processing in that both assume that the processes that are active at the time of testing match those that were active at the time of encoding. Although at first blush, the processes associated with perception and reflection seem similar to data-driven and conceptually-driven processing, respectively, they are quite different. For one thing, MEM subsystems and processes interact, so that memory performance rarely reflects only perception or reflection, but memory performance by the transfer-appropriate processing account is attributed to one type of processing or the other. In addition, reflection and perception both contribute to processing that is considered to be conceptually-driven (for discussion, see Johnson & Hirst 1993).

In addition, MEM is more complex than the transfer-appropriate processing framework; as a result, it can account for more complex cognitive performance. For the same reason, it is better equipped to account for deficits in cognition. Because combinations of component processes comprise functional subsystems, a breakdown in any process could disrupt any of the subsystems to which that component contributed and, as a result, could produce a variety of patterns of functional deficit. Neuroanatomical data that localize the brain regions or pathways that may be implicated in the different component processes further increase MEM's potential explanatory value. Evidence of an impaired ability to bind item and location information in amnesia (Chalfonte, Verfaellie, Johnson & Reiss 1996), for example, suggests that damage to the hippocampal structure disrupts *reactivating* (Johnson & Chalfonte 1994). Likewise, frontal-lobe damage, which often results in confabulation (profound source confusion), led to ERP (event-related potential) studies that implicated the right prefrontal cortex in the evaluation of automatically activated information (familiarity, perceptual detail), which is necessary for both recognition and source identification (Johnson, Kounios & Nolde 1996; Johnson & Raye 1998). Neuroimaging studies, in turn, have implicated the left prefrontal cortex in both the reflectively guided retrieval of specific details and the more difficult, systematic evaluation of confirming and disconfirming information, which are necessary for source attributions (Nolde, Johnson & D'Esposito 1998). Being so general, the transfer-appropriate processing framework cannot provide as satisfactory an account for the data of amnesics as either MEM or structural accounts (Roediger et al. 1989a, 1990).

MEM and implicit/explicit memory

According to MEM, dissociations on implicit and explicit memory tasks simply reflect the fact that the tasks tap entries in different processing subsystems. Because many tasks involve processes from most or all of the subsystems, the extent to which a task relies more heavily on processes from one system or another usually determines whether it is described as implicit or explicit. As we have seen, few if any implicit and explicit tasks are process-pure (Jacoby 1991). Thus, an implicit memory test such as perceptual identification of a degraded picture would rely heavily on component processes from the perception system (P-1, P-2) to process the physical features or structure of the stimulus but would also be likely to engage component processes from the reflective system (e.g., noting relationships between parts, shifting attention from one aspect of the figure to another). Conversely, an explicit version of the test would rely more heavily on component processes from the reflection system, but the component processes from the perception system would still be recruited to process the physical features of the stimulus.

Accordingly, a memory dissociation on implicit and explicit tasks does not mean that the two tasks depend on different underlying processes. Rather, it means that implicit and explicit tasks reflect the relative *reliance* of different tasks on different perceptual or reflective subprocesses. As Shimamura (1990) argued, if memory performance on a particular implicit task is not impaired by a given experimental manipulation or subject variable (age, amnesia), but memory performance on a particular explicit task is, then this dissociation can be taken as evidence that the implicit task recruited a particular process that the explicit task did not. Because many of the other processes recruited in both tasks are the same, however, the products they generate may not be accurately characterized as different or independent forms of memory.

Developmental sequence of MEM subsystems

Johnson and colleagues described the developmental sequence of the four subsystems from infancy to adulthood as P-1, P-2, R-1, and R-2 and speculated that the four subsystems may have evolved in the same sequence (Johnson 1991a; Johnson & Chalfonte 1994; Johnson & Hirst 1993). As we observed earlier, however, evolution is not linear (see *Functional Incompatibility of Operations*, this chapter).

As an example that P-1 develops before P-2, Johnson and Hirst (1993) noted that infants engage in visual tracking before they can recognize something as familiar. Evidence for this example and others that one might think of, however, is either absent or contradictory. Although newborn infants can track a visual stimulus, they can also distinguish their mother's voice from that of a stranger — and prefer it (DeCasper & Fifer 1980). Moreover, newborns tested 33 hours after birth can distinguish a tape-recording of their mother reading a *familiar* Dr. Seuss passage (i.e., one that she had read aloud for 20 min a day during the last 6 weeks of gestation) from a tape-recording of their mother reading a *novel* Dr. Seuss passage (DeCasper & Spence 1986). Further, newborns prefer the familiar passage.

In the same chapter, however, Johnson and Hirst acknowledged that a particular memory subsystem or process should not be associated with a particular age:

> "it would be a mistake simply to characterize a human infant as 'having' only P-1 and P-2 subsystems, or to characterize a young child as 'getting' R-2 processes at some particular age. For example, some aspects of reflective processes (e.g., *reactivation*) may operate from quite early on (Rovee-Collier 1990). Furthermore, specific learning occurs in all subsystems throughout the lifespan. Acquisition of new information in any particular subsystem depends on acquisition of prior information. Consequently, differences in 'sophistication' of the subsystems at a given age are partly the consequence of what has already been learned by the different subsystems. One might have a knowledgeable P-1 system and a less educated R-2 system or vice versa" (Johnson & Hirst 1993, pp. 252-253).

MEM and infant memory

MEM offers a number of distinct advantages for analyses of infant memory. First, it captures the complexity of memory without requiring that particular neural mechanisms be functionally mature. Because the developmental timetable by which different brain mechanisms become *functionally* mature in humans is behaviorally based and largely unknown, MEM's reliance on cognitive processes rather than neural systems eliminates this problem. Second, by emphasizing the interaction between different subsystems and processes in most tasks, MEM does not associate a particular type of task with an underlying process (i.e., does not make the flawed assumption that a task is process-pure). Third, MEM eliminates conscious awareness as a defining (or ill-defined) characteristic of explicit memory. Fourth, it allows the different subsystems to develop at different rates depending on an individual's prior experiences. Fifth, MEM does not grant special status to autobiographical memory. Of course, whether the R-2 component processes are within the capability of preverbal infants will remain in the realm of speculation until someone figures out how to measure introspective processes in nonverbal organisms, which seems unlikely. Nonetheless, the bulk of measurable memory phenomena in preverbal infants is readily accommodated by the P-1, P-2, and R-1 subsystems and their component processes.

MEM is generally consistent with research findings from infants. Johnson and Hirst (1993) observed, for example, that reactivating in MEM (an R-1 process) may be analogous to reactivation in infant memory studies. In fact, for subjects of all ages, reactivating an inactive memory makes it available for integration with other memories, distortion, and so forth. There are, however, some problems with this analogy. In the infant literature, reactivation is considered to be an implicit, automatic priming process that is either directly or indirectly (as in mediated priming) cued by an external stimulus (for review, see Chapter 7). Johnson and Chalfonte (1994), however, defined reactivation as an *internally generated* repetition of a memory. Even if the R-1 subsystem were to develop relatively early in infancy, however, this would not challenge Johnson and Hirst's (1993) proposal that the *sequence* of development of the subsystems is P-1, P-2, R-1, and R-2.

Three lines of evidence from reactivation studies with infants lead us to conclude that the R-1 subsystem does develop early in the first year of life. First, memories can be reactivated in infants as young as 2 months of age (Davis & Rovee-Collier 1983; Rovee-Collier, Hartshorn & DiRubbo 1999). Second, Barr and Vieira (1999) found that previously associated information that had become inactive (the memory of the train) could be reactivated by exposing infants to either member in the association — either the puppet or the train. Exposing infants to a partial puppet demonstration, for example, reactivated the forgotten memory of the train that was associated with it; as a result, infants again responded to the train during the ensuing long-term memory test. This example exactly parallels one of the examples of R-1 reactivating that was cited in Johnson and Chalfonte (1994) and confirms that the R-1 subsystem is active by at least 6 months of age. And third, the memory of kicking to move a mobile in a distinctive context was reactivated 2, 3, and 4 weeks after it was forgotten by exposing infants to only the distinctive context — the mobile was not present at the time of the exposure (Hayne & Findlay 1995;

Rovee-Collier et al. 1985a). This example also exactly parallels one of the examples of R-1 reactivating that was cited in Johnson and Chalfonte (1994) and confirms that the R-1 subsystem is active by at least 3 months of age. In the preceding examples, we cannot say whether infants' memories were indirectly reactivated in response to *internally-generated* cues, as is required of reactivating in MEM. However, we can say that reactivation in examples 2 and 3 was indirect and mediated by a prior association.

If *reactivating* in MEM and reactivation in infants and animals are the same, then the proposed appearance of the four memory subsystems in phylogeny must be rethought. Johnson and Chalfonte (1994) cited evidence of reactivating (MEM) in rats, but reactivation effects have been documented in organisms at all phyletic levels — from the sea snail *Hermissenda* (Matzel, Collin & Alkon 1992) to humans (see Chapter 7).

Conclusions

Both of the two major multiple-memory-systems accounts that have been advanced to explain the functional memory dissociations that are exhibited by brain-damaged and normal (instructed) adults hold that the memory system that mediates explicit memory (i.e., episodic or declarative memory) develops quite late in the infancy period relative to the memory system that mediates implicit memory (i.e., semantic or procedural memory), but data obtained directly from infants indicate otherwise (see Chapter 7). In contrast, the transfer-appropriate processing account does not presume a particular developmental sequence. Because infants' study and test materials are identical, it adequately explains infants' memory performance in delayed recognition tasks; however, its account of their memory performance in reactivation tasks is less clear-cut. The MEM model postulates that the processing components develop sequentially, with the perceptual processes (P1, P2) developing earlier than reflective processes (R1, R2). Recently, the authors of this model acknowledged that some processing subcomponents of the reflective system (reactivation) might appear relatively early in the infancy period. They use the term *reactivation* differently than it is used in the infant literature, however, where it refers exclusively to automatic (*nonreflective*) perceptual processing. In short, no theoretical models — either multiple-memory-systems models or processing models — have yet provided a fully satisfactory account of the functional dissociations in infant memory.

CHAPTER 9

Interactions between Implicit and Explicit Memories in Infants

This chapter considers the fate of implicit memories after they have been primed, the effect of priming when a memory is active versus when it is not, and the effect of priming with a novel stimulus after delays when a memory can still be explicitly retrieved. The data in this chapter were obtained exclusively from infants, but they have major implications for everyday memory in individuals of all ages.

In laboratory experiments on implicit and explicit memory, individuals study a list of words or pictures and then are asked a simple question to which they typically respond with an item from the study list whether instructed to do so (the explicit memory task) or not (the implicit memory task). Even though the same response may be expressed on both types of test, different theoretical models propose that the memory which is retrieved is different. Squire (1992a), for example, proposed that the declarative and nondeclarative systems encode different memories, and so the memories that are expressed on the explicit and implicit tests that tap those systems would be different. Mandler (1980), however, argued for a single memory system in which a memory is either automatically activated without contextual information or intentionally retrieved with contextual information. By this account, the implicit memory would presumably be a leaner version of the explicit memory. Johnson (1983; Johnson & Hirst 1993), who also proposed a theoretical account based on a unitary memory system, differentiated the memories that are expressed on implicit and explicit tests in terms of the combinations of subprocesses that create them. Strategic R-2 processes are more likely to be engaged on an explicit memory test, whereas nonstrategic R-1 processes are more likely to be engaged on an implicit memory test (see Chapter 8). Because interactions involving R-2 processes endow a memory with different qualities than R-1 processes alone, the product of these subprocesses should also differ.

In some ways, however, the distinction between explicit and implicit memories is not so clear-cut. Adults' memories that were originally explicit, for example, can eventually become automatic — a defining characteristic of implicit memories (Mandler 1985) — if they are repeatedly practiced or retrieved (Logan 1988, 1990, 1992; Logan & Klapp 1991; Willingham & Goedert-Eschmann 1999). Logan (1988), for example, proposed that specific instances of past encounters with a given stimulus and the response that was made to it are stored as episodic memories that are retrieved when the stimulus is presented on a future occasion. Over repeated retrievals of prior processing episodes involving the same stimulus and response (i.e., practice), memory performance becomes faster and more automatized. Thus, learning to drive a car with a standard transmission initially requires a great deal of focused attention, and the dos-and-don'ts from specific prior training episodes are recalled and rehearsed during later practice sessions. Eventually, however, clutching, shifting, accelerating, braking, turning on the turn signals or wind-shield wipers, and steering are performed automatically and effortlessly in a coordinated manner.

Although some researchers might classify learning to drive as a skill or procedural memory (Squire 1992a), more complex behavioral acts that defy simple classification as procedural memories also can become automatic. A common experience such as driving the car to work — which may require more than an hour, traverse many miles, and require negotiating all manner of traffic and hazards, can become frighteningly automatized. Although we arrive safely at the office, we have no recollection of getting there or what we saw or did en route.

In everyday life, implicit and explicit memories presumably guide our normal commerce with the environment and influence our understanding. Although the long-term effects of retrieving implicit and explicit memories are clearly important for our future behavior, memory studies with adults have given little consideration to whether these effects are the same or different. Whereas instructing normal adults to respond with the first word that comes to mind (an implicit memory task) yields immediate memory performance that is similar to that of amnesics, the long-term effect of priming on the subsequent memory performance of normal and abnormal populations surely differs. When this question has been asked of normal adults, it has been framed only in terms of the effect of retrieving explicit memories on future retrieval. In addition to becoming automatized (Logan 1988), this effect is to facilitate present understanding (Ross & Bradshaw 1994), produce forgetting of the memory content that was not previously retrieved (Anderson, Bjork & Bjork 1994; Loftus & Loftus 1974), and protract retention within a limited period of time (Bjork 1975; Schmidt & Bjork 1992; Roediger & Payne 1982). In contrast, the long-term effect of priming has gone largely unstudied.

One potentially important factor that distinguishes priming in amnesics from priming in normal adults is that amnesics are *incapable* of recognizing the target item at the time of priming, but normal (instructed) adults are. Although amnesics are brain-damaged, whether the memory is recognizable at the time of priming may also affect how long it is subsequently remembered by normal adults. The duration for which normal adults remember an explicit memory, for example, increases with the effortfulness or difficulty of its retrieval, which is operationally defined as the time between original encoding and subsequent retrieval (Bjork 1975; Schmidt & Bjork 1992). Although the duration for which an implicit memory is subsequently remembered is unknown, it might also be affected differently by when the prime was encountered. On the other hand, because the retrieval of an implicit memory is effortless and automatic (Besson et al. 1992; Hasher & Zacks 1977; Mandler 1980; Musen & Treisman 1990), its effect on subsequent retention may be independent of the retention interval.

Conversely, the long-term consequences of priming when the memory is still recognizable (as it is in priming studies with normal adults) has also not been explored. Nor have researchers studied the long-term consequences of priming with a novel stimulus. In the adult literature, priming has been described as hyperspecific (Tulving & Schacter 1990). Changes in the physical appearance of a previously studied object usually — but not always — reduce the amount of priming (see Richardson-Klavehn & Bjork 1988, for review). The specificity that characterizes effective primes for adults is also found in reactivation studies with infants whose memories have been forgotten (see Chapter 7). Given that exactly the same stimulus rarely recurs in nature twice (Wyers, Peeke & Herz 1973), however, we should ask whether an incidental encounter with a slightly different stimulus might implicitly prime a memory that can still be retrieved on a recognition test, and, if so, how that encounter affects future retention.

Given the evidence presented in previous chapters that memory processing by preverbal infants and healthy adults is qualitatively the same, infants may be an ideal population for answering some of the questions that are less amenable to experimental study with adults. Because 3-month-olds forget within only 1 week, and 6-month-olds forget within only 3 weeks, their subsequent retention following administration of a prime after the original memory was forgotten can be assessed within a reasonable time frame. In addition, the functional significance of priming when the memory is active versus when it is not, as well as the effect of priming with a novel stimulus when the memory is active, can be studied with relative ease. The results of studies with infants that addressed some of these questions are reviewed below.

Similarities between infants' implicit and explicit memories

Despite the numerous functional dissociations that have been found between implicit and explicit memories in infants (see Chapter 7), other aspects of their implicit and explicit memories are very similar.

Magnitude of retention

The magnitude of explicit memories declines as the interval between training and recognition testing increases for both infants (Hartshorn et al. 1998b; Hill et al. 1988; Sullivan et al. 1979) and adults (Cave 1997; Tulving et al. 1982). In contrast, the initial magnitude of implicit (reactivated) memories is independent of the interval between training and priming for both adults (Tulving et al. 1982) and infants (Davis & Rovee-Collier 1983; Hayne 1990; Hayne & Findlay 1995; Hildreth & Rovee-Collier 1999a; Sheffield & Hudson 1994). These data suggest that explicit and implicit memories are different. Once an implicit memory has been reactivated, however, its subsequent magnitude declines with the time since reactivation, just as the magnitude of an explicit memory declines with the time since training (Hildreth & Rovee-Collier 1999b). In this regard, then, explicit and implicit memories are similar.

Duration of retention

The duration of retention of explicit memories in both delayed recognition and deferred imitation tests increases linearly with age (Hartshorn et al. 1998b;

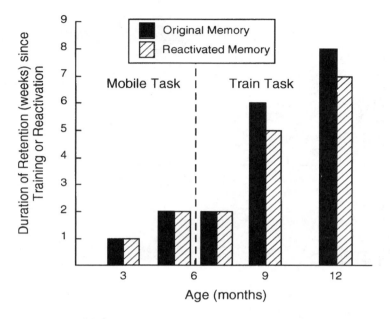

Figure 9.1. The duration of retention between 3 and 12 months of age after original training (*dark bars*) and after reactivation (*striped bars*). In both cases, the duration of retention increases linearly with age.

Hayne et al. 1997; Herbert & Hayne 2000), and the duration of retention of implicit (reactivated) memories does as well. As can be seen in Figure 9.1, the duration of a reactivated memory increased linearly between 3 and 12 months of age in both the mobile and train tasks (Hildreth & Rovee-Collier 1999b).

Rate of forgetting

Since the time of Ebbinghaus (1885), forgetting has been recognized as the most ubiquitous characteristic of adult memory. This characteristic describes infant memory as well. Over the first year of life, infants gradually forget explicit memories over the interval between training and the delayed recognition test, and they gradually forget implicit (reactivated) memories over the interval between priming and testing as well. Figure 9.2 shows that the rate of forgetting explicit and implicit memories was the same over the first year of life, whether infants were studied with mobiles or trains (Hildreth & Rovee-

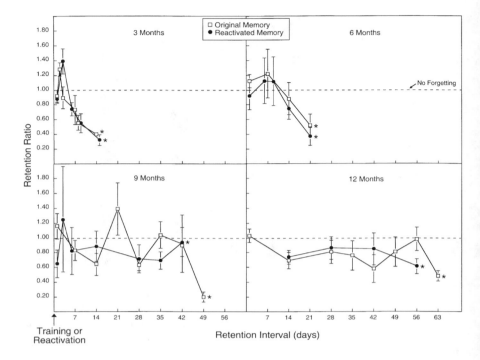

Figure 9.2. The rate at which infants between 3 and 12 months of age forget the original memory (*open squares*) and the reactivated memory (*filled squares*). At each age, the memory prime was administered 1 week after infants of a given age last remembered the task. Asterisks indicate no retention (*M* baseline ratio not significantly > 1.00).

Collier 1999b). This common pattern occurred despite the fact that both explicit and implicit memories were forgotten over increasingly longer periods of time with age. A cursory inspection of Figure 9.2 offers no clue as to which function represents infants' forgetting of the reactivated memory.

The preceding results are particularly impressive when one considers that the forgotten memory was always reactivated 1 week after infants of a given age last remembered the task. When this 1-week delay is taken into account, we see that exposing infants to a single memory prime at least doubles the accessibility of the memory over the entire first year of life (see Figure 9.3). The robustness of this effect encourages us that it probably occurs for older individuals as well.

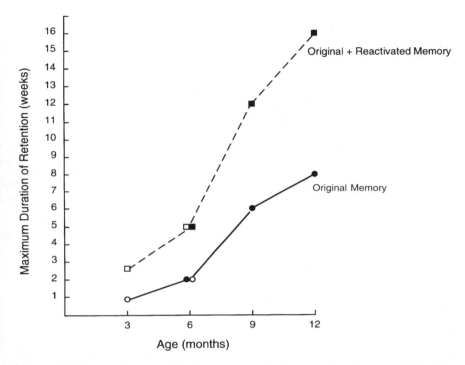

Figure 9.3. The retention benefit of a single reactivation over the first year of life. The maximum duration of retention (weeks) of the training memory is shown before reactivation (*solid line*; see Figure 6.6) and after reactivation (*dashed line*). The single memory prime was given 1 week after infants of each age last remembered the task.

Although a single memory prime appears to *recycle* a forgotten memory so that it is remembered again for as long as it originally was, presenting additional primes may protract its duration even more. Hayne (1990) gave one, two, or three reactivation treatments to 3-month-olds. During each reactivation treatment, she merely showed infants the training mobile, in motion, for 3 min. As expected, infants recognized the mobile for as long after a single reactivation as they had after original training, whether the forgotten memory was reactivated 2 weeks or 3 weeks after training. After being primed once, the reactivated memory persisted for 3 days but not for 1 week, but after being primed twice, the reactivated memory persisted for 2 weeks but not 3 weeks. Moreover, the retention-enhancing effect of the second prime occurred whether it was presented 3 weeks or 4 weeks after training. In the latter instance, retention was still seen 6 weeks after infants were initially trained — a period almost half again their life-time. After being primed three times, however, infants' retention was no longer than when they were primed only once.

Although Hayne found that three reactivations were not as effective as two, we have found that whether additional reactivations can protract retention even longer depends on their timing. In a subsequent mobile study with infants who were only 2 months old when they were trained, we gave infants the same reactivation treatments as Hayne but spaced them every 3 weeks through 26 weeks of age (Rovee-Collier et al. 1999). Immediately preceding each reactivation treatment, we administered a 3-min delayed recognition test in order to determine whether or not infants exhibited retention. After three to five reactivations, these younger infants eventually exhibited significant retention 3 weeks after their last reactivation.

Taken together, these data reveal that the durations of explicit and implicit memories differ after a memory has been multiply primed.

Accessibility of different types of memory attributes

Recall that the specific details of both the original mobile and the encoding context are represented in infants' training memory. As the interval between training and testing increases, infants progressively forget the specific details of the original mobile but continue to remember its general features or gist, thereby generalizing to novel test mobiles (Rovee-Collier & Sullivan 1980). If infants are trained and tested in a highly distinctive context, however, the context primes these forgotten details via a serial attention-gating mechanism. As a result, infants are able to discriminate the original mobile from a novel one after longer delays, when they can still recognize the context (Butler & Rovee-Collier 1989). Likewise, at both 3 and 6 months of age, an implicit memory is also highly specific to the details of the original cue and context (Hartshorn & Rovee-Collier 1997; Hayne & Rovee-Collier 1995; Shields & Rovee-Collier 1992). In this respect, then, explicit and implicit memories are similar.

After the implicit memory has been forgotten, however, the memory attributes that represented the details of the encoding context are apparently lost, because the second time the memory is reactivated, the context can be different. Moreover, after the twice-reactivated memory has been forgotten, the memory attributes that represented the details of the original mobile apparently are lost, because the twice-reactivated and twice-forgotten memory can be reactivated a third time by a different cue as well as in a different context (Hitchcock & Rovee-Collier 1996). These data reveal that explicit and implicit memories differ in the accessibility of their different attributes after they have been multiply primed, perhaps because multiply primed memories are older, and older memories are more fragile.

In 1972, Tulving proposed that information is more readily lost from the episodic than from the semantic memory system. Furlong (1951, cited in Tulving 1983, p. 17) had similarly hypothesized that retrospective [i.e., epi-sodic] memory became nonretrospective [i.e., semantic] memory *as the context faded*. These statements are consistent with the preceding evidence that contextual information becomes lost from infants' memories over the course of repeated reactivations. If an episodic memory eventually becomes context free because its details pertaining to the time and place of its origin have been lost, however, then this raises questions about the usefulness of distinguishing different memory systems in the first place. Does, for example, an episodic memory become a semantic one, shifting memory systems, *after* this informa-tion has been lost? Or does context-specific information become lost *because* a memory has been transferred from the episodic to the semantic memory system? Or does such a transfer even occur? The loss of context specificity seems to be better accommodated by envisioning memory as a single system that is characterized by different degrees of specificity, different routes of access, and so forth (e.g., Mandler 1985).

The effect of priming an active memory on retention

The effect of priming (reactivation) on subsequent retention also depends on the state of the memory when the prime is administered. Recall that Hayne (1990) found that two reactivation treatments, each given when the memory was inactive (13 and 20 days after training), protracted retention for 2 weeks, whereas a single reactivation treatment given 20 days after training protracted retention for less than 1 week. She also found that three reactivations given 6, 13, and 20 days after training were no more effective than one (see Fig-ure 9.4). Hayne speculated that the third reactivation may have lost some of its effectiveness because it was given only 1 week after the second reactivation treatment — a point when the twice-reactivated memory was still active. But why would the state of the memory make a difference?

The answer was suggested a number of years ago by a study in which researchers used memory primes of different durations. Gordon, Smith and Katz (1979) reported that exposing adult rats to a memory prime for 15 s reactivated a memory of active avoidance, whereas exposing rats to the prime for 75 s extinguished it. Subsequently, Arnold and Spear (1993) obtained a similar result with preweanling rat pups: Exposing pups to a memory prime for 5 s or 15 s reactivated the forgotten training memory, but exposing them to the prime for 30 s did not. Given evidence that a memory can be modified only when it is active (Lewis 1979), Gordon (1981) had hypothesized that reactivation of a memory begins when a prime is initially exposed and that, after the memory has been reactivated, the continued presence of the prime can lead to new learning that can modify it. By this account, then, a lengthy prime provides an opportunity for the reactivated memory to be modified counteracting the original effectiveness of the prime.

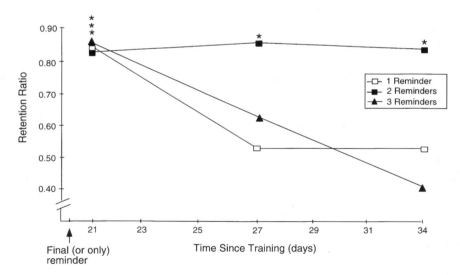

Figure 9.4. The duration of retention (days) following one, two, or three reactivation treatments at 3 months of age. An asterisk indicates significant retention.

In fact, Hayne (1990) observed this result in a control group that was included to determine whether the retention benefit of two reactivations resulted because the memory prime was presented twice or because the total duration of priming was twice as long. When Hayne had exposed infants to two 3-min primes — each when the memory was inactive, their forgotten mobile memory had not only been reactivated but had been protracted for 2 weeks. When she exposed infants to one 6-min prime — also when the memory was inactive, however, infants exhibited no retention at all only 24 hours later. By Gordon's (1981) account, the 6-min prime initially reactivated the inactive memory, but its continued exposure enabled new learning that either competed with or subtracted from what infants had learned before.

If a lengthy exposure to the prime once the memory is inactive can impair retention, then a shorter exposure to the prime when the memory is already active should have a similar effect. In fact, when Hayne (1990) gave infants a third 3-min reactivation treatment only 1 week after the second reactivation treatment — a time when the twice-reactivated memory was still highly accessible, infants exhibited excellent retention 1 day later but none 1 week later — when the benefit of two reactivations had still been seen. Apparently, presenting the 3-min prime when the memory was still accessible was long enough to partially counteract the retention benefit produced by the second reactivation but not so long that it eliminated the effectiveness of the second reactivation altogether.

As another test of the effect of priming on an accessible memory, Adler et al. (2000) gave 3-month-olds an initial 3-min reactivation treatment either immediately (0 days) or 3 days after training — when the original memory was still relatively accessible — and asked how it affected infants' subsequent retention. Although 3-month-olds can remember an explicit memory for 5 but not 6 days after training is over (Hayne 1990), infants who were primed for 3 min immediately after training exhibited significant retention 6 but not 7 days later; and infants who were primed 3 days after training exhibited significant retention 7 but not 9 days after training. Thus, priming an accessible memory provided a slight memory boost that increased with the delay between training and priming. Priming when the original memory was active, however, did not boost retention nearly as long as priming when it was not (e.g., Hayne 1990; Hildreth & Rovee-Collier 1999b).

The effect of a novel prime on retention of an active memory

In the preceding study, Adler et al. (2000) presented the prime 3 days after training. Because 3-month-old infants have forgotten the specific details of their original training mobile after this delay, we speculated that the effect of the prime on the active memory might be different if it were novel. Previously, we found that priming with a novel mobile for 3 min immediately after training (day 0), when the memory does not have to be retrieved at all, retroactively interfered with infants' recognition of the original mobile the next day, but this effect was temporary and disappeared within 2 days (Rossi-George & Rovee-Collier 1999). The same interference phenomenon had occurred when infants were primed with a novel mobile 3 days after training and tested with the original mobile the next day (Rovee-Collier et al. 1994). This phenomenon was also temporary: Although infants who were primed with a novel mobile 3 days after training had failed to recognize the training mobile 1 day later, Adler et al. found that they did recognize it 7 days but not 9 days afterward. Thus, as before, a 3-min exposure to a novel prime temporarily interfered with the original memory. Because priming the active memory with either a novel mobile or the original mobile 3 days after training protracted retention for the same duration (i.e., for an additional 2 days), Adler et al. concluded that the common retention boost was mediated by the general features that the novel mobile shared with the original one. (Recall that priming occurred at a time when infants could not behaviorally differentiate a novel mobile from the training one.) In other words, the prime in Adler et al. did not protract retention because it was novel but because it was effectively the same as the training mobile.

Because the original memory becomes progressively less accessible over time until it finally cannot be retrieved on a delayed recognition test at all, we thought that what infants actually learned about a novel prime might be analyzed in more depth if it were exposed at more points along the original forgetting function. To do this, we had to turn to older infants, who remember longer. Therefore, we trained 6-month-olds in the mobile task and primed them with a novel mobile (mobile B) after delays ranging from 1 to 13 days, testing them with either the training mobile (mobile A) or mobile B 24 hours later (Muzzio & Rovee-Collier 1996).

Previously, Boller et al. (1995) had primed 6-month-olds with a novel mobile immediately after training (day 0) and had found that they recognized *both mobile A and mobile B* 24 hours later. In the present study, we found that if 6-month-olds were primed with a novel mobile after delays ranging from 1 to 8 days, then they subsequently recognized *only mobile B but not mobile A*; but if they were primed with a novel mobile after delays ranging from 9 to 13 days, then they subsequently recognized *neither mobile A nor mobile B* (see Figure 9.5). Because unprimed infants of this age can recognize mobile A for 14 days and can also discriminate it from mobile B after that same delay, we concluded that priming with the novel mobile after delays longer than 1 day had interfered with their recognition of mobile A whether they had recognized mobile B 24 hours later or not.

In addition, both mobile A and mobile B reactivated the training memory 3 weeks later if the novel prime was exposed only 1 day after training, but only mobile B reactivated the memory if the novel prime was exposed 13 days after

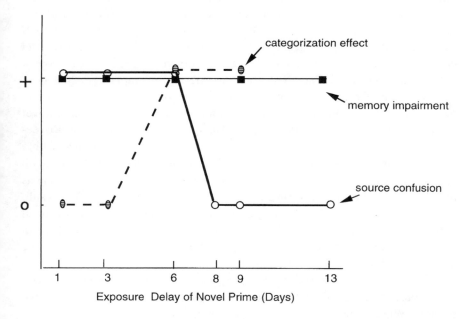

Figure 9.5. The time line for the onset (+) of three qualitatively different consequences of priming an active memory — memory impairment, source confusion (memory facilitation), and categorization. After training in the mobile task for 2 days, 6-month-olds were primed for 2 min with a novel mobile after different delays (*exposure delay*) between 1 and 14 days and were tested 1 day later.

training. These data are intriguing because infants who were primed with mobile B after either delay had not recognized mobile A 24 hours later. This result suggested that mobile A was still represented in the training memory after the 1-day novel prime but was not after the 13-day novel prime. Because other attempts to demonstrate that mobile A was still represented in the training memory after being primed with mobile B after a long delay also failed, we concluded that its details had probably been *replaced* in the training memory by mobile B. These data, like the data of Hitchock and Rovee-Collier (1996), suggest that older memories are more fragile.

The preceding results reveal that priming with a novel mobile when infants' training memory is still relatively accessible can produce either *memory facilitation* (i.e., facilitated recognition of the novel prime) or *memory impairment* (i.e., impaired recognition of original mobile), depending on the timing of the prime in relation to the original training event. However, a third effect of priming a relatively accessible memory with a novel stimulus can also occur — a *categorization* effect. Exposing adults to at least two different exemplars of a category facilitates their subsequent responding to novel category members (e.g., Flannagan, Fried & Holyoak 1986; Fried & Holyoak 1984), and exposing infants to at least two different exemplars of a category has the same effect. After being trained with mobile A in one session and mobile B in another, for example, both 3- and 6-month-olds recognize a novel category member (mobile C) 1 day later (Hayne et al. 1987; Shields & Rovee-Collier 1992). The same result occurs when 3-month-olds are primed with a novel mobile (mobile B) immediately after being trained for 2 days with mobile A. Apparently, the prior memory of training with mobile A that is retrieved at the outset of session 2 is recoded to include mobile B. As a result, infants subsequently behave to mobile C as if they had actually been trained with two different mobiles in the first place (Rovee-Collier et al. 1993a). Otherwise, infants trained for 2 days with the same mobile would have discriminated the novel test mobile (mobile C).

Muzzio and Rovee-Collier (1996) found a similar categorization effect, but it too depended on when the prime was presented in relation to original training. When 6-month-olds were primed with mobile B after delays of 1, 3, 6, or 9 days, they responded to mobile C after the two longest priming delays (6 and 9 days) but not after the two shortest ones (see Figure 9.5). The fact that infants responded to a completely novel test mobile means that their memory of mobile A was still intact after 9 days (i.e., the interference by mobile B after delays up to this point had been temporary) and distinguishes their memory performance as a genuine categorization effect (recall that categorization requires exposure to two different category members — A and B).

An important finding of this study is that failing to observe an effect of recently encountered information or observing one effect (e.g., memory impairment) but not another (e.g., memory facilitation or categorization) cannot be taken as evidence that priming an accessible memory with a novel stimulus has no other effects. Here, after priming delays when infants subsequently recognized neither mobile A nor mobile B (i.e., 9 days), they still recognized mobile C. Had they not previously been primed with mobiles A and B, then they would not have responded to mobile C. Likewise, after priming delays when they recognized neither mobile A nor mobile C, they recognized mobile B. This study clearly demonstrates that the effect of a prime when the memory is accessible is strictly determined by the point on the forgetting function at which it is presented.

Conclusions

Studies with infants have answered several questions about the relation between implicit and explicit memories that are difficult to address with adults. They have revealed that implicit memories assume a number of the characteristics of explicit memories. Over the first year of life, for example, implicit memories that were forgotten before they were primed are remembered for as long as explicit memories, and their pattern of forgetting is also the same. Memories that are still accessible at the time of priming are not remembered as long as memories that are forgotten. Nonetheless, the extent to which an already accessible memory is protracted by priming varies with the delay between training and priming as it does with the delay between training and recognition testing, even though the duration of retention after priming is not as great when the memory is accessible. Finally, we previously found that implicit and explicit memories enter into the same functional relationships with the context at 3 and 6 months of age (Borovsky & Rovee-Collier 1990; Butler & Rovee-Collier 1989; Hartshorn & Rovee-Collier 1997; Hayne & Rovee-Collier 1995; Shields & Rovee-Collier 1992).

Taken together, these findings seem inconsistent with the notion that explicit and implicit memories are distinctly different memories that are encoded by structurally different memory systems (Squire 1992a). Rather, because explicit and implicit memories appear to be the same once they have been retrieved and reactivated, respectively, we propose that they are not different memories at all but are actually the same memory that has been retrieved via different routes — either *implicitly* or *explicitly* (see also Crowder 1988; Mandler 1985). Speaking colloquially, "If it walks like a duck and quacks like a duck, then it must be a duck!" Whether these different routes of access are parts of different memory systems, however, remains unanswered.

CHAPTER 10

Epilogue

In this chapter, we summarize our basic conclusions and reflect on some of the popular notions that are based on earlier assumptions about the development of implicit and explicit memory. Finally, we consider the implications of recent memory research with infants for theory and research on memory in general.

The practice of attributing cognitive competencies to immature organisms without actually studying them is not new. In 1885, Wilhelm Preyer, who pioneered the study of human embryonic development, wrote:

> "For thousands of years children have been born and lovingly tended and watched by their mothers, and for thousands of years learned men have disputed over the mental growth of the child, without even studying the children. As a rule, the experimental physiologist seldom visits the nursery, even when he is a father."

This practice is nowhere more apparent than in the field of memory development, where the central problem is to specify how the superior memory of adults evolves from the memory abilities of infants. Where do we stand today in terms of its solution? In one proposed solution, adult memory is cast as the product of multiple memory systems that develop hierarchically during the infancy period (Bachevalier & Mishkin 1984; Schacter & Moscovitch 1984; Squire 1987, 1992a; Tulving 1983, 1993). In the preceding chapters, however, we reviewed evidence that this solution is not correct for either human or animal infants, primate or nonprimate. Even if adults possess multiple memory systems that decline sequentially, those systems most certainly do not develop hierarchically.

In the face of mounting evidence against it, some scientists have continued to defend the hierarchical development hypothesis. Why? We can only speculate that they are either philosophically committed to this solution, have ignored the overwhelming evidence against it, or have not understood it. One clear source of misunderstanding has centered on the kinds of memory that are measured in studies of mobile conjugate reinforcement. Nelson (1995), for example, likened infants' conditioned footkicks during delayed recognition tests to the conditioned limb flexion response of the cat. Given that limb flexion is reflexively elicited by electrical shock, this analogy is obviously incorrect. Operant kicks are not elicited, and their magnitude obviously cannot depend on the parameters of the eliciting stimulation. Unlike conditioned limb reflexes, whether the infant kicks above baseline during a delayed recognition test depends on the *informational content* of the test stimulus and the test context. Moreover, prior to 1 year of age, young infants do not immediately respond to a priming stimulus, whereas elicited reflexes occur within milliseconds. In fact, an infant's conditioned kicking or lever-pressing is no different from an adult's pressing a response key, touching a video screen, circling a word on a piece of paper, or verbalizing "yes" or "no" as an index of recognition.

For others, whether infants are capable of explicit memory or behave like amnesics seems to boil down to the question of whether they can consciously recollect having seen a stimulus before — a question that cannot be directly answered. This stance is reflected in the following quote from Eacott (1999, p. 47):

> "...a behavioral measure of recall, such as lever pressing, presents a problem, as all memory abilities may not be alike. An ability to recall facts and events has been contrasted to the ability to learn and remember how to use skills and strategies. Memories of facts and events can be brought to mind and be made consciously available, whereas skills and strategies are often implicit and not accessible to consciousness. These two aspects of memory are called declarative and nondeclarative (procedural) memory, respectively. The long-term memory abilities demonstrated in infants may be an example of nondeclarative memory. If so, it may be that they do not have...a late-developing declarative memory system (Bachevalier & Mishkin 1984)."

In the preceding quote, Eacott classified infants' kicks and lever presses on retention tests as skills. Then, asserting that memory for skills does not require conscious recollection, she concluded that infants' memory performance — like that of amnesics — lacks conscious awareness. Bjorklund (2000) expressed the same view in his text on children's thinking:

> "...conditioning experiments with infants do not seem to require conscious awareness. That is, unlike most of the memory we will discuss in this chapter,

it was not *explicit* — it did not involve children consciously retrieving information from their long-term stores" (p. 239).

In the same chapter, he described an increase in the duration of retention with age as a unique characteristic of explicit memory. Yet, infants between 2 and 18 months of age exhibit delayed recognition for increasingly longer durations in conditioning studies, as do infants between 6 and 24 months of age in studies of deferred imitation (see Chapters 6, 7, and 9). We assume, therefore, that the underlying distinction still boils down to the question of conscious awareness.

In the same vein, Mandler has complained that mobile studies cannot possibly reveal anything about human memory (or any other higher-level cognitive process) because they measure "only conditioning," and even "cockroaches" (1990, p. 515) and "the lowly flatworm" (1998, p. 296) can be conditioned. This complaint similarly rests on a commitment to conscious awareness as the *sine qua non* of explicit memory and the conclusion that conditioning is devoid of such awareness. In her basic argument, however, Mandler failed to distinguish between the *learning process,* which entails associating the representations of two events in short-term memory and may well be automatic, and the *memory process*, which entails retrieving information from long-term memory back into short-term memory and may or may not be automatic. Operant conditioning, however, is not even an underlying learning process — it is a *procedure* whose underlying mechanisms are not yet understood.

As it turns out, a major obstacle to gaining a conceptual handle on the development of implicit and explicit memory has been the eagerness of scientists to label the tasks that have been used with infants as either implicit or implicit. Response-to-novelty tasks, for example, which used to be considered as implicit tasks (Nelson 1995), are now described as explicit memory tasks; operant conditioning tasks, as procedural (implicit) memory tasks; imitation tasks, as declarative (explicit) memory tasks, and so forth. Tasks per se, however, are neither one nor the other. Just as adults can complete a word stem or word fragment either implicitly or explicitly, for example, so can infants perform an imitation, conditioning, or response-to-novelty task either implicitly or explicitly. As in studies with adults, whether a particular memory task is implicit or explicit depends on *how it is solved.* If a memory task is solved by infants or adults via a prior-cuing procedure, or priming, then it is an implicit memory task. If a memory task is solved by infants or adults via a contemporaneous-cuing procedure (which, for adults, requires instructions to respond on the basis of a particular prior experience), then it is an explicit memory task. Thus, for example, a word stem could be used as either a memory prime in an implicit task or a retrieval cue in an explicit task, depending on the instructions. The failure of researchers to recognize this very fundamental fact has obfuscated the analysis of infant memory.

A look to the future

Studies with infants have yielded novel findings about basic memory phenomena that are difficult to study with older children and impractical to study with adults. These studies have revealed, for example, that implicit and explicit memories "behave" identically after they have been retrieved. This finding suggests that implicit and explicit memories are not different memories from different systems (Squire 1992a) nor even different forms of memory (Graf & Schacter 1985) but are the same memory that has simply been retrieved via different routes — either implicitly or explicitly (Crowder 1988; Mandler 1985). Another finding from studies with infants pertains to the functional significance of retrieving implicit and explicit memories. Memories that have been primed remain accessible for as long as they were originally, being forgotten only gradually and at the same rate. Priming the memory when it is active, however, has different consequences than priming the memory when it is not, and refreshing the memory has different consequences yet. All prolong the life of a memory, but some conditions are more likely to facilitate its distortion. These findings have major implications for whether and for how long we can access and use that memory in the future. Finally, if a memory is repeatedly retrieved either explicitly or implicitly, its contents will change. New information can be added, and old information can be lost — and some kinds of information are added and lost more readily. These changes distort both the specificity and accuracy of the memory that was originally encoded and thereby will impact what we remember and understand in the future.

These and other findings from studies of infant memory speak directly to the three major phenomena that, according to Estes (1997), any satisfactory theory of memory must address — memory retrieval, forgetting, and memory distortions. Memory theories that have been formulated solely from adult data and that do not accommodate new findings from infants are incomplete and inadequate. In the past, memory data from infants have been put through a sieve that lets pass only those fragments that are commensurate with preestablished notions of how memory works at different ages or what different tasks or procedures can reveal. This is wrong — and it is bad Science. Data from critically controlled studies with infants must be taken at face value as evidence of what organisms can and cannot do and how their prior experiences affect their current behavior.

Let us be clear: We do not seek more satisfactory theories of *memory development* — such theories inevitably turn out to be theories of language development. If not, then, what? We seek more satisfactory *theories of memory*. Although major aspects of both the brain and behavior change dramatically over ontogeny, the *basic processes* of learning and memory and the *general principles* that describe them do not. Only by drawing on a complete data base will memory theorists be able to test the generality and affirm the validity of their predictions. Only from such a rich data base will psychologists be able to construct a truly satisfactory theory of memory.

References

Abravanel, E., Levan-Goldschmidt, E., & Stevenson, M.B. 1976. Action imitation: The early phase of infancy. *Child Development, 47,* 1032–1044.

Adler, S.A., Gerhardstein, P., & Rovee-Collier, C. 1998. Levels-of-processing effects in infant memory? *Child Development, 69,* 280–294.

Adler, S.A., & Rovee-Collier, C. 1994. The memorability and discriminability of primitive perceptual units in infancy. *Vision Research, 34,* 449–459.

Adler, S.A., Wilk, A., & Rovee-Collier, C. 2000. Effects of reinstatement and reactivation on active memory in infants, *Journal of Experimental Child Psychology, 75,* 93–115.

Adolphs, R., Tranel, D., Damasio, H., & Damasio, A.R. 1994. Impaired recognition of emotion in facial expressions following bilateral damage to the human amygdala. *Nature, 372,* 669–672.

Agayoff, J.L., Sheffield, E.G., & Hudson, J.A. 1999, April. *Effects of video reminders on young children's long-term recall.* Symposium paper presented at the meeting of the Society for Research in Child Development, Albuquerque, NM.

Ajuriaguerra, J. de, Rey-Bellet-Muller, M., & Tissot, R. 1964. A propos de quelques problemes poses par le deficit operatoire des vieillards atteints de demence degenerative en debut d'evolution. *Cortex, 1,* 232–256.

Alberts, J.R. 1984. Sensory-perceptual development in the Norway rat: A view toward comparative studies. In R. Kail & N.E. Spear (Eds.), *Comparative perspectives on the development of memory* (pp. 65–101). Hillsdale, NJ: Lawrence Erlbaum Associates.

Allen, S.W., & Jacoby, L.L. 1990. Reinstating study context produces unconscious influences of memory. *Memory & Cognition, 18,* 270–278.

Alvarez, P., Zola-Morgan, S., & Squire, L.R. 1994. The animal model of human amnesia: Long-term memory impaired and short-term memory intact. *Proceedings of the National Academy of Sciences, (USA), 91,* 5637–5641.

Alvarez, P., Zola-Morgan, S., & Squire, L.R. 1995. Damage limited to the hippocampal region produces long-lasting memory impairment in monkeys. *Journal of Neuroscience, 15,* 3796–3807.

Alvarez-Royo, P., Clower, R.P., Zola-Morgan, S.M., & Squire, L.R. 1991. Stereotaxic lesions of the hippocampus in monkeys: Determination of surgical coordinates and analysis of lesions using magnetic resonance imaging. *Journal of Neuroscience Methods, 38,* 223–232.

Amabile, T.A., & Rovee-Collier, C. 1991. Contextual variation and memory retrieval at six months. *Child Development, 62,* 1155–1166.

Anderson, J.R., & Ross, B.H. 1980. Evidence against a semantic-episodic distinction. *Journal of Experimental Psychology: Human Learning and Memory, 6,* 441–465.

Anderson, M.C., Bjork, R.A., & Bjork, E.L. 1994. Remembering can cause forgetting: Retrieval dynamics in long-term memory. *Journal of Experimental Psychology: Learning, Memory, and Cognition, 20*, 1063–1087.

Angeli, S.J., Murray, E.A., & Mishkin, M.M. 1993. Hippocampectomized monkeys can remember one place but not two. *Neuropsychologia, 31*, 1021–1030.

Anglin, J.M. 1977. *Word, object, and conceptual development.* New York: W.W. Norton.

Angulo Y Gonzales, A.W. 1932. The prenatal development of behavior in the albino rat. *Journal of Comparative Neurology, 55*, 395–442.

Arnold, H.M., & Spear, N.E. 1993. Order and duration of stimuli are important determinants of reactivation. *Animal Learning and Behavior, 21*, 391–398.

Atkinson, R.C., & Joula, J.F. 1973. Factors influencing speed and accuracy of word recognition. In S. Kornblum (Ed.), *Attention and performance* (Vol. 4, pp. 583–612). New York, NY: Academic Press.

Babkin, P.S. 1960. The establishment of reflex activity in early postnatal life. *Fiziologii Zhurnal USSR, 44*(10), 922–927. [The establishment of reflex activity in early postnatal life. In *The central nervous system and behavior*, pp. 24–41, trans. by the Russian Scientific Translation Program, National Institutes of Health, Bethesda, MD.]

Bachevalier, J. 1990. Ontogenetic development of habit and memory formation in primates. In A. Diamond (Ed.), *The development and neural bases of higher cognitive functions* (Vol. 608, pp. 457–477), *Annals of the New York Academy of Sciences.* New York: New York Academy of Sciences.

Bachevalier, J. 1992. Cortical versus limbic immaturity: Relationship to infantile amnesia. In M.R. Gunnar & C.A. Nelson (Eds.), *Developmental behavioral neuroscience* (pp. 129–153). Hillsdale, NJ: Lawrence Erlbaum Associates.

Bachevalier, J., Beauregard, M., & Alvarado, M.C. 1999. Long-term effects of neonatal damage to the hippocampal formation and amygdaloid complex on object discrimination and object recognition in rhesus monkeys (Macaca mulatta). *Behavioral Neuroscience, 113*, 1127–1151.

Bachevalier, J., Brickson, M., & Hagger, C. 1993. Limbic-dependent recognition memory in monkeys develops early in infancy. *NeuroReport, 4*, 77–80.

Bachevalier, J., Brickson, M., Hagger, C., & Mishkin, M.M. 1990. Age and sex differences in the effects of selective temporal lobe lesions on the formation of visual discrimination habits in rhesus monkeys (*Macaca mulatta*). *Behavioral Neuroscience, 104*, 885–899.

Bachevalier, J., Malkova, L., & Beauregard, M. 1996. Multiple memory systems: A neuropsychological and developmental perspective. In L.G. Reid & N.E. Krasnegor (Eds.), *Attention, memory, and executive function* (pp. 185–198). Baltimore, MD: Paul H. Brookes Publishing Co.

Bachevalier, J., & Mishkin, M.M. 1984. An early and a late developing system for learning and retention in infant monkeys. *Behavioral Neuroscience, 98*, 770–778.

Bachevalier, J., & Mishkin, M.M. 1994. Effects of selective neonatal temporal lobe lesions on visual recognition memory in rhesus monkeys. *Journal of Neuroscience, 14*, 2128–2139.

Bachevalier, J., Ungerleider, L.G., O'Neill, J.B., & Friedman, D.P. 1986. Regional distribution of [3H]naloxone binding in the brain of a newborn rhesus monkey. *Developmental Brain Research, 25*, 302–308.

Baddeley, A. 1984. Neuropsychological evidence and the semantic/episodic distinction. *Behavioral and Brain Sciences, 7*, 238–239.

Baddeley, A., & Warrington, E.K. 1970. Amnesia and the distinction between long- and short-term memory. *Journal of Verbal Learning and Verbal Behavior, 9*, 176–189.

Bahrick, L.E., Hernandez-Reif, M., & Pickens, J. 1997. The effect of retrieval cues on visual preferences and memory in infancy: Evidence for a four-phase attention function. *Journal of Experimental Child Psychology, 67*, 1–20.

Bahrick, L.E., & Pickens, J. 1995. Infant memory for object motion across a period of three months: Implications for a four-phase attention function. *Journal of Experimental Child Psychology, 59*, 343–371.

Baillargeon, R., DeVos, J., & Graber, M. 1989. Location memory in 8-month-old infants in a non-search AB̄ task: Further evidence. *Cognitive Development, 4*, 345–367.

Baillargeon, R., & Graber, M. 1988. Evidence of location memory in 8-month-old infants in a non-search AB̄ task. *Developmental Psychology, 24*, 502–511.

Barnat, S.A., Klein, P.J., & Meltzoff, A.N. 1996. Deferred imitation across changes in context and object: Memory and generalization in 14-month-old infants. *Infant Behavior and Development, 19*, 241–251.

Barnes, J.M., & Underwood, B. 1959. "Fate" of first-list associations in transfer theory. *Journal of Experimental Psychology, 58*, 97–105.

Barr, R. 1997, April. *Monkey see or monkey do: The effect of practice on memory processing in infancy*. Paper presented at the meeting of the Society for Research in Child Development, Washington, DC.

Barr, R., Dowden, A., & Hayne, H. 1996. Developmental changes in deferred imitation by 6- to 24-month-old infants. *Infant Behavior and Development, 19*, 159–170.

Barr, R., & Hayne, H. 1996. The effect of event structure on imitation in infancy: Practice makes perfect? *Infant Behavior and Development, 19*, 253–257.

Barr, R., & Hayne, H. 2000. Age-related changes in imitation: Implications for memory development. In C. Rovee-Collier, L.P. Lipsitt, & H. Hayne (Eds.), *Progress in infancy research* (Vol. 1, pp. 21–67). Hillsdale, NJ: Lawrence Erlbaum Associates.

Barr, R., & Vieira, A. 1999, January. *Piggybacking the puppet onto the train: Associated memories form across experimental paradigms in 6-month-old infants*. Paper presented at the New England Mini-Conference on Infant Studies, Providence, RI.

Bartus, R.T., Dean, R.L., Goas, J.A., & Lippa, A.S. 1980. Age-related changes in passive-avoidance retention: Modulation with dietary choline. *Science, 209*, 301–303.

Bauer, P.J. 1996. What do infants recall of their lives? Memory for specific events by one- to two-year-olds. *American Psychologist, 51*, 29–41.

Bauer, P.J., & Hertsgaard, L.A. 1993. Increasing steps in recall of events: Factors facilitating immediate and long-term memory in 13.5- and 16.5-month-old children. *Child Development, 64*, 1204–1223.

Bauer, P.J., Hertsgaard, L.A., & Dow, G.A. 1994. After 8 months have passed: Long-term recall of events by 1- to 2-year-old children. *Memory, 2*, 353–382.

Bauer, P.J., Hertsgaard, L.A., & Wewerka, S.S. 1995. Effects of experience and reminding on long-term recall in children: Remembering not to forget. *Journal of Experimental Child Psychology, 59*, 260–298.

Bauer, P.J., & Mandler, J.M. 1989. One thing follows another: Effects of temporal structure on 1- to 2-year-olds' recall of events. *Developmental Psychology, 25*, 197–206.

Bauer, P.J., & Shore, C.M. 1987. Making a memorable event: Effects of familiarity and organization on young children's recall of action sequences. *Cognitive Development, 2*, 327–338.

Bechara, A., Tranel, D., Damasio, H., Adolphs, R., Rockland, C., & Damasio, A.R. 1995. Double dissociation of conditioning and declarative knowledge relative to the amygdala and hippocampus in humans. *Science, 269*, 1115–1118.

Beck, A.T., Ward, C.H., Mendelson, M., Mock, J., & Erbaugh, J. 1961. An inventory for measuring depression. *Archives of General Psychiatry, 4*, 561–571.

Bentin, S., & Moscovitch, M. 1988. The time course of repetition effects for words and unfamiliar faces. *Journal of Experimental Psychology, 117*, 148–160.

Berntson, C.G., Tuber, D.S., Ronca, A.E., & Bachman, D.S. 1983. The decerebrate human: Associative learning. *Experimental Neurology, 81*, 77–88.

Besson, M., Fischler, I., Boaz, T., & Raney, G. 1992. Effects of automatic associative activation on explicit and implicit memory tests. *Journal of Experimental Psychology: Learning, Memory, and Cognition, 18*, 89–105.

Best, C.T. 1995. Learning to perceive the sound pattern of English. In C. Rovee-Collier & L.P. Lipsitt (Eds.), *Advances in infancy research* (Vol. 9, pp. 217–304). Norwood, NJ: Ablex Publishing Corporation.

Bhatt, R.S. 1997, April. *Determinants of memory modification in infancy: The strength of the interfering experience.* Paper presented at the meeting of the Society for Research in Child Development, Washington, D.C.

Bhatt, R.S., & Rovee-Collier, C. 1994. Perception and 24-hour retention of feature relations in infancy. *Developmental Psychology, 30*, 142–150.

Bhatt, R.S., & Rovee-Collier, C. 1996. Infants' forgetting of correlated attributes and object recognition. *Child Development, 67*, 172–187.

Bhatt, R.S., & Rovee-Collier, C. 1997. Dissociation between features and feature relations in infant memory: Effect of memory load. *Journal of Experimental Child Psychology, 67*, 69–89.

Bhatt, R.S., Rovee-Collier, C., & Weiner, S. 1994. Developmental changes in the interface between perception and memory retrieval. *Developmental Psychology, 30*, 151–162.

Biederman, I., & Cooper, E.E. 1991. Evidence for complete translational and reflectional invariance in visual object priming. *Perception, 20*, 585–593.

Biederman, I., & Cooper, E.E. 1992. Size invariance in visual object priming. *Journal of Experimental Psychology: Human Perception and Performance, 18*, 121–133.

Bjork, R.A. 1975. Retrieval as a memory modifier: An interpretation of negative recency and related phenomena. In R.L. Solso (Ed.), *Information processing and cognition: The Loyola symposium* (pp. 123–144). Hillsdale, NJ: Lawrence Erlbaum Associates.

Bjorklund, D.F. 2000. *Children's thinking: Developmental function and individual differences.* Belmont, CA: Wadsworth.

Blaney, P.H. 1986. Affect and memory: A review. *Psychological Bulletin, 99*, 229–246.

Blaxton, T.A. 1989. Investigating dissociations among memory measures: Support for a transfer-appropriate processing framework. *Journal of Experimental Psychology: Learning, Memory, and Cognition, 15*, 657–668.

Bolhuis, J.J. Stewart, C.A., & Forrest, E.M. 1994. Retrograde amnesia and memory reactivation in rats with ibotenate lesions to the hippocampus and subiculum. *Quarterly Journal of Experimental Psychology, 47B*, 129–150.

Boller, K. 1997. Preexposure effects on infant learning and memory. *Developmental Psychobiology, 31,* 93–105.

Boller, K., Grabelle, M., & Rovee-Collier, C. 1995. Effects of postevent information on infants' memory for a central target. *Journal of Experimental Child Psychology, 59,* 372–396.

Boller, K., & Rovee-Collier, C. 1992. Contextual coding and recoding of infants' memories. *Journal of Experimental Child Psychology, 53,* 1–23.

Boller, K., Rovee-Collier, C., Borovsky, D., O'Connor, J., & Shyi, G.C.-W. 1990. Developmental changes in the time-dependent nature of memory retrieval. *Developmental Psychology,* 26, 770–779.

Boller, K., Rovee-Collier, C., Gulya, M., & Prete, K. 1996. Infants' memory for context: Timing effects of postevent information. *Journal of Experimental Child Psychology, 63,* 583–602.

Boniface, J., Barr, R., MacDonald, S., & Hayne, H. 1996, April. *Developmental changes in generalization: Implications for memory development.* Poster presented at the International Conference on Infant Studies, Providence, RI.

Borovsky, D., & Rovee-Collier, C. 1990. Contextual constraints on memory retrieval at 6 months. *Child Development, 61,* 1569–1583.

Bousfield, W.A., Whitmarsh, G.A., & Esterson, J. 1958. Serial position effects and the "Marbe effect" in the free recall of meaningful words. *Journal of General Psychology, 59,* 255–262.

Bouton, M.E., & Bolles, R.C. 1985. Contexts, event-memories, and extinction. In P.D. Balsam & A. Tomie (Eds.), *Context and learning* (pp. 133–166). Hillsdale, NJ: Lawrence Erlbaum Associates.

Bower, B. 1995. Conscious memories may emerge in infants. *Science News, 148 (17),* 86.

Bower, G.H. 1981. Mood and memory. *American Psychologist, 36,* 129–148.

Bridges, K. 1932. Emotional development in early infancy. *Child Development, 3,* 324–341.

Brody, L.R. 1981. Visual short-term cued recall memory in infancy. *Child Development, 52,* 242–250.

Brogden, W.J. 1939. Sensory preconditioning. *Journal of Experimental Psychology, 25,* 323–332.

Brooks, B.M. 1994. A comparison of serial position effects in implicit and explicit word-stem completion. *Psychonomic Bulletin & Review, 1,* 264–268.

Butler, J., & Rovee-Collier, C. 1989. Contextual gating of memory retrieval. *Developmental Psychobiology, 22,* 533–552.

Butters, N., Wolfe, J., Martone, M., Granholm, E., & Cermak, L.S. 1985. Memory disorders associated with Huntington's disease: Verbal recall, verbal recognition, and procedural memory. *Neuropsychologia, 23,* 729–743.

Caldwell, D.F., & Werboff, J. 1962. Classical conditioning in newborn rats. *Science, 136,* 1118–1119.

Campbell, B.A., & Alberts, J.R. 1979. Ontogeny of long-term memory for learned taste aversions. *Behavioral and Neural Biology, 25,* 139–156.

Campbell, B.A., & Campbell, E.H. 1962. Retention and extinction of learned fear in infant and adult rats. *Journal of Comparative and Physiological Psychology, 55,* 1–8.

Campbell, B.A., & Coulter, X. 1976. Neural and psychological processes underlying the development of learning and memory. In T.J. Tighe & R.N. Leaton (Eds.), *Habituation* (pp. 129–157). Hillsdale, NJ: Lawrence Erlbaum Associates.

Campbell, B.A., Krauter, E.E., & Wallace, J.E. 1980. Animal models of aging: Sensory-motor and cognitive function in the aged rat. In D.G. Stein (Ed.), *The psychobiology of aging: Problems and perspectives* (pp. 201–226). North Holland: Elsevier Science Publishers.

Campbell, B.A., Misanin, J.R., White, B.C., & Lytle, L.D. 1974. Species differences in ontogeny of memory: Indirect support for neural maturation as a determinant of forgetting. *Journal of Comparative and Physiological Psychology, 87*, 193–202.

Campbell, B.A., Sananes, C.B., & Gaddy, J.R. 1984. Animal models of infantile amnesia, benign senescent forgetfulness, and senile dementia. *Neurobehavioral Toxicology and Teratology, 6*, 467–471.

Campbell, B.A., Sananes, C.B., & Gaddy, J.R. 1985. Animal models of Jacksonian dissolution of memory in the aged. In J. Traber & W.H. Gispen (Eds.), *Senile dementia of the Alzheimer type* (pp. 283–291). Berlin: Springer-Verlag.

Campbell, B.A., & Spear, N.E. 1972. Ontogeny of memory. *Psychological Review, 79*, 215–236.

Carroll, M., Byrne, B., & Kirsner, K. 1985. Autobiographical memory and perceptual learning: A developmental study using picture recognition, naming latency, and perceptual identification. *Memory & Cognition, 13*, 273–279.

Cave, C.B. 1997. Very long-lasting priming in picture naming. *Psychological Science, 8*, 322–325.

Cave, C.B., Blake, R., & McNamara, T.P. 1998. Binocular rivalry disrupts visual priming. *Psychological Science, 9*, 299–302.

Cave, C.B., Bost, P.R., & Cobb, R.I. 1996. Effects of color and pattern on implicit and explicit picture memory. *Journal of Experimental Psychology: Learning, Memory, and Cognition, 22*, 639–653.

Cave, C.B., & Squire, L.R. 1992. Intact and long-lasting repetition priming in amnesia. *Journal of Experimental Psychology: Learning, Memory, and Cognition, 18*, 509–520.

Cermak, L.S. 1984. The episodic-semantic distinction in amnesia. In L.S. Squire & N. Butters (Eds.), *Neuropsychology of memory* (pp. 55–62). New York: Guilford Press.

Chalfonte, B.L., & Johnson, M.K. 1996. Feature memory and binding in young and old adults. *Memory & Cognition, 24*, 403–416.

Chalfonte, B.L., Verfaellie, M., Johnson, M.K., & Reiss, L. 1996. Spatial location memory in amnesia: Binding item and location information under incidental and intentional encoding conditions. *Memory, 4*, 591–614.

Cho, Y.H., Kesner, R.P., & Brodale, S. 1995. Retrograde and anterograde amnesia for spatial discrimination in rats: Role of hippocampus, entorhinal cortex, and parietal cortex. *Psychobiology, 23*, 185–194.

Clark, H.H., & Carlson, T.B. 1981. Context for comprehension. In J. Long & A. Baddeley (Eds.), *Attention and performance IX* (pp. 313–330). Hillsdale, NJ: Lawrence Erlbaum Associates.

Clayton, K., Habibi, A., & Bendele, M.S. 1995. Recognition priming effects following serial learning: Implications for episodic priming effects. *American Journal of Psychol-*

ogy, 108, 547–561.

Clower, R.P., Alvarez-Royo, P., Zola-Morgan, S.M., & Squire, L.R. 1991. Recognition memory impairment in monkeys with selective hippocampal lesions. *Society for Neuroscience Abstracts, 17,* 338.

Coghill, G.E. 1916. Correlated anatomical and physiological studies of the growth of the nervous system of Amphibia. II. The afferent system of the head of Amblystoma. *Journal of Comparative Neurology, 26,* 247–340.

Coghill, G.E. 1929. *Anatomy and the problem of behaviour.* London: Cambridge University Press.

Cohen, L.B., DeLoache, J.S., & Pearl, R.A. 1977. An examination of interference effects in infants' memory for faces. *Child Development, 48,* 88–96.

Cohen, L.B., & Gelber, E.R. 1975. Infant visual memory. In L.B. Cohen & P. Salapatek (Eds.), *Infant perception: From sensation to cognition. Vol. 1. Basic visual processes* (pp. 347–403). New York: Academic Press.

Cohen, N.J. 1984. Preserved learning capacity in amnesia: Evidence for multiple memory systems. In L. Squire & N. Butters (Eds.), *Neuropsychology of memory* (pp. 83–103). New York: Guilford Press.

Cohen, N.J., & Corkin, S. 1981. The amnesic patient H.M.: Learning and retention of a cognitive skill. *Society for Neuroscience Abstracts, 7,* 235.

Cohen, N.J., & Eichenbaum, H. 1993. *Memory, amnesia, and the hippocampal system.* Cambridge, MA: MIT Press.

Cohen, N.J., & Squire, L.R. 1980. Preserved learning and retention of pattern analyzing skill in amnesia: Dissociation of knowing how and knowing that. *Science, 210,* 207–210.

Cohen, R.L. 1985. On the generality of the laws of memory. In L.-G. Nilsson & T. Archer (Eds.), *Perspectives on learning and memory* (pp. 247–277). Hillsdale, NJ: Lawrence Erlbaum Associates.

Collie, R., & Hayne, H. 1999. Deferred imitation by 6- and 9-month-old infants: More evidence for declarative memory. *Developmental Psychobiology, 35,* 83–90.

Collins, A.M., & Loftus, E.F. 1975. A spreading-activation theory of semantic processing. *Psychological Review, 82,* 407–428.

Collins, A.M., & Quillian, M.R. 1969. Retrieval time from semantic memory. *Journal of Verbal Learning and Verbal Behavior, 8,* 240–247.

Colombo, J., & Bundy, R.S. 1983. Infant response to auditory familiarity and novelty. *Infant Behavior and Development, 6,* 305–311.

Colombo, M., Cawley, S., & Broadbent, N. 1997. The effects of hippocampal and area parahippocampalis lesions in pigeons. II. Concurrent discrimination and spatial memory. *Quarterly Journal of Experimental Psychology, 50B,* 172–189.

Colombo, M., D'Amato, M.R., Rodman, H.R., & Gross, C.G. 1990. Auditory association cortex lesions impair auditory short-term memory in monkeys. *Science, 247,* 336–338.

Colombo, M., Rodman, H.R., & Gross, C.G. 1996. The effects of superior temporal cortex lesions on the processing and retention of auditory information in monkeys (*Cebus apella*). *Journal of Neuroscience, 16,* 4501–4517.

Cooper, E.H., & Pantle, A.J. 1967. The total-time hypothesis in verbal learning. *Psychological Bulletin, 68,* 221–234.

Cooper, L.A., Schacter, D.L., Ballesteros, S., & Moore, C. 1992. Priming and recognition of transformed three-dimensional objects: Effects of size and reflection. *Journal of Experimental Psychology: Learning, Memory, and Cognition, 18*, 43–57.

Cooper, L.A., Schacter, D.L., & Moore, C. 1991, November. *Orientation affects both structural and episodic representations of three-dimensional objects.* Paper presented at the meeting of the Psychonomic Society, San Francisco, CA.

Cooper, R.L., McNamara, M.C., Thompson, W.C., & Marsh, G.R. 1980. Vasopressin modulation of learning and memory in the rat. In L. Poon (Ed.), *Aging in the 1980's: Psychological issues* (pp. 201–211). Washington, D.C.: American Psychological Association.

Corkin, S. 1968. Acquisition of motor skill after bilateral medial temporal-lobe excision. *Neuropsychologia, 6*, 255–265.

Corkin, S. 1984. Lasting consequences of bilateral medial temporal lobectomy: Clinical course and experimental findings in H.M. *Seminars in Neurology, 4*, 249–259.

Cornell, E.H. 1974. Infants' discrimination of photographs of faces following redundant presentations. *Journal of Experimental Child Psychology, 18*, 98–106.

Cornell, E.H. 1979. Infants' recognition memory, forgetting, and savings. *Journal of Experimental Child Psychology, 28*, 359–374.

Cornell, E.H. 1980. Distributed study facilitates infants' delayed recognition memory. *Memory & Cognition, 8*, 539–542.

Cornell, E.H. 1984. Developmental continuity of memory mechanisms: Suggestive phenomena. In R. Kail, Jr., & N.E. Spear (Eds.), *Comparative perspectives on the development of memory* (pp. 287–316). Hillsdale, NJ: Lawrence Erlbaum Associates.

Cornell, E.H., & Bergstrom, L.I. 1983. Serial-position effects in infants' recognition memory. *Memory & Cognition, 11*, 494–499.

Correll, R.E., & Scoville, W.B. 1965. Performance on delayed match following lesions of medial temporal lobe structures. *Journal of Comparative and Physiological Psychology, 60*, 360–367.

Coulter, X. 1979. The determinants of infantile amnesia. In N.E. Spear & B.A. Campbell (Eds.), *Ontogeny of learning and memory* (pp. 245–270). Hillsdale, NJ: Lawrence Erlbaum Associates.

Craik, F.I.M. 1983. On the transfer of information from temporary to permanent memory. *Philosophical Transactions of the Royal Society of London, 302B*, 341–359.

Craik, F.I.M., & Lockhart, R.S. 1972. Levels of processing: A framework for memory research. *Journal of Verbal Learning and Verbal Behavior, 11*, 671–684.

Craik, F.I.M., & Tulving, E. 1975. Depth of processing and the retention of words in episodic memory. *Journal of Experimental Psychology: General, 104*, 268–294.

Crowder, R.G. 1976. *Principles of learning and memory.* Hillsdale, NJ: Lawrence Erlbaum Associates.

Crowder, R.G. 1988. Modularity and dissociations in memory systems. In H.L. Roediger, III, & F.I.M. Craik (Eds.), *Varieties of memory and consciousness: Essays in honour of Endel Tulving* (pp. 271–294). Hillsdale, NJ: Lawrence Erlbaum Associates.

Cuddy, L.J., & Jacoby, L.L. 1982. When forgetting helps memory: An analysis of repetition effects. *Journal of Verbal Learning and Verbal Behavior, 21*, 451–467.

Cummings, J.L., Tomiyasu, U., Read, S., Benson, D.F. 1984. Amnesia with hippocampal lesions after cardiopulmonary arrest. *Neurology, 34*, 679–681.

Curran, T. 1998. Implicit sequence learning from a cognitive neuroscience perspective: What, how, and where? In M.A. Stadler & P.A. French (Eds.), *Handbook of implicit learning* (pp. 365–400). Thousand Oaks, CA: Sage Publications.

D'Amato, M.R. 1973. Delayed matching and short-term memory in monkeys. In G.H. Bower (Ed.), *The psychology of learning and motivation* (Vol. 7, pp. 227–269). New York: Academic Press.

Davis, H.P., Idowu, A., & Gibson, G.E. 1983. Improvement of 8-arm maze performance in aged Fischer 344 rats with 3,4-diaminopyridine. *Experimental Aging Research, 9*, 211–214.

Davis, J., & Rovee-Collier, C. 1983. Alleviated forgetting of a learned contingency in 8-week-old infants. *Developmental Psychology, 19*, 353–365.

Dean, R.L., III., Scozzafava, J.A., Goas, J.A., Regan, R., Beer, B., & Bartus, R.T. 1981. Age-related differences in behavior across the lifespan of the C57BL/6J mouse. *Experimental Aging Research, 78*, 427–451.

Debner, J.A., & Jacoby, L.L. 1994. Unconscious perception: Attention, awareness, and control. *Journal of Experimental Psychology: Learning, Memory, and Cognition, 20*, 304–317.

DeCasper, A.J., & Fifer, W.P. 1980. Of human bonding: Newborns prefer their mothers' voices. *Science, 208*, 1174–1176.

DeCasper, A.J., & Spence, M.J. 1986. Prenatal maternal speech influences newborns' perception of speech sounds. *Infant Behavior and Development, 9*, 133–150.

Denny, E.B., & Hunt, R.R. 1992. Affective valence and memory in depression: Dissociation of recall and fragment completion. *Journal of Abnormal Psychology, 101*, 575–580.

de Vries, J.I.P., Visser, G.H.A., & Prechtl, H.F.R. 1984. Fetal motility in the first half of pregnancy. In H.F.R. Prechtl (ed.), *Continuity of neural functions from prenatal to postnatal life. Clinics in developmental medicine* (vol 94, pp. 46–64). Philadelphia, PA: Lippincott.

Diamond, A. 1985. Development of the ability to use recall to guide action, as indicated by infants' performance on AB̄. *Child Development, 56*, 868–883.

Diamond, A. 1990a. Rate of maturation of the hippocampus and the developmental progression of children's performance on the delayed non-matching-to-sample and visual-paired comparison tasks. In A. Diamond (Ed.), *The development and neural bases of higher cognitive functions* (Vol. 608, pp. 394–426), *Annals of the New York Academy of Sciences*. New York: New York Academy of Sciences.

Diamond, A. 1990b. The development and neural bases of memory functions as indexed by the AB̄ and delayed response tasks in human infants and infant monkeys. In A. Diamond (Ed.), *The development and neural bases of higher cognitive functions* (Vol. 608, pp. 267–309), *Annals of the New York Academy of Sciences*. New York: New York Academy of Sciences.

Diamond, A. 1995. Evidence of robust recognition memory early in life even when assessed by reaching behavior. *Journal of Experimental Child Psychology, 59*, 419–456.

Diamond, A., Churchland, A., Cruess, L., & Kirkham, N.Z. 1999. Early developments in the ability to understand the relation between stimulus and reward. *Developmental Psychology, 35*, 1507–1517.

Diamond, A., Cruttenden, L, & Niederman, D. 1989. Why have studies found better performance with multiple wells than with only two wells on AB̄? *Society for Research in Child Development Abstracts, 6,* 227.

Diamond, A., & Doar, B. 1989. The performance of human infants on a measure of frontal cortex function, the delayed response task. *Developmental Psychobiology, 22,* 271–294.

Diamond, A., Towle, C., & Boyer, K. 1994. Young children's performance on a task sensitive to the memory functions of the medial temporal lobe in adults: The delayed nonmatching-to-sample task reveals problems that are due to non-memory-related task demands. *Behavioral Neuroscience, 108,* 659–680.

Dienes, Z., & Berry, D. 1997. Implicit learning: Below the subjective threshold. *Psychonomic Bulletin & Review, 4,* 3–23.

DiGiulio, D.V., Seidenberg, M., O'Leary, D.S., & Raz, N. 1994. Procedural and declarative memory: A developmental study. *Brain and Cognition, 25,* 79–91.

Dominowski, R.L., & Ekstrand, B.R. 1967. Direct and associative priming in anagram solving. *Journal of Experimental Psychology, 74,* 84–86.

Dorfman, J., Kihlstrom, J.F., Cork, R.C., & Misiaszek, J. 1995. Priming and recognition in ECT-induced amnesia. *Psychonomic Bulletin & Review, 2,* 244–248.

Dritschel, B.H., Williams, J.M.G., Baddeley, A.D., & Nimmo-Smith, I. 1992. Autobiographical fluency: A method for the study of personal memory. *Memory & Cognition, 20,* 133–140.

Eacott, M.J. 1999. Memory for the events of early childhood. *Current Directions in Psychological Science, 8,* 46–49.

Earley, L.A., Bhatt, R.S., & Rovee-Collier, C. 1995. Developmental changes in the contextual control of recognition. *Developmental Psychobiology, 28,* 27–43.

Ebbinghaus, H. 1885/1964. *Memory: A contribution to experimental psychology.* (H.A. Ruger & C.E. Bussenius, Trans.) New York: Dover.

Eich, E., Macaulay, D., & Ryan, L. 1994. Mood dependent memory for events of the personal past. *Journal of Experimental Psychology: General, 123,* 201–215.

Eichenbaum, H., Otto, T., & Cohen, N.J. 1994. Two functional components of the hippocampal memory system. *Behavioral and Brain Sciences, 17,* 449–518.

Engen, T., & Ross, B.M. 1973. Long-term memory of odors with and without verbal descriptions. *Journal of Experimental Psychology, 100,* 221–227.

Estes, W.K. 1997. Processes of memory loss, forgetting, and distortion. *Psychological Review, 104,* 148–169.

Fagan, J.F., III. 1970. Memory in the infant. *Journal of Experimental Child Psychology, 9,* 217–226.

Fagan, J.F., III. 1973. Infants' delayed recognition memory and forgetting. *Journal of Experimental Child Psychology, 16,* 424–450.

Fagan, J.F., III. 1990. Discussion of J.M. Mandler, "Recall of events by preverbal children." In A. Diamond (Ed.), *The development and neural bases of higher cognitive functions* (Vol. 608, pp. 503–516), *Annals of the New York Academy of Sciences.* New York: New York Academy of Sciences.

Fagen, J.W., Morrongiello, B.A., Rovee-Collier, C., & Gekoski, M.J. 1984. Expectancies and memory retrieval in 3-month-old infants. *Child Development, 55,* 936–943.

Fagen, J.W., Ohr, P.S., Fleckenstein, L.K., & Ribner, D.R. 1985. The effect of crying on long-term memory in infancy. *Child Development, 56,* 1584–1592.

Fagen, J.W., Ohr, P.S., Singer, J.M., & Klein, S.J. 1989. Crying and retrograde amnesia in young infants. *Infant Behavior and Development, 12,* 13–24.

Fagen, J.W., & Prigot, J.A. 1993. Negative affect and infant memory. In C. Rovee Collier & L.P. Lipsitt (Eds.), *Advances in infancy research* (Vol. 8, pp. 169–216). Norwood, NJ: Ablex Publishing Corporation.

Fagen, J.W., & Rovee-Collier, C. 1983. Memory retrieval: A time-locked process in infancy. *Science, 222,* 1349–1351.

Fagen, J.W., Yengo, L.A., Rovee-Collier, C., & Enright, M.K. 1981. Reactivation of a visual discrimination in early infancy. *Developmental Psychology, 17,* 266–274.

Fantz, R.L. 1956. A method for studying early visual development. *Perceptual and Motor Skills, 6,* 13–15.

Field, T.M., Cohen, D., Garcia, R., & Greenberg, R. 1984. Mother-stranger face discrimination by the newborn. *Infant Behavior and Development, 7,* 19–25.

Feigenbaum, J.D., Polkey, C.E., & Morris, R.G. 1996. Deficits in spatial working memory after unilateral temporal lobectomy in man. *Neuropsychologia, 34,* 163–176.

Fivush, R., Kuebli, J., & Clubb, P.A. 1992. The structure of events and event representation: A developmental analysis. *Child Development, 63,* 188–201.

Flannagan, M.J., Fried, L.S., & Holyoak, K.J. 1986. Distributional expectations and the induction of category structure. *Journal of Experimental Psychology: Learning, Memory, and Cognition, 12,* 241–256.

Fox, N.J., Kagan, J., & Weiskopf, S. 1979. The growth of memory during infancy. *Genetic Psychology Monographs, 99,* 91–130.

Freud, S. 1935. *A general introduction to psychoanalysis.* New York: Clarion Books.

Fried, L.S., & Holyoak, K.J. 1984. Induction of category distributions: A framework for classification learning. *Journal of Experimental Psychology: Learning, Memory, and Cognition, 10,* 234–257.

Gabrieli, J.D.E., Brewer, J.B., & Poldrack, R.A. 1998. Images of medial temporal lobe functions in human learning and memory. *Neurobiology of Learning and Memory, 70,* 275–283.

Gabrieli, J.D.E., Cohen, N.J., & Corkin, S. 1988. The impaired learning of semantic knowledge following bilateral medial temporal-lobe resection. *Brain and Cognition, 7,* 157–177.

Gabrieli, J.D.E., Fleischman, D.A., Keane, M.M., Reminger, S.L., & Morrell, F. 1995. Double dissociation between memory systems underlying explicit and implicit memory in the human brain. *Psychological Science, 6,* 76–82.

Gage, F.J., Dunnett, S.B., & Bjorklund, A. 1984. Spatial learning and motor deficits in aged rats. *Neurobiology of Aging, 5,* 43–48.

Gardiner, J.M., & Java, R.I. 1993. Recognising and remembering. In A.F. Collins, S.E. Gathercole, M.A. Conway, & P.E. Morris (Eds.), *Theories of memory* (pp. 163–188). Hillsdale, NJ: Lawrence Erlbaum Associates.

Gazzaniga, M.S. 1972. One brain — two minds? *American Scientist, 60,* 311–317.

Gekoski, M.J., Fagen, J.W., & Pearlman, M.A. 1984. Early learning and memory in the preterm infant. *Infant Behavior and Development, 7,* 267–276.

Gerhardstein, P., Adler, S.A., & Rovee-Collier, C. 2000. A dissociation in infants' memory for stimulus size: Evidence for the early development of multiple memory systems. *Developmental Psychobiology, 36,* 123–135.

Gershberg, F.B., & Shimamura, A.P. 1994. Serial position effects in implicit and explicit tests of memory. *Journal of Experimental Psychology: Learning, Memory, and Cognition, 20*, 1370–1378.

Gibson, E.J. 1969. *Principles of perceptual learning and development.* New York: Appleton-Century-Crofts.

Gold, P.E., McGaugh, J.L., Hankins, L.L., Rose, R.P., & Vasquez, B.J. 1981. Age-dependent changes in retention in rats. *Experimental Aging Research, 8*, 53–58.

Gordon, W.C. 1979. Age: Is it a constraint on memory content? In N.E. Spear & B.A. Campbell (Eds.), *Ontogeny of learning and memory* (pp. 271–287). Hillsdale, NJ: Lawrence Erlbaum Associates.

Gordon, W.C. 1981. Mechanisms of cue-induced retention enhancement. In N.E. Spear & R.R. Miller (Eds.), *Information processing in animals: Memory mechanisms* (pp. 319–339). Hillsdale, NJ: Lawrence Erlbaum Associates.

Gordon, W.C., Smith, G.J., & Katz, D.S. 1979. Dual effects of response blocking following avoidance learning. *Behavior Research and Therapy, 17*, 479–487.

Gottlieb, G. 1971. Ontogenesis of sensory function in birds and mammals. In E. Tobach, L.R. Aronson, & E. Shaw (Eds.), *The biopsychology of development* (pp. 67–128). New York: Academic Press.

Goubet, N., & Clifton, R.K. 1998. Object and event representation in 61/2-month-old infants. *Developmental Psychology, 34*, 63–76.

Gould, S.J. 1998, April. *Ontogeny and phylogeny revisited, or why the child is not the evolutionary father to the man.* Address presented at the International Conference on Infant Studies, Atlanta, GA.

Graf, P. 1988, November. *Implicit and explicit remembering in same and different environments.* Paper presented at the meeting of the Psychonomic Society, Chicago, IL.

Graf, P. 1990. Life-span changes in implicit and explicit memory. *Bulletin of the Psychonomic Society, 28*, 353–358.

Graf, P., & Mandler, G. 1984. Activation makes words more accessible, but not necessarily more retrievable. *Journal of Verbal Learning and Verbal Behavior, 23*, 553–568.

Graf, P., Mandler, G., & Haden, P. 1982. Simulating amnesic symptoms in normal subjects. *Science, 218*, 1243–1244.

Graf, P., & Schacter, D.L. 1985. Implicit and explicit memory for new associations in normal and amnesic patients. *Journal of Experimental Psychology: Learning, Memory, and Cognition, 11*, 501–518.

Graf, P., & Schacter, D.L. 1987. Selective effects of interference on implicit and explicit memory for new associations. *Journal of Experimental Psychology: Learning, Memory, and Cognition, 13*, 45–53.

Graf, P., Squire, L.R., & Mandler, G. 1984. The information that amnesic patients do not forget. *Journal of Experimental Psychology: Learning, Memory, and Cognition, 10*, 164–178.

Gratch, G., & Landers, W.F. 1971. Stage IV of Piaget's theory of infants' object concepts: A longitudinal study. *Child Development, 42*, 359–372.

Greco, C., & Daehler, M.W. 1985. Immediate and long-term retention of basic-level categories in 24-month-olds. *Infant Behavior and Development, 8*, 459–474.

Greco, C., Hayne, H., & Rovee-Collier, C. 1990. The roles of function, reminding, and variability in categorization by 3-month-old infants. *Journal of Experimental Psychology: Learning, Memory, and Cognition, 16,* 617–633.

Greenbaum, J.L., & Graf, P. 1989. Preschool period development of implicit and explicit remembering. *Bulletin of the Psychonomic Society, 27,* 417–420.

Greene, R.L. 1986. Word stems as cues in recall and completion tasks. *Quarterly Journal of Experimental Psychology, 38,* 663–673.

Greene, R.L. 1990. Spacing effects on implicit memory tests. *Journal of Experimental Psychology: Learning, Memory, and Cognition, 16,* 1004–1011.

Gregg, B.E., Kittrell, M.W., Domjan, M., & Amsel, A. 1978. Ingestional aversion learning in preweanling rats. *Journal of Comparative and Physiological Psychology, 92,* 785–795.

Griffin, D.R. 1976. *The question of animal awareness: Evolutionary continuity of mental experience.* New York: Rockefeller University Press.

Guanowsky, V., & Misanin, J.R. 1983. Retention of conditioned taste aversion in weanling, adult and old-age rats. *Behavioral and Neural Biology, 37,* 173–178.

Gulya, M., Rossi-George, A., Hartshorn, K., Rovee-Collier, C., Johnson, M.K., & Chalfonte, B.L. submitted. *Development of feature memory over the life span.*

Gulya, M., Rossi-George, A., & Rovee-Collier, C. 1999, April. *Time-dependent retroactive interference on a recognition task.* Paper presented at the meeting of the Eastern Psychological Association, Providence, RI.

Gulya, M., Rovee-Collier, C., Galluccio, L., & Wilk, A. 1998. Memory processing of a serial list by young infants. *Psychological Science, 9,* 303–307.

Gulya, M., Sweeney, B., & Rovee-Collier, C. 1999. Infants' memory processing of a serial list: List length effects. *Journal of Experimental Child Psychology, 73,* 72–91.

Gunderson, V.M., & Sackett, G.P. 1984. Development of pattern recognition in infant pigtailed macaques (*Macaca nemestrina*). *Developmental Psychology, 20,* 418–426.

Gunderson, V.M., & Swartz, K.B. 1986. Effects of familiarization time on visual recognition memory in infant pigtailed macaques (*Macaca nemestrina*). *Developmental Psychology, 22,* 477–480.

Hanna, E., & Meltzoff, A.N. 1993. Peer imitation by toddlers in laboratory, home, and daycare contexts: Implications for social learning and memory. *Developmental Psychology, 29,* 701–710.

Hartshorn, K., & Rovee-Collier, C. 1997. Infant learning and long-term memory at 6 months: A confirming analysis. *Developmental Psychobiology, 30,* 71–85.

Hartshorn, K., Rovee-Collier, C., Gerhardstein, P.C., Bhatt, R.S., Klein, P.J., Aaron, F., Wondoloski, T.L., & Wurtzel, N. 1998a. Developmental changes in the specificity of memory over the first year of life. *Developmental Psychobiology, 33,* 61–78.

Hartshorn, K., Rovee-Collier, C., Gerhardstein, P.C, Bhatt, R.S., Wondoloski, T.L., Klein, P., Gilch, J., Wurtzel, N., & Campos-de-Carvalho, M. 1998b. Ontogeny of long-term memory over the first year-and-a-half of life. *Developmental Psychobiology, 32,* 69–89.

Hartshorn, K., Wilk, A., Muller, K., & Rovee-Collier, C. 1998c. An expanding training series protracts retention for 3-month-old infants. *Developmental Psychobiology, 33,* 271–282.

Hasher, L., & Zacks, R.T. 1979. Automatic and effortful processes in memory. *Journal of Experimental Psychology: General, 108,* 356–388.

Hayman, C.A.G., & Tulving, E. 1989. Is priming in fragment completion based on a "traceless" memory system? *Journal of Experimental Psychology: Learning, Memory, & Cognition, 15*, 941–956.

Hayne, H. 1990. The effect of multiple reminders on long-term retention in human infants. *Developmental Psychobiology, 23*, 453–477.

Hayne, H. 1996. Categorization in infancy. In C. Rovee-Collier & L.P. Lipsitt (Eds.), *Advances in infancy research* (Vol. 10, pp. 79–120). Norwood, NJ: Ablex Publishing Corporation.

Hayne, H., Boniface, J., & Barr, R. 2000a. The development of declarative memory in human infants: Age-related changes in deferred imitation. *Behavioral Neuroscience, 114*, 77–83.

Hayne, H., & Campbell, B.A. 1997, October. *Declarative memory during the first year of life*. Paper presented at the meeting of the Society for Neuroscience, New Orleans, LA.

Hayne, H., & Findlay, N. 1995. Contextual control of memory retrieval in infancy: Evidence for associative priming. *Infant Behavior and Development, 18*, 195–207.

Hayne, H., Greco, C., Earley, L.A., Griesler, P.C., & Rovee-Collier, C. 1986. Ontogeny of early event memory: II. Encoding and retrieval by 2- and 3-month-olds. *Infant Behavior and Development, 9*, 461–472.

Hayne, H., Greco-Vigorito, C., & Rovee-Collier, C. 1993. Forming contextual categories in infancy. *Cognitive Development, 8*, 63–82.

Hayne, H., Gross, J., Hildreth, K., & Rovee-Collier, C. 2000b. Repeated reminders increase the speed of memory retrieval in 3-month-old infants. *Developmental Science, 3*, 312–318.

Hayne, H., MacDonald, S., & Barr, R. 1997. Developmental changes in the specificity of memory over the second year of life. *Infant Behavior and Development, 20*, 233–245.

Hayne, H., & Rovee-Collier, C. 1995. The organization of reactivated memory in infancy. *Child Development, 66*, 893–906.

Hayne, H., Rovee-Collier, C., & Borza, M. 1991. Infant memory for place information. *Memory & Cognition, 19*, 378–386.

Hayne, H., Rovee-Collier, C., & Perris, E.E. 1987. Categorization and memory retrieval in 3-month-olds. *Child Development, 58*, 750–767.

Heimann, M., & Nilheim, K. 1999, September. *Deferred imitation in 6-month-old infants*. Paper presented at the IXth European Conference on Developmental Psychology, Spetses, Greece.

Heindel, W.C., Butters, N., & Salmon, D.P. 1988. Impaired learning of a motor skill in patients with Huntington's disease. *Behavioral Neuroscience, 102*, 141–147.

Herbert, J., & Hayne, H. 2000. The ontogeny of long-term retention during the second year of life. *Developmental Science, 3*, 50–56.

Hermann, D.J. 1982. The semantic-episodic distinction and the history of long-term memory typologies. *Bulletin of the Psychonomic Society, 20*, 207–210.

Hertel, P.T., & Hardin, T.S. 1990. Remembering with and without awareness in a depressed mood: Evidence of deficits in initiative. *Journal of Experimental Psychology: General, 119*, 45–59.

Hildreth, K. 1999, June. *Reactivating forgotten memories: Priming latency and reforgetting over the first year of life*. Symposium paper presented at the meeting of the

American Psychological Society, Denver, CO.

Hildreth, K., & Rovee-Collier, C. 1999a. Decreases in the response latency to priming over the first year of life. *Developmental Psychobiology, 35,* 276–290.

Hildreth, K., & Rovee-Collier, C. 1999b, October. *Reforgetting of reactivated memories over the first year of life.* Paper presented at the meeting of the International Society for Developmental Psychobiology, Coral Gables, FL.

Hill, W.H., Borovsky, D., & Rovee-Collier, C. 1988. Continuities in infant memory development over the first half-year. *Developmental Psychobiology, 21,* 43–62.

Hintzman, D.L. 1984. Episodic versus semantic memory: A distinction whose time has come — and gone? *Behavioral and Brain Sciences, 7,* 240–241.

Hintzman, D.L. 1990. Human learning and memory: Connections and dissociations. *Annual Review of Psychology, 41,* 109–139.

Hirsh, R. 1974. The hippocampus and contextual retrieval of information from memory: A theory. *Behavioral Biology, 12,* 421–444.

Hitchcock, D.F.A., & Rovee-Collier, C. 1996. The effect of repeated reactivations on memory specificity in infants. *Journal of Experimental Child Psychology, 62,* 378–400.

Honig, W.K. 1978. Studies of working memory in the pigeon. In S.H. Hulse, H. Fowler, & W.K. Honig (Eds.), *Cognitive processes in animal behavior* (pp. 211–248). Hillsdale, NJ: Lawrence Erlbaum Associates.

Hood, B., & Willatts, P. 1986. Reaching in the dark to an object's remembered position: Evidence for object permanence in 5-month-old infants. *British Journal of Developmental Psychology, 4,* 57–65.

Hooker, D. 1952. *The prenatal origin of behavior.* Lawrence, KS: University of Kansas Press.

Hubbard, J.I. 1975. *The biological basis of mental activity.* Reading, MA: Addison-Wesley.

Hudson, J. 1994, August. *Reinstatement of toddlers' event memory: A matter of timing.* Paper presented at the Practical Aspects of Memory Conference, College Park, MD.

Humphrey, T. 1969. Postnatal repetition of human prenatal activity sequences with some suggestions of their neuroanatomical basis. In R.J. Robinson (Ed.), *Brain and early behaviour* (pp. 43–84). London: Academic Press.

Hunt, J.McV. 1970. Attentional preference and experience: I. Introduction. *Journal of Genetic Psychology, 117,* 99–107.

Hunt, J.McV., & Uzgiris, I.C. 1964, September. *Cathexis from recognitive familiarity.* Paper presented at the meeting of the American Psychological Association, Los Angeles, CA.

Hunter, M.A., & Ames, E.W. (1988). A multifactor model of infant preferences for novel and familiar stimuli. In C. Rovee-Collier & L.P. Lipsitt (Eds.), *Advances in infancy research* (Vol. 5, pp. 69–95). Norwood, NJ: Ablex Publishing Corporation.

Hunter, W.S. 1913. The delayed reaction in animals and children. *Behavioral Monographs, 2,* 52–62.

Hunter, W.S. 1917. The delayed reaction in a child. *Psychological Review, 24,* 74–87.

Isingrini, M., Vazoiu, F., & Leroy, P. 1995. Dissociation of implicit and explicit memory tests: Effect of age and divided attention on category exemplar generation and cued recall. *Memory & Cognition, 23,* 462–467.

Izard, C.E., Dougherty, L.M., & Hembree, E.A. 1980. *A system for identifying affect expressions by holistic judgments (Affex)*. Newark, DE: University of Delaware Instructional Resources Center.

Jackson, J.H. 1880. Essays on the dissolution of the nervous system. *Lancet.*

Jackson, J.H. 1884. Croonian lectures on evolution and dissolution of the nervous system. *British Medical Journal, 1*, 591. [Reprinted in J.E. Taylor (Ed.), *Selected writings of John Hughlings Jackson* (Vol. 2, pp. 45–75). London: Staples Press, 1958.]

Jacobs, W.J., & Nadel, L. 1985. Stress-induced recovery of fears and phobias. *Psychological Review, 92*, 512–531.

Jacoby, L.L. 1978. On interpreting the effects of repetition: Solving a problem versus remembering a solution. *Journal of Verbal Learning and Verbal Behavior, 17*, 649–667.

Jacoby, L.L. 1983. Perceptual enhancement: Persistent effects of an experience. *Journal of Experimental Psychology: Learning, Memory, and Cognition, 9*, 21–38.

Jacoby, L.L. 1984. Incidental versus intentional retrieval: Remembering and awareness as separate issues. In L.R. Squire & N. Butters (Eds.), *Neuropsychology of memory* (pp. 145–156). New York: Guilford Press.

Jacoby, L.L. 1991. A process dissociation framework: Separating automatic from intentional uses of memory. *Journal of Memory and Language, 30*, 513–541.

Jacoby, L.L., & Dallas, M. 1981. On the relationship between autobiographical memory and perceptual learning. *Journal of Experimental Psychology: General, 110*, 306–340.

Jacoby, L.L., Toth, J.P., & Yonelinas, A.P. 1993. Separating conscious and unconscious influence of memory: measuring recollection. *Journal of Experimental Psychology: General, 122*, 139–154.

Jacoby, L.L., & Witherspoon, D. 1982. Remembering without awareness. *Canadian Journal of Psychology, 36*, 300–324.

Jarrard, L.E., & Moise, S.L. 1971. Short-term memory in the monkey. In L.E. Jarrard (Ed.), *Cognitive processes of nonhuman primates* (pp. 1–24). New York: Academic Press.

Jarvik, M.E., Goldfarb, T.L., & Carley, J.L. 1969. Influence of interference on delayed matching in monkeys. *Journal of Experimental Psychology, 81*, 1–6.

Java, R.I., & Gardiner, J.M. 1991. Priming and aging: Further evidence of preserved memory function. *American Journal of Psychology, 104*, 89–100.

Jensen, R.A., Martinez, J.L., Jr., McGaugh, J.L., Messing, R.B., & Vasquez, B.J. 1980. The psychobiology of aging. In G.J. Meletta & F.J. Pirozzolo (Eds.), *The aging nervous system* (pp. 110–125). New York: Praeger.

Johnson, M.K. 1983. A multiple-entry, modular memory system. In G.H. Bower (Ed.), *The psychology of learning and motivation* (Vol. 17, pp. 81–123). New York: Academic Press.

Johnson, M.K. 1991a. Reality monitoring: Evidence from confabulation in organic brain disease patients. In G.P. Prigatano & D.L. Schacter (Eds.), *Awareness of deficit after brain injury* (pp. 176–197). New York: Oxford University Press.

Johnson, M.K. 1991b. Reflection, reality monitoring, and the self. In R. Kunzendorf (Ed.), *Mental imagery: Proceedings of the Eleventh Annual Conference of the American Association for the Study of Mental Imagery* (pp. 3–16). New York: Plenum Publishing Corporation.

Johnson, M.K. 1992. MEM: Mechanisms of recollection. *Journal of Cognitive Neuro-*

science, 4, 268–280.

Johnson, M.K., & Chalfonte, B.L. 1994. Binding complex memories: The role of reactivation and the hippocampus. In D.L. Schacter & E. Tulving (Eds.), *Memory systems 1994* (pp. 311–350). Cambridge, MA: MIT Press.

Johnson, M.K., & Hasher, L. 1987. Human learning and memory. *Annual Review of Psychology, 38,* 631–668.

Johnson, M.K., & Hirst, W. 1991. Processing subsystems of memory. In R.G. Lister & H.J. Weingartner (Eds.), *Perspectives on cognitive neuroscience* (pp. 197–217). New York: Oxford University Press.

Johnson, M.K., & Hirst, W. 1993. MEM: Memory subsystems as processes. In A.F. Collins, S.E. Gathercole, M.A. Conway, & P.E. Morris (Eds.), *Theories of memory* (pp. 241–286). Hillsdale, NJ: Lawrence Erlbaum Associates.

Johnson, M.K., Kounios, J., & Nolde, S.F. 1996. Electrophysiological brain activity and memory source monitoring. *NeuroReport, 7,* 2929–2932.

Johnson, M.K., & Raye, C.L. 1981. Reality monitoring. *Psychological Review, 88,* 67–85.

Johnson, M.K., & Raye, C.L. 1998. False memories and confabulation. *Trends in Cognitive Sciences, 2,* 137–145.

Jolicoeur, P. 1987. A size-congruency effect in memory for visual shape. *Memory & Cognition, 15,* 531–543.

Jones, H.E. 1930. The retention of conditioned emotional reactions in infancy. *Journal of Genetic Psychology, 37,* 485–498.

Jones, E.G., & Powell, T.P.S. 1970. An anatomical study of converging sensory pathways within the cerebral cortex of the monkey. *Brain, 93,* 793–820.

Kagan, J. 1984. *The nature of the child.* New York: Basic Books.

Kagan, J., & Hamburg, M. 1981. The enhancement of memory in the first year. *Journal of Genetic Psychology, 138,* 3–14.

Kandel, E.R., & Hawkins, R.D. 1992. The biological basis of learning and individuality. *Scientific American, 267(3),* 79–86.

Kantrow, R.W. 1937. An investigation of conditioned feeding responses and concomitant adaptive behavior in young infants. *University of Iowa Studies in Child Welfare, 13,* 3.

Kaplan, M.G. 1967. *Infant visual preferences: The role of familiarity and responsiveness.* Unpublished master's thesis, University of Illinois, Champaign, IL.

Karmiloff-Smith, A. 1998. Is atypical development necessarily a window on the normal mind/brain? The case of William's syndrome. *Developmental Science, 1,* 273–277.

Kesner, R.P. 1980. An attribute analysis of memory: The role of the hippocampus. *Physiological Psychology, 8,* 189–197.

Kihlstrom, J.F., Schacter, D.L., Cork, R.C., Hurt, C.A., & Behr, S.E. 1990. Implicit and explicit memory following surgical anesthesia. *Psychological Science, 1,* 303–306.

Kim, J.J., & Fanselow, M.S. 1992. Modality specific retrograde amnesia of fear. *Science, 256,* 675–677.

Kimble, G. (Ed.) 1961. *Hilgard & Marquis' conditioning and learning.* New York: Appleton-Century-Crofts.

Kinsbourne, M., & Wood, F. 1982. Theoretical considerations regarding the episodic-semantic distinction. In L. Cermak (Ed.), *Human memory and amnesia* (pp. 195–218). Hillsdale, NJ: Lawrence Erlbaum Associates.

Kintsch, W. 1974. *The representation of meaning in memory*. Hillsdale, NJ: Lawrence Erlbaum Associates.

Klein, P.J., & Meltzoff, A.N. 1999. Long-term memory, forgetting, and deferred imitation in 12-month-old infants. *Developmental Science, 2*, 102–113.

Klein, S.B., Mikulka, P.J., Domato, G.C., & Haklstead, C. 1977. Retention of internal experiences in juvenile and young rats. *Journal of Comparative and Physiological Psychology, 5*, 63–66.

Knopman, D.S., & Nissen, M.J. 1987. Implicit learning in patients with probable Alzheimer's disease. *Neurology, 37*, 784–788.

Knowlton, B.J., Mangels, J.A., & Squire, L.R. 1996. A neostriatal habit learning system in humans. *Science, 273*, 1399–1402.

Komatsu, S.I., & Ohta, N. 1984. Priming effects in word-fragment completion for short and long retention intervals. *Japanese Psychological Research, 26*, 194–200.

Kunst-Wilson, W.R., & Zajonc, R.B. 1980. Affective discrimination of stimuli that cannot be recognized. *Science, 207*, 557–558.

Landauer, T.K., & Bjork, R.A. 1978. Optimum rehearsal patterns and name learning. In M.M. Gruneberg, P.E. Norris, & R.N. Sykes (Eds.), *Practical aspects of memory* (pp. 625–632). London: Academic Press.

Lewandowsky, S., Kirsner, K., & Bainbridge, V. 1989. Context effects in implicit memory: A sense-specific account. In S. Lewandowsky, J.C. Dunn, & K. Kirsner (Eds.), *Implicit memory: Theoretical issues* (pp. 185–198). Hillsdale, NJ: Lawrence Erlbaum Associates.

Lewis, D.J. 1979. Psychobiology of active and inactive memory. *Psychological Bulletin, 86*, 1054–1083.

Light, L.L., & Albertson, S.A. 1989. Direct and indirect tests of memory for category exemplars in young and older adults. *Psychology & Aging, 4*, 487–492.

Light, L.L., & Lavoie, D. 1993. Direct and indirect measures of memory in old age. In P. Graf & M.E.J. Masson (Eds.), *Implicit memory: New directions in cognition, development, and neuropsychology* (pp. 207–230). Hillsdale, NJ: Lawrence Erlbaum Associates.

Light, L.L., & Singh, A. 1987. Implicit and explicit memory in young and older adults. *Journal of Experimental Psychology: Learning, Memory, and Cognition, 13*, 531–541.

Lindberg, M.A. 1980. Is knowledge-base development a necessary and sufficient condition for memory development? *Journal of Experimental Child Psychology, 30*, 401–410.

Little, A.H. 1970. *Eyelid conditioning in the human infant as a function of the interstimulus interval*. Unpublished master's thesis, Brown University, Providence, RI.

Little, A.H., Lipsitt, L.P., & Rovee-Collier, C. 1984. Classical conditioning and retention of the infant's eyelid response: Effects of age and interstimulus interval. *Journal of Experimental Child Psychology, 37*, 512–524.

Loftus, G.R., & Loftus, E.F. 1974. The influence of one memory retrieval on a subsequent memory retrieval. *Memory & Cognition, 2*, 467–471.

Logan, G.D. 1988. Skill and automaticity: Relations, implications, and future directions. *Canadian Journal of Psychology, 39*, 367–386.

Logan, G.D. 1990. Toward an instance theory of automatization. *Psychological Review, 95*, 492–527.

Logan, G.D. 1992. Repetition priming and automaticity: Common underlying mechanisms? *Cognitive Psychology, 22,* 1–35.

Logan, G.D., & Klapp, S.T. 1991. Automatizing alphabet arithmetic: I. Is extended practice necessary to produce automaticity? *Journal of Experimental Psychology: Learning, Memory, and Cognition, 17,* 179–195.

Macaulay, D., Ryan, L., & Eich, E. 1993. Mood dependence in implicit and explicit memory. In P. Graf & M.E.J. Masson (Eds.), *Implicit memory: New directions in cognition, development, and neuropsychology* (pp. 75–94). Hillsdale, NJ: Lawrence Erlbaum Associates.

Madigan, S. 1983. Picture memory. In J.C. Yuille (Ed.), *Imagery, memory, and cognition: Essays in honor of Allan Paivio* (pp. 65–69). Hillsdale, NJ: Lawrence Erlbaum Associates.

Malamut, B.L., Saunders, R.C., & Mishkin, M.M. 1984. Monkeys with combined amygdalo-hippocampal lesions succeed in object discrimination learning despite 24-hour intertrial intervals. *Behavioral Neuroscience, 98,* 759–769.

Malkova, L., Bachevalier, J., Webster, M., & Mishkin, M.M. in press. Effects of neonatal inferior prefrontal and medial temporal lesions on learning the rule for delayed nonmatching-to-sample. *Developmental Neuropsychology.*

Malkova, L., Mishkin, M.M., & Bachevalier, J. 1995. Long-term effects of selective neonatal temporal lobe lesions on learning and memory in monkeys. *Behavioral Neuroscience, 109,* 212–226.

Mandler, G. 1980. Recognizing: The judgment of previous occurrence. *Psychological Review, 87,* 252–271.

Mandler, G. 1985. *Cognitive psychology: An essay in cognitive science.* Hillsdale, NJ: Lawrence Erlbaum Associates.

Mandler, G. 1989. Memory: Conscious and unconscious. In P.R.Solomon, G.R. Goethals, C.M. Kelley, & R.B. Stephens (Eds.), *Perspectives on memory* (pp. 84–106). New York: Springer-Verlag.

Mandler, G., Nakamura, Y., & Van Zandt, B.J.S. 1987. Nonspecific effects of exposure on stimuli that cannot be recognized. *Journal of Experimental Psychology: Learning, Memory, and Cognition, 13,* 646–648.

Mandler, J.M. 1984. Representation and recall in infancy. In M. Moscovitch (Ed.), *Advances in the study of communication and affect. Vol. 9: Infant memory* (pp. 75–101). New York: Plenum Publishing Corporation.

Mandler, J.M. 1986. The development of event memory. In F. Klix & H. Hagendorf (Eds.), *Human memory and cognitive capabilities: Mechanisms and performance* (pp. 459–467). New York: Elsevier Science Publishers.

Mandler, J.M. 1988. How to build a baby: On the development of an accessible representational system. *Cognitive Development, 3,* 113–136.

Mandler, J.M. 1990. Recall of events by preverbal children. In A. Diamond (Ed.), *The development and neural bases of higher cognitive functions* (Vol. 608, pp. 485–503), *Annals of the New York Academy of Sciences.* New York: New York Academy of Sciences.

Mandler, J.M. 1998. Representation. In W. Damon (Ed.), *Handbook of child psychology: Cognition, perception, & language* (Vol. 2, pp. 255–307). New York: John Wiley & Sons.

Marrott, H., Barr, R., & Rovee-Collier, C. 2000, March. *Sensory preconditioning facilitates deferred imitation by 6-month-olds*. Paper presented at the meeting of the Eastern Psychological Association, Baltimore, MD.

Martone, M., Butters, N., Payne, M., Becker, J. T., & Sax, D. S. 1984. Dissociations between skill learning and verbal recognition in amnesia and dementia. *Archives of Neurology, 41*, 965–970.

Matzel, L.D., Collin, C., & Alkon, D.L. 1992. Biophysical and behavioral correlates of memory storage: Degradation and reactivation. *Behavioral Neuroscience, 106*, 954–963.

McCall, R.B., Kennedy, C.B., & Dodds, C. 1977. The interfering effect of distracting stimuli on the infant's memory. *Child Development, 48*, 79–87.

McCall, R.B., Parke, R.D., & Kavanaugh, R.D. 1977. Imitation of live and televised models by children one to three years of age. *Monographs of the Society for Research in Child Development, 42* (5, Serial No. 173).

McDonald, R.J., & White, N. M. 1993. A triple dissociation of memory systems: Hippocampus, amygdala, and dorsal striatum. *Behavioral Neuroscience, 107*, 3–22.

McDonough, L., Mandler, J.M., McKee, R.D., & Squire, L.R. 1995. The deferred imitation task as a nonverbal measure of declarative memory. *Proceedings of the National Academy of Sciences (USA), 92*, 7580–7584.

McDougall, W. 1923. *Outline of psychology*. New York: Scribner.

McFarland, D.J. 1977. Decision making in animals. *Nature, 269*, 15–21.

McKee, R.D., & Squire, L.R. 1993. On the development of declarative memory. *Journal of Experimental Psychology: Learning, Memory, and Cognition, 19*, 397–404.

McKenzie, W.A., & Humphries, M.S. 1991. Recency effects in direct and indirect memory tasks. *Memory & Cognition, 19*, 321–331.

McKoon, G., Ratcliff, R., & Dell, G.S. 1986. A critical evaluation of the semantic-episodic distinction. *Journal of Experimental Psychology: Learning, Memory, and Cognition, 12*, 295–306.

Meltzoff, A.N. 1988a. Infant imitation and memory: Nine-month-olds in immediate and deferred tests. *Child Development, 59*, 217–225.

Meltzoff, A.N. 1988b. Imitation of televised models by infants. *Child Development, 59*, 1221–1229.

Meltzoff, A.N. 1990. Towards a developmental cognitive science: The implications of cross-modal matching and imitation for the development of representation and memory in infancy. In A. Diamond (Ed.), *The development and neural bases of higher cognitive functions* (Vol. 608, pp. 1–37), *Annals of the New York Academy of Sciences*. New York: New York Academy of Sciences.

Meltzoff, A.N. 1995a. What infant memory tells us about infantile amnesia: Long-term recall and deferred imitation. *Journal of Experimental Child Psychology, 59*, 497–515.

Meltzoff, A.N. 1995b. Understanding the intentions of others: Re-enactment of intended acts by 18-month-old children. *Developmental Psychology, 31*, 838–850.

Meltzoff, A.N., & Moore, M.K. 1994. Imitation, memory, and the representation of persons. *Infant Behavior and Development, 17*, 83–99.

Merriman, J., & Rovee-Collier, C. 1994, June. *Developmental changes in infants' sensitivity to temporal order*. Paper presented at the International Conference on Infant Studies, Paris, France.

Merriman, J., Rovee-Collier, C., & Wilk, A. 1997. Exemplar spacing and infants' memory for category information. *Infant Behavior and Development, 20,* 219–232.

Meulemans, T., Van der Linden, M., & Perruchet, P. 1998. Implicit sequence learning in children. *Journal of Experimental Child Psychology, 69,* 199–221.

Milliken, B., & Jolicoeur, P. 1992. Size effects in visual recognition memory are determined by perceived size. *Memory & Cognition, 20,* 83–95.

Milner, B. 1962. Les troubles de la memoire accompagnant des lesions hippocampiques bilaterales. In P. Passouant (Ed.), *Physiologie de l'hippocampe* (pp. 257–272). Paris: Editions du Centre National de la Recherche Scientifique.

Milner, B. 1965. Memory disturbance after bilateral hippocampal lesions. In P.M. Milner & S.E. Glickman (Eds.), *Cognitive processes and the brain* (pp. 97–111). Princeton, NJ: D. Van Nostrand Company, Inc.

Milner, B. 1972. Disorders of learning and memory after temporal lobe lesions in man. *Clinical Neurosurgery, 19,* 421–446.

Milner, B., Corkin, S., & Teuber, H.L. 1968. Further analysis of the hippocampal amnesic syndrome: Fourteen year follow-up study of H.M. *Neuropsychologia, 6,* 215–234.

Milner, B., Squire, L.R., & Kandel, E.R. 1998. Cognitive neuroscience and the study of memory. *Neuron, 20,* 445–468.

Mishkin, M.M. 1978. Memory in monkeys is severely impaired by combined but not by separate removal of amygdala and hippocampus. *Nature, 273,* 297–298.

Mishkin, M.M. 1982. A memory system in the monkey. *Philosophical Transactions of the Royal Society of London, 298B,* 85–92.

Mishkin, M.M., & Delacour, J. 1975. An analysis of short-term visual memory in the monkey. *Journal of Experimental Psychology: Animal Behavior Processes, 1,* 326–334.

Mishkin, M.M., Malamut, B.L., & Bachevalier, J. 1984. Memories and habits: Two neural systems. In G. Lynch, J.L. McGaugh, & N.M. Weinberger (Eds.), *Neurobiology of learning and memory* (pp. 65–77). New York: Guilford Press.

Mishkin, M.M., & Petri, H.L. 1984. Memories and habits: Some implications for the analysis of learning and retention. In L.R. Squire & N. Butters (Eds.), *Neuropsychology of memory* (pp. 287–296). New York: Guilford Press.

Mishkin, M.M, & Phillips, R.R. 1990. A corticolimbic memory path revealed through its disconnection. In C.B. Trevarthen (Ed.), *Brain circuits and functions of the mind: Essays in honor of Roger W. Sperry* (pp. 196–210). New York, NY: Cambridge University Press.

Mitchell, D.B. 1993. Implicit and explicit memory for pictures: Multiple views across the lifespan. In P. Graf & M.E.J. Masson (Eds.), *Implicit memory: New directions in cognition, development, and neuropsychology* (pp. 171–190). Hillsdale, NJ: Lawrence Erlbaum Associates.

Mitchell, D.B., & Brown, A.S. 1988. Persistent repetition priming in picture naming and its dissociation from recognition memory. *Journal of Experimental Psychology: Learning, Memory, and Cognition, 14,* 213–222.

Mitchell, D.B., Brown, A.S., & Murphy, D.R. 1990. Dissociations between procedural and episodic memory: Effects of time and aging. *Psychology & Aging, 5,* 264–276.

Morris, R. 1984. Development of a water-maze procedure for studying spatial learning in the rat. *Journal of Neuroscience Methods, 11,* 47–60.

Morris, R.G.M. 1981. Spatial localization does not require the presence of local cues. *Learning and Motivation, 12,* 239–260.

Morris, R.G.M., Garrud, P., Rawlins, J.N.P., & O'Keefe, J. 1982. Place navigation impaired in rats with hippocampal lesions. *Nature, 297,* 681–683.

Moscovitch, M. 1982. A neuropsychological approach to perception and memory in normal and pathological aging. In F.I.M. Craik & S. Trehub (Eds.), *Aging and cognitive processes* (pp. 55–78). New York: Plenum Publishing Corporation.

Moscovitch, M. 1985. Memory from infancy to old age. Implications for theories of normal and pathological memory. In D.S. Olton, E. Gamzy, & S. Corkin (Eds.), *Memory dysfunctions: An integration of animal and human research from preclinical and clinical perspectives* (Vol 444, pp. 78–96). *Annals of the New York Academy of Sciences.* New York: New York Academy of Sciences.

Moscovitch, M. 1994. Memory and working with memory: Evaluation of a component process model and comparisons with other models. In D.L. Schacter & E. Tulving (Eds.), *Memory systems 1994* (pp. 269–310). Cambridge, MA: MIT Press.

Mulligan, N.W. 1997. Attention and implicit memory tests: The effects of varying attentional load on conceptual priming. *Memory & Cognition, 25,* 11–17.

Mulligan, N.W., & Hartman, M. 1996. Divided attention and indirect memory tests. *Memory & Cognition, 24,* 453–465.

Mumby, D.G., & Pinel, J.P.J. 1994. Rhinal cortex lesions and object recognition in rats. *Behavioral Neuroscience, 108,* 11–18.

Mumby, D.G., Wood, E.R., & Pinel, J.P.J. 1992. Object-recognition memory is only mildly impaired in rats with lesions of the hippocampus and amygdala. *Psychobiology, 20,* 18–27.

Murdock, B.B. 1962. The serial position effect of free recall. *Journal of Experimental Psychology, 64,* 482–488.

Murdock, B.B. 1988. The past, the present, and the future: Comments on Section 1. In H.L. Roediger, III., & F.I.M. Craik (Eds.), *Varieties of memory and consciousness: Essays in honour of Endel Tulving* (pp. 93–98). Hillsdale, NJ: Lawrence Erlbaum Associates.

Murray, E.A. 1996. What have ablation studies told us about the neural substrates of stimulus memory? *Seminars in the Neurosciences, 8,* 13–22.

Murray, E.A., & Mishkin, M.M. 1998. Object recognition and location memory in monkeys with excitotoxic lesions of the amygdala and hippocampus. *Journal of Neuroscience, 18,* 6568–6582.

Musen, G. 1991. Effects of verbal labeling and exposure duration on implicit memory for visual patterns. *Journal of Experimental Psychology: Learning, Memory, and Cognition, 17,* 954–962.

Musen, G., & Treisman, A. 1990. Implicit and explicit memory for visual patterns. *Journal of Experimental Psychology: Learning, Memory, and Cognition, 16,* 127–137.

Muzzio, I.A., & Rovee-Collier, C. 1996. Timing effects of postevent information on infant retention. *Journal of Experimental Child Psychology, 63,* 212–238.

Nadel, L. 1990. Varieties of spatial cognition: Psychological considerations. In A. Diamond (Ed.), *The development and neural bases of higher cognitive functions* (Vol. 608, pp. 613–626), *Annals of the New York Academy of Sciences.* New York: New York Academy of Sciences.

Nadel, L. 1992. Multiple memory systems: What and why. *Journal of Cognitive Neuroscience, 4,* 179–188.

Nadel, L. 1994. Multiple memory systems: What and why, an update. In D.L. Schacter & E. Tulving (Eds.), *Memory systems 1994* (pp. 39–63). Cambridge, MA: MIT Press.

Nadel, L., & Zola-Morgan, S.M. 1984. Infantile amnesia: A neurobiological perspective. In M. Moscovitch (Ed.), *Advances in the study of communication and affect. Vol. 9: Infant memory* (pp. 145–172). New York: Plenum Publishing Corporation.

Nagy, Z.M. 1979. Development of learning and memory processes in infant mice. In N.E. Spear & B.A. Campbell (Eds.), *Ontogeny of learning and memory* (pp. 101–133). Hillsdale, NJ: Lawrence Erlbaum Associates.

Nagy, Z.M., Misanin, J.R., Newman, J.A., Olsen, P.L., & Hinderliter, C.F. 1972. Ontogeny of memory in the neonatal mouse. *Journal of Comparative and Physiological Psychology, 81,* 380–393.

Naito, M. 1990. Repetition priming in children and adults: Age-related dissociation between implicit and explicit memory. *Journal of Experimental Child Psychology, 50,* 462–484.

Naito, M., & Komatsu, S.I. 1993. Processes involved in childhood development of implicit memory. In P. Graf & M.E.J. Masson (Eds.), *Implicit memory: New directions in cognition, development, and neuropsychology* (pp. 231–260). Hillsdale, NJ: Lawrence Erlbaum Associates.

Neely, J.H. 1989. Experimental dissociations and the episodic/semantic memory distinction. In H.L. Roediger, III., & F.I.M. Craik (Eds.), *Varieties of memory and consciousness: Essays in honour of Endel Tulving* (pp. 229–270). Hillsdale, NJ: Lawrence Erlbaum Associates.

Neely, J.H., & Durgunoglu, A. 1985. Dissociative episodic and semantic priming effects in episodic recognition and lexical decision tasks. *Journal of Memory and Language, 24,* 466–489.

Neill, W.T., Beck, J.L., Bottalico, K.S., & Molloy, R.D. 1990. Effects of intentional versus incidental learning on explicit and implicit tests of memory. *Journal of Experimental Psychology: Learning, Memory, and Cognition, 16,* 457–463.

Nelson, C.A. 1995. The ontogeny of human memory: A cognitive neuroscience perspective. *Developmental Psychology, 31,* 723–738.

Nelson, C.A. 1997. The neurobiological basis of early memory development. In N. Cowan (Ed.), *The development of memory in early childhood* (pp. 41–82). Hove East Sussex, UK: Psychology Press.

Nelson, C.A. 1998. The nature of early memory. *Preventive Medicine, 27,* 172–179.

Nelson, D.L., Keelean, M.J., & Negrao, M. 1989. Word-fragment cuing: The lexical search hypothesis. *Journal of Experimental Psychology: Learning, Memory, and Cognition, 15,* 388–397.

Nelson, D.L., LaLomia, P.D., & Canas, J.J. 1991. Dissociative effects in different prime domains. *Memory & Cognition, 19,* 44–62.

Nelson, K. 1984. The transition from infant to child memory. In M. Moscovitch (Ed.), *Advances in the study of communication and affect. Vol. 9: Infant memory* (pp. 103–130). New York: Plenum Publishing Corporation.

Nelson, K. 1990. Remembering, forgetting, and childhood amnesia. In R. Fivush & J.A.

Hudson (Eds.), *Knowing and remembering in young children* (pp. 301–316). Cambridge: Cambridge University Press.

Nelson, K., & Brown, A.L. 1978. The semantic-episodic distinction in memory development. In P. Ornstein (Ed.), *Memory development in children* (pp. 233–241). Hillsdale, NJ: Lawrence Erlbaum Associates.

Nelson, K., & Kosslyn, S. 1975. Semantic retrieval in children and adults. *Developmental Psychology, 11*, 807–813.

Nissen, M.J., & Bullemer, P.T. 1987. Attentional requirements of learning: Evidence from performance measures. *Cognitive Psychology, 19*, 1–32.

Nissen, M.J., Knopman, D.S., & Schacter, D.L. 1987. Neurochemical dissociation of memory systems. *Neurology, 37*, 789–794.

Nissen, M.J., Willingham, D., & Hartman, M. 1989. Explicit and implicit remembering: When is learning preserved in amnesia? *Neuropsychologia, 27*, 341–352.

Nolde, S.F., Johnson, M.K., & D'Esposito, M. 1998. Left prefrontal activation during episodic remembering: An event-related fMRI study. *Neuroreport, 9*, 3509-3514.

Nolde, S.F., Johnson, M.K., & Raye, C.L. 1998. The role of prefrontal cortex during tests of episodic memory. *Trends in Cognitive Sciences, 2*, 399–405.

Nyberg, L. 1994. A structural equation modeling approach to the multiple memory systems question. *Journal of Experimental Psychology: Learning, Memory, and Cognition, 20*, 485–491.

Oakley, D.A. 1983. The varieties of memory: A phylogenetic approach. In A. Mayes (Ed.), *Memory in animals and humans:* Some comparisons and their theoretical implications (pp. 20–82). Cambridge, UK: Van Nostrand Reinhold.

Ogilvie, J.C., Tulving, E., Paskowitcz, S., & Jones, G.V. 1980. Three-dimensional memory traces: A model and its application to forgetting. *Journal of Verbal Learning and Verbal Behavior, 19*, 405–415.

Ohr, P., Fagen, J.W., Rovee-Collier, C., Hayne, H., & Vander Linde, E. 1989. Amount of training and retention by infants. *Developmental Psychobiology, 22*, 69–80.

O'Keefe, J., & Nadel, L. 1978. *The hippocampus as a cognitive map.* Oxford: Clarendon Press.

Olson, G.M., & Strauss, M.S. 1984. The development of infant memory. In M. Moscovitch (Ed.), *Advances in the study of communication and affect. Vol. 9: Infant memory* (pp. 29–48). New York: Plenum Publishing Corporation.

Olton, D.S. 1989. Inferring psychological dissociations from experimental dissociations: The temporal context of episodic memory. In H.L. Roediger, III., & F.I.M. Craik (Eds.), *Varieties of memory and consciousness: Essays in honour of Endel Tulving* (pp. 161–177). Hillsdale, NJ: Lawrence Erlbaum Associates.

Olton, D.S., Becker, J.T., & Handelmann, G.E. 1979. Hippocampus, space, and memory. *Behavioral and Brain Sciences, 2*, 313–365.

Olton, D.S., & Samuelson, R.J. 1976. Remembrance of places passed: Spatial memory in rats. *Journal of Experimental Psychology: Animal Behavior Processes, 2*, 97–116.

O'Neill, J.B., Friedman, J., Bachevalier, J., & Ungerleider, L.G. 1986. Distribution of muscarinic cholinergic receptors in the brain of a newborn monkey. *Society for Neuroscience Abstracts, 12*, 809.

Orbach, J., Milner, B., & Rasmussen, T. 1960. Learning and retention in monkeys after amygdala-hippocampal resection. *Archives of Neurology, 3*, 230–251.

Oscar-Berman, M., & Bonner, R.T. 1985. Matching- and delayed matching-to-sample performance as measures of visual processing, selective attention, and memory in aging and alcoholic individuals. *Neuropsychologia, 23*, 639–651.

Oscar-Berman, M., & Zola-Morgan, S.M. 1980. Comparative neuropsychology and Korsakoff's syndrome. II. Two-choice visual discrimination learning. *Neuropsychologia, 18*, 513–525.

Overman, W., Bachevalier, J., Turner, M., & Peuster, A. 1992. Object recognition versus object discrimination: Comparison between human infants and infant monkeys. *Behavioral Neuroscience, 106*, 15–29.

Packard, M.G., & McGaugh, J.L. 1992. Double dissociation of fornix and caudate nucleus lesions on acquisition of two water maze tasks: Further evidence for multiple memory systems. *Behavioral Neuroscience, 106*, 439–446.

Packard, M.G., & White, N.M. 1991. Dissociation of hippocampus and caudate nucleus memory systems by posttraining intracerebral injection of dopamine agonists. *Behavioral Neuroscience, 105*, 295–306.

Packard, M.G., Hirsh, R., & White, N.M. 1989. Differential effects of fornix and caudate nucleus lesions on two radial maze tasks: Evidence for multiple memory systems. *Journal of Neuroscience, 9*, 1465–1472.

Paivio, A. 1971. *Imagery and verbal processes*. New York: Holt.

Pan, S. 1926. The influence of context upon learning and recall. *Journal of Experimental Psychology, 9*, 468–491.

Pandya, D.N., & Kuypers, H.G.J.M. 1969. Cortico-cortical connections in the rhesus monkey. *Brain Research, 13*, 13–36.

Parkin, A.J. 1989. The development and nature of implicit memory. In S. Lewandowsky, C., Dunn, & K. Kirsner (Eds.), *Implicit memory: Theoretical issues* (pp. 231–240). Hillsdale, NJ: Lawrence Erlbaum Associates.

Parkin, A.J. 1993. Implicit memory across the lifespan. In P. Graf & M.E.J. Masson (Eds.), *Implicit memory: New directions in cognition, development, and neuropsychology* (pp. 191–206). Hillsdale, NJ: Lawrence Erlbaum Associates.

Parkin, A.J. 1997. The development of procedural and declarative memory. In N. Cowan (Ed.), *The development of memory in childhood* (pp. 113–137). Hove East Sussex, UK: Psychology Press.

Parkin, A.J., & Streete, S. 1988. Implicit and explicit memory in young children and adults. *British Journal of Psychology, 79*, 361–369.

Parkinson, J.K., Murray, E.A., & Mishkin, M.M. 1988. A selective mnemonic role for the hippocampus in monkeys: Memory for the location of objects. *Journal of Neuroscience, 8*, 4159–4167.

Pascalis, O., & DeSchonen, S. 1994. Recognition memory in 3- to 4-day-old human neonates. *NeuroReport, 5*, 1721–1724.

Pascalis, O., DeSchonen, S., Morton, J., Deruelle, C., & Fabre-Grenet, M. 1995. Mother's face recognition by neonates: A replication and an extension. *Infant Behavior and Development, 18*, 79–85.

Paulson, G.W. 1977. The neurological examination in dementia. In C.E. Wells (Ed.), *Dementia* (pp. 169–188). Philadelphia, PA: Davis.

Paulson, G., & Gotlieb, G. 1968. Development of reflexes: The reappearance of foetal and neonatal reflexes in aged patients. *Brain, 91*, 37–52.

Pavlov, I.P. 1927. *Conditioned reflexes.* (Translated by G.V. Anrep.) London: Oxford University Press.

Perris, E.E., Myers, N.A., & Clifton, R.K. 1990. Long-term memory for a single infancy experience. *Child Development, 61*, 1796–1807.

Perruchet, P. 1989. The effect of spaced practice on explicit and implicit memory. *British Journal of Psychology, 80*, 113–130.

Perruchet, P., & Baveux, P. 1989. Correlational analyses of explicit and implicit memory performance. *Memory & Cognition, 17*, 77–86.

Petri, H.L., & Mishkin, M. 1994. Behaviorism, cognitivism and the neuropsychology of memory. *American Scientist, 82*, 30–37.

Piaget, J. 1952. *The origins of intelligence in children.* New York: International Universities Press.

Piaget, J. 1954. *The construction of reality in the child.* New York: Basic Books.

Piaget, J. 1962. *Play, dreams and imitation in childhood.* New York: Norton.

Piaget, J., & Inhelder, B. 1973. *Memory and intelligence.* New York: Basic Books.

Postman, L., & Underwood, B. 1973. Critical issues in interference theory. *Memory & Cognition, 1*, 19–40.

Preyer, W. 1885. *Spezielle physiologie des embryo.* Leipsig: Grieben.

Quinn, P.C., & Eimas, P.D. 1996. Perceptual organization and categorization in young infants. In C. Rovee-Collier & L.P. Lipsitt (Eds.), *Advances in infancy research* (Vol. 10, pp. 1–36). Norwood, NJ: Ablex Publishing Corporation.

Radvansky, G.A. 1999. Aging, memory, and comprehension. *Current Directions in Psychological Science, 8*, 49–53.

Radvansky, G.A., Zacks, R.T., & Hasher, L. 1996. Fact retrieval in younger and older adults: The role of mental models. *Psychology and Aging, 11*, 258–271.

Rajaram, S. 1993. Remembering and knowing: Two means of access to the personal past. *Memory & Cognition, 21*, 89–102.

Rakic, P., & Nowakowski, R.S. 1981. The time of origin of neurons in the hippocampal region of the rhesus monkey. *Journal of Comparative Neurology, 196*, 99–128.

Ramos, J.M.J. 1998. Retrograde amnesia for spatial information: A dissociation between intra- and extramaze cues following hippocampus lesions in rats. *European Journal of Neuroscience, 10*, 3295–3301.

Ramsay, D.S., & Campos, J.J. 1978. The onset of representation and entry into Stage 6 of object permanence development. *Developmental Psychology, 14*, 79–86.

Ratcliff, R., & McKoon, G. 1986. More on the distinction between episodic and semantic memories. *Journal of Experimental Psychology: Learning, Memory, and Cognition, 12*, 312–313.

Ratcliff, R., & Murdock, B.B., Jr. 1976. Retrieval processes in recognition memory. *Psychological Review, 83*, 190–214.

Ratcliff, R., Van Zandt, T., & McKoon, G. 1995. Process dissociation, single-process theories, and recognition memory. *Journal of Experimental Psychology: General, 124*, 352–374.

Ratner, H., Smith, B., & Dion, S. 1986. Development of memory for events. *Journal of*

Experimental Child Psychology, 41, 411–428.

Rauch, S.L., & Raskin, L.A. 1984. Cholinergic mediation of spatial memory in the preweanling rat: Application of the radial arm maze paradigm. *Behavioral Neuroscience, 98,* 35–43.

Rea, C.P., & Modigliani, V. 1985. The effect of expanded versus massed practice on the retention of multiplication facts and spelling lists. *Human Learning, 4,* 11–18.

Reeves, A., & Sperling, G. 1986. Attention gating in short-term visual memory. *Psychological Review, 93,* 180–206.

Reinitz, M.T., & Alexander, R. 1996. Mechanisms of facilitation in primed perceptual identification. *Memory & Cognition, 24,* 129–135.

Reinitz, M.T., & Demb, J.B. 1994. Implicit and explicit memory for compound words. *Memory & Cognition, 22,* 687–694.

Rheingold, H.L., Gewirtz, J.L., & Ross, H.W. 1959. Social conditioning of vocalizations in the infant. *Journal of Comparative & Physiological Psychology, 52,* 68–73.

Ribot, T.A. 1882. *The diseases of memory.* New York: Appleton & Co.

Riccio, D.C., Ackil, J., & Burch-Vernon, A. 1992. Forgetting of stimulus attributes: Methodological implications for assessing associative phenomena. *Psychological Bulletin, 112,* 433–445.

Richardson, R., Riccio, D.C., & McKenney, M. 1988. Stimulus attributes of reactivated memory: Alleviation of ontogenetic forgetting in rats is context specific. *Developmental Psychobiology, 21,* 135–143.

Richardson-Klavehn, A., & Bjork, R.A. 1988. Measures of memory. *Annual Review of Psychology, 39,* 475–543.

Roberts, W.A. 1972a. Spatial separation and visual differentiation of cues as factors influencing short-term memory in the rat. *Journal of Comparative and Physiological Psychology, 78,* 284–291.

Roberts, W.A. 1972b. Free recall of word lists varying in length and rate of presentation: A test of total-time. *Journal of Experimental Psychology, 92,* 365–372.

Roberts, W.A. 1974. Spaced repetition facilitates short-term retention in the rat. *Journal of Comparative and Physiological Psychology, 86,* 164–171.

Roberts, W.A., & Grant, D.S. 1976. Studies of short-term memory in the pigeon using the delayed matching-to-sample procedure. In D.L. Medin, W.A. Roberts, & R.T. Davis (Eds.), *Processes of animal memory* (pp. 79–112). Hillsdale, NJ: Lawrence Erlbaum Associates.

Roediger, H.L., III. 1984. Does current evidence from dissociation experiments favor the episodic/semantic distinction? *Behavioral and Brain Sciences, 7,* 252–254.

Roediger, H.L., III. 1990a. Implicit memory: A commentary. *Bulletin of the Psychonomic Society, 28,* 373–380.

Roediger, H.L., III. 1990b. Implicit memory: Retention without remembering. *American Psychologist, 45,* 1043–1056.

Roediger, H.L., III., & Blaxton, T.A. 1987. Effects of varying modality, surface features, and retention interval on priming in word-fragment completion. *Memory & Cognition, 15,* 379–388.

Roediger, H.L., III., & Payne, D.G. 1982. Hypermnesia: The role of repeated testing. *Journal of Experimental Psychology: Learning, Memory, and Cognition, 8,* 66–72.

Roediger, H.L., III., Rajaram, S., & Srinivas, K. 1990. Specifying criteria for postulating memory systems. In A. Diamond (Ed.), *The development and neural bases of higher cognitive functions* (Vol. 608, pp. 572–589), *Annals of the New York Academy of Sciences*. New York: New York Academy of Sciences.

Roediger, H.L., III., & Srinivas, K. 1993. Specificity of operations in perceptual priming. In P. Graf & M.E.J. Masson (Eds.), *Implicit memory: New directions in cognition, development, and neuropsychology* (pp. 17–48). Hillsdale, NJ: Lawrence Erlbaum Associates.

Roediger, H.L., III., Srinivas, K., & Weldon, M.S. 1989a. Dissociations between implicit measures of memory. In S. Lewandowsky, J.C. Dunn, & K. Kirsner (Eds.), *Implicit memory: Theoretical issues* (pp. 67–84). Hillsdale, NJ: Lawrence Erlbaum Associates.

Roediger, H.L., III., & Weldon, M.S. 1987. Reversing the picture superiority effect. In M.A. McDaniel & M. Pressley (Eds.), *Imagery and related mnemonic processes: Theories, individual differences, and applications* (pp. 151–174). New York: Springer-Verlag.

Roediger, H.L., III., Weldon, M.S., & Challis, B.H. 1989b. Explaining dissociations between implicit and explicit measures of retention: A processing account. In H.L. Roediger, III., & F.I.M. Craik (Eds.), *Varieties of memory and consciousness: Essays in honour of Endel Tulving* (pp. 3–41). Hillsdale, NJ: Lawrence Erlbaum Associates.

Roediger, H.L., III., Weldon, M.S., Stadler, M.L., & Riegler, G L. 1992. Direct comparison of two implicit memory tests: Word fragment and word stem completion. *Journal of Experimental Psychology: Learning, Memory, and Cognition, 18*, 1251–1269.

Rose, S.A. 1981. Developmental changes in infants' retention of visual stimuli. *Child Development, 52*, 227–233.

Ross, B.H., & Bradshaw, G.L. 1994. Encoding effects of remindings. *Memory & Cognition, 22*, 591–605.

Rossi-George, A., & Rovee-Collier, C. 1999. Retroactive interference in 3-month-old infants. *Developmental Psychobiology, 35*, 167–177.

Rovee, C.K., & Fagen, J.W. 1976. Extended conditioning and 24-hour retention in infants. *Journal of Experimental Child Psychology, 21*, 1–11.

Rovee, C.K., & Rovee, D.T. 1969. Conjugate reinforcement of infant exploratory behavior. *Journal of Experimental Child Psychology, 8*, 33–39.

Rovee-Collier, C. 1984. The ontogeny of learning and memory in human infancy. In R. Kail, & N.E. Spear (Eds.), *Comparative perspectives on the development of memory* (pp. 103–134). Hillsdale, NJ: Lawrence Erlbaum Associates.

Rovee-Collier, C. 1990. The "memory system" of prelinguistic infants. In A. Diamond (Ed.), *The development and neural bases of higher cognitive functions* (Vol. 608, pp. 517–536), *Annals of the New York Academy of Sciences*. New York: New York Academy of Sciences.

Rovee-Collier, C. 1995. Time windows in cognitive development. *Developmental Psychology, 31*, 147–169.

Rovee-Collier, C. 1997. Dissociations in infant memory: Rethinking the development of implicit and explicit memory. *Psychological Review, 104*, 467–498.

Rovee-Collier, C., Adler, S.A., & Borza, M.A. 1994. Substituting new details for old? Effects of delaying postevent information on infant memory. *Memory & Cognition, 22*, 644–656.

Rovee-Collier, C., Bhatt, R.S., & Chazin, S. 1996. Set size, novelty, and visual pop-out in infancy. *Journal of Experimental Psychology: Human Perception and Performance, 22*, 1178–1187.

Rovee-Collier, C., & Boller, K. 1995. Current theory and research on infant learning and memory: Application to early intervention. *Infants and Young Children, 7*, 1–12.

Rovee-Collier, C., Borza, M.A., Adler, S.A., & Boller, K. 1993a. Infants' eyewitness testimony: Effects of postevent information on a prior memory representation. *Memory & Cognition, 21*, 267–279.

Rovee-Collier, C., & DuFault, D. 1991. Multiple contexts and memory retrieval at 3 months. *Developmental Psychobiology, 24*, 39–49.

Rovee-Collier, C., Earley, L.A., & Stafford, S. 1989. Ontogeny of early event memory: III. Attentional determinants of retrieval at 2 and 3 months. *Infant Behavior and Development, 12*, 147–161.

Rovee-Collier, C., Enright, M.K., Lucas, D., Fagen, J.W., & Gekoski, M.J. 1981. The forgetting of newly acquired and reactivated memories of 3-month-old infants. *Infant Behavior and Development, 4*, 317–331.

Rovee-Collier, C., Evancio, S., & Earley, L.A. 1995. The time window hypothesis: Spacing effects. *Infant Behavior and Development, 18*, 69–78.

Rovee-Collier, C., Greco-Vigorito, C., & Hayne, H. 1993b. The time-window hypothesis: Implications for categorization and memory modification. *Infant Behavior and Development, 16*, 149–176.

Rovee-Collier, C., Griesler, P.C., & Earley, L.A. 1985a. Contextual determinants of retrieval in three-month-old infants. *Learning and Motivation, 16*, 139–157.

Rovee-Collier, C., Hankins, E., & Bhatt, R.S. 1992a. Textons, visual pop-out effects, and object recognition in infancy. *Journal of Experimental Psychology: General, 121*, 435–445.

Rovee-Collier, C., Hartshorn, K., & DiRubbo, M. 1999. Long-term maintenance of infant memory. *Developmental Psychobiology, 35*, 91–102.

Rovee-Collier, C., & Hayne, H. 1987. Reactivation of infant memory: Implications for cognitive development. In H.W. Reese (Ed.), *Advances in child development and behavior* (Vol. 20, pp. 185–238). New York: Academic Press.

Rovee-Collier, C., & Hayne, H. 2000. Memory in infancy and early childhood. In E. Tulving & F.I.M. Craik (Eds.), *The Oxford handbook of memory.* (pp. 267–282). New York: Oxford University Press.

Rovee-Collier, C., Patterson, J., & Hayne, H. 1985b. Specificity in the reactivation of infant memory. *Developmental Psychobiology, 18*, 559–574.

Rovee-Collier, C., Schechter, A., Shyi, G.C-W., & Shields, P. 1992b. Perceptual identification of contextual attributes and infant memory retrieval. *Developmental Psychology, 28*, 307–318.

Rovee-Collier, C., & Sullivan, M.W. 1980. Organization of infant memory. *Journal of Experimental Psychology: Human Learning and Memory, 6*, 798–807.

Rovee-Collier, C., Sullivan, M.W., Enright, M.K., Lucas, D., & Fagen, J.W. 1980. Reactivation of infant memory. *Science, 208*, 1159–1161.

Rozin, P. 1976. The psychobiological approach to human memory. In M.R. Rosenzweig & E.L. Bennett (Eds.), *Neural mechanisms of learning and memory* (pp. 3–48). Cambridge, MA: MIT Press.

Rudy, J.W. 1991. Elemental and configural associations, the hippocampus, and development. *Developmental Psychobiology, 24*, 219–236.

Rudy, J.W., & Sutherland, R.J. 1989. The hippocampal formation is necessary for rats to learn and remember configural discriminations. *Behavioral Brain Research, 34*, 97–109.

Ruggiero, F.T., & Flagg, S.F. 1976. *Do animals have memory?* In D.L. Medin, W.A. Roberts, & R.T. Davis (EDs.), Processes of animal memory (pp. 1–19). Hillsdale, NJ: Lawrence Erlbaum Associates.

Russo, R., & Parkin, A.J. 1993. Age differences in implicit memory: More apparent than real. *Memory & Cognition, 21*, 73–80.

Russo, R., Nichelli, P., Gibertoni, M., & Cornia, C. 1995. Developmental trends in implicit and explicit memory: A picture completion study. *Journal of Experimental Child Psychology, 59*, 566–578.

Rybash, J.M., & Osborne, J.L. 1991. Implicit memory, the serial position effect, and test awareness. *Bulletin of the Psychonomic Society, 29*, 327–330.

Saint-Cyr, J.A., Taylor, A.E., & Lang, A.E. 1988. Procedural learning and neostriatal dysfunction in man. *Brain, 111*, 941–959.

Sameroff, A.J. 1968. The components of sucking in the human newborn. *Journal of Experimental Child Psychology, 6*, 607–623.

Schacter, D.L. 1985. Priming of old and new knowledge in amnesic patients and normal subjects. In D.S. Olton, E. Gamzu, & S. Corkin (Eds.), *Memory dysfunctions: An integration of animal and human research from preclinical and clinical perspectives* (vol 444, pp. 44–53). Annals of the New York Academy of Sciences. New York: New York Academy of Science..

Schacter, D.L. 1987. Implicit memory: History and current status. *Journal of Experimental Psychology: Learning, Memory, and Cognition, 13*, 501–518.

Schacter, D.L. 1989. On the relation between memory and consciousness: Dissociable interactions and conscious experience. In H.L. Roediger, III., & F.I.M. Craik (Eds.), *Varieties of memory and consciousness: Essays in honour of Endel Tulving* (pp. 355–389). Hillsdale, NJ: Lawrence Erlbaum Associates.

Schacter, D.L. 1990. Perceptual representation systems and implicit memory: Toward a resolution of the multiple memory systems debate. In A. Diamond (Ed.), *The development and neural bases of higher cognitive functions* (Vol. 608, pp. 543–567), *Annals of the New York Academy of Sciences*. New York: New York Academy of Sciences.

Schacter, D.L. 1992. Priming and multiple memory systems: Perceptual mechanisms of implicit memory. *Journal of Cognitive Neuroscience, 4*, 244–256.

Schacter, D.L. 1994. Priming and multiple memory systems: Perceptual mechanisms of implicit memory. In D.L. Schacter & E. Tulving (Eds.), *Memory systems 1994* (pp. 233–268). Cambridge, MA: MIT Press.

Schacter, D.L. 1997. The cognitive neuroscience of memory: Perspectives from neuroimaging research. *Philosophical Transactions of the Royal Society of London, 352B*, 1689–1695.

Schacter, D.L., Alpert, N.M., Savage, C.R., Rauch, S.L., & Albert, M.S. 1996. Conscious recollection and the human hippocampal formation: Evidence from positron emission tomography. *Proceedings of the National Academy of Sciences (USA), 93*, 321–325.

Schacter, D.L., Bowers, J., & Booker, J. 1989. Intention, awareness, and implicit memory: The retrieval intentionality criterion. In S. Lewandowsky, J.C. Dunn, & K. Kirsner (Eds.), *Implicit memory: Theoretical issues* (pp. 47–65). Hillsdale, NJ: Lawrence Erlbaum Associates.

Schacter, D.L., Chiu, C.Y.P., & Ochsner, K.N. 1993a. Implicit memory: A selective review. *Annual Review of Neuroscience, 16,* 159–182.

Schacter, D.L., & Cooper, L.A. 1993. Implicit and explicit memory for novel visual objects: Structure and function. *Journal of Experimental Psychology: Learning, Memory, and Cognition, 19,* 995–1009.

Schacter, D.L., Cooper, L.A., & Delaney, S.M. 1990. Implicit memory for unfamiliar objects depends on access to structural descriptions. *Journal of Experimental Psychology: General, 119,* 5–24.

Schacter, D.L., Cooper, L.A., Delaney, S.M., Peterson, M.A., & Tharan, M. 1991a. Implicit memory for possible and impossible objects: Constraints on the construction of structural descriptions. *Journal of Experimental Psychology: Learning, Memory, and Cognition, 17,* 3–19.

Schacter, D.L., Cooper, L.A., Tharan, M., & Rubens, A.B. 1991b. Preserved priming of novel objects in patients with memory disorders. *Journal of Cognitive Neuroscience, 3,* 118–131.

Schacter, D.L., Cooper, L.A., & Treadwell, J. 1993b. Preserved priming of novel objects across size transformation in amnesic patients. *Psychological Science, 4,* 331–335.

Schacter, D.L., & Moscovitch, M. 1984. Infants, amnesics, and dissociable memory systems. In M. Moscovitch (Ed.), *Advances in the study of communication and affect. Vol. 9: Infant memory* (pp. 173–216). New York: Plenum Publishing Corporation.

Schacter, D.L., & Tulving, E. 1994. What are the memory systems of 1994? In D.L. Schacter & E. Tulving (Eds.), *Memory systems 1994* (pp. 1–38). Cambridge, MA: MIT Press.

Schenk, F., Inglin, F., & Morris, R.G.M. 1983. Place navigation in rats as a function of age. *Society of Neuroscience Abstracts, 9,* 332.

Schmidt, R.A., & Bjork, R.A. 1992. New conceptualizations of practice: Common principles in three paradigms suggest new concepts for training. *Psychological Science, 3,* 207–217.

Schulenberg, C.J., Riccio, D.C., & Stikes, E.S. 1971. Acquisition and retention of a passive-avoidance response as a function of age in rats. *Journal of Comparative and Physiological Psychology, 74,* 75–83.

Schwartz, B.L., & Hashtroudi, S. 1991. Priming is independent of skill learning. *Journal of Experimental Psychology: Learning, Memory, and Cognition, 17,* 1177–1187.

Schweitzer, L., & Green, L. 1982. Acquisition and extended retention of a conditioned taste aversion in preweanling rats. *Journal of Comparative and Physiological Psychology, 96,* 791–806.

Scott, S.K., Young, A.W., Calder, A.J., Hellawell, D.J., Aggleton, J.P., & Johnson, M. 1997. Impaired auditory recognition of fear and anger following bilateral amygdala lesions. *Nature, 385,* 254–257.

Scoville, W.B., & Milner, B. 1957. Loss of recent memory after bilateral hippocampal lesions. *Journal of Neurology, Neurosurgery, and Psychiatry, 20,* 11–21.

Searle, J.R. 1983. *Intentionality: An essay in the philosophy of mind.* Cambridge, UK: Cambridge University Press.

Searle, J.R. 1984. *Minds, brains, and science.* Cambridge: Harvard University Press.

Searle, J.R. 1995. The mystery of consciousness. *New York Review of Books, 42(17),* 60–66.

Searle, J.R. 1998. *Mind, language, and society.* New York: Basic Books.

Shallice, T. 1988. *From neuropsychology to mental structure.* Cambridge, UK: Cambridge University Press.

Shapiro, M.L., & Olton, D.S. 1994. Hippocampal function and interference. In D.L. Schacter & E. Tulving (Eds.), *Memory systems 1994* (pp. 87–117). Cambridge, MA: MIT Press.

Sheffield, E.G., & Hudson, J.A. 1994. Reactivation of toddlers' event memory. *Memory, 2,* 447–465.

Sherry, D.F., & Schacter, D.L. 1987. The evolution of multiple memory systems. *Psychological Review, 94,* 439–454.

Shields, P.J., & Rovee-Collier, C. 1992. Long-term memory for context-specific category information at 6 months. *Child Development, 63,* 245–259.

Shimamura, A.P. 1985. Problems with the finding of stochastic independence as evidence for multiple memory systems. *Bulletin of the Psychonomic Society, 23,* 506–508.

Shimamura, A.P. 1986. Priming effects in amnesia. Evidence for a dissociable memory function. *Quarterly Journal of Experimental Psychology, 38A,* 619–644.

Shimamura, A.P. 1990. Forms of memory: Issues and directions. In J.L. McGaugh, N.M. Weinberger, & G. Lynch (Eds.), *Brain organization and memory: Cells, systems and circuits* (pp. 159–173). New York: Oxford University Press.

Shimamura, A.P., Janowsky, J.S., & Squire, L.R. 1991. What is the role of frontal lobe damage in memory disorders? In H.S. Levin, H.M. Eisenberg, & A.L.Benton (Eds.), *Frontal lobe function and dysfunction* (pp. 173–195). New York: Oxford University Press.

Shimamura, A.P., & Squire, L.R. 1984. Paired-associate learning and priming effects in amnesia: A neuropsychological study. *Journal of Experimental Psychology: General, 113,* 556–570.

Shimp, C.P., & Moffitt, M. 1974. Short-term memory in the pigeon: Stimulus-response associations. *Journal of the Experimental Analysis of Behavior, 22,* 507–512.

Sidman, M., Stoddard, L.T., & Mohr, J.P. 1968. Some additional quantitative observations of immediate memory in a patient with bilateral hippocampal lesions. *Neuropsychologia, 6,* 245–254.

Singer, J.M., & Fagen, J.W. 1992. Negative affect, emotional expression, and forgetting in young infants. *Developmental Psychology, 28,* 48–57.

Skinner, B.F. 1953. *Science and human behavior.* New York: Macmillan.

Skinner, B.F. 1957. *Verbal behavior.* New York: Appleton-Century-Crofts.

Sloman, S.A., Hayman, C.A.G., Ohta, N., Law, J., & Tulving, E. 1988. Forgetting in primed fragment completion. *Journal of Experimental Psychology: Learning, Memory, and Cognition, 14,* 223–239.

Smith, M.L., & Milner, B. 1981. The role of the right hippocampus in the recall of spatial location. *Neuropsychologia, 19,* 781–793.

Smith, S.M., Heath, F.R., & Vela, E. 1990. Environmental context-dependent homophone spelling. *American Journal of Psychology, 103*, 229–242.

Snodgrass, J.G. 1989. Sources of learning in the picture fragment completion task. In S. Lewandowsky, J.C. Dunn, & K. Kirsner (Eds.), *Implicit memory: Theoretical issues* (pp. 259–282). Hillsdale, NJ: Lawrence Erlbaum Associates.

Snodgrass, J.G., & Feenan, K. 1990. Priming effects in picture fragment completion: Support for the perceptual closure hypothesis. *Journal of Experimental Psychology: General, 119*, 276–296.

Snodgrass, J.G., Smith, B., Feenan, K., & Corwin, J. 1987. Fragmenting pictures on the Apple Macintosh computer for experimental and clinical applications. *Behavior Research Methods, Instruments & Computers, 19*, 270–274.

Snodgrass, J.G., & Vanderwart, M. 1980. A standardized set of 260 pictures: Norms for name agreement, image agreement, familiarity, and visual complexity. *Journal of Experimental Psychology: Human Learning and Memory, 6*, 174–215.

Sokolov, E.N. 1963. Higher nervous functions: The orienting reflex. *Annual Review of Physiology, 25*, 545–580.

Solomon, P.R., Groccia-Ellison, M., Levine, E., Blanchard, S., & Pendlebury, W.W. 1990. Do temporal relationships in conditioning change across the life span? Perspectives from eyeblink conditioning in humans and rabbits. In A. Diamond (Ed.), *The development and neural bases of higher cognitive functions* (Vol. 608, pp. 212–232), *Annals of the New York Academy of Sciences*. New York: New York Academy of Sciences.

Solomon, P.R., Pomerleau, D., Bennett, L., James, J., & Morse, D.L. 1989. Acquisition of the classically conditioned eyeblink response in humans over the lifespan. *Psychology & Aging, 4*, 34–41.

Spear, N.E. 1973. Retrieval of memories in animals. *Psychological Review, 80*, 163–194.

Spear, N.E. 1978. *The processing of memories: Forgetting and retention*. Hillsdale, NJ: Lawrence Erlbaum Associates.

Spear, N.E., & Kucharski, D. 1984. Ontogenetic differences in stimulus selection during conditioning. In R. Kail, & N.E. Spear (Eds.), *Comparative perspectives on the development of memory* (pp. 227–252). Hillsdale, NJ: Lawrence Erlbaum Associates.

Spear, N.E., & Parsons, P.J. 1976. Analysis of a reactivation treatment: Ontogenetic determinants of alleviated forgetting. In D.L. Medin, W.A. Roberts, & R.T. Davis (Eds.), *Processes of animal memory* (pp. 135–165). Hillsdale, NJ: Lawrence Erlbaum Associates.

Squire, L.R. 1986. Mechanisms of memory. *Science, 232*, 1612–1619.

Squire, L.R. 1987. *Memory and brain*. New York: Oxford University Press.

Squire, L.R. 1992a. Declarative and nondeclarative memory: Multiple brain systems supporting learning and memory. *Journal of Cognitive Neuroscience, 4*, 232–243.

Squire, L.R. 1992b. Memory and the hippocampus: A synthesis from findings with rats, monkeys, and humans. *Psychological Review, 99*, 195–231.

Squire, L.R. 1994. Declarative and nondeclarative memory: Multiple brain systems supporting learning and memory. In D.L. Schacter & E. Tulving (Eds.), *Memory Systems 1994* (pp. 203–231). Cambridge, MA: MIT Press.

Squire, L.R., Knowlton, B., & Musen, G. 1993. The structure and organization of memory. *Annual Review of Psychology, 44*, 453–495.

Squire, L.R., Ojemann, J.G., Miezin, F.M., Petersen, S.E., Videen, T.O., & Raichle, M.E. 1992. Activation of the hippocampus in normal humans: A functional anatomical study of memory. *Proceedings of the National Academy of Sciences (USA), 89*, 1837–1841.

Squire, L.R., & Slater, P.C. 1975. Forgetting in very long-term memory as assessed by an improved questionnaire technique. *Journal of Experimental Psychology, 1*, 50–54.

Squire, L.R., & Zola-Morgan, S.M. 1991. The medial temporal lobe memory system. *Science, 253*, 1380–1386.

Squire, L.R., Zola-Morgan, S.M., & Chen, K.S. 1988. Human amnesia and animal models of amnesia: Performance of amnesic patients on tests designed for the monkey. *Behavioral Neuroscience, 102*, 210–221.

Srinivas, K. 1996. Contrast and illumination effects on explicit and implicit measures of memory. *Journal of Experimental Psychology: Learning, Memory, and Cognition, 22*, 1123–1135.

Srinivas, K., & Roediger, H.L., III. 1990. Classifying implicit memory tests: Category association and anagram solution. *Journal of Memory and Language, 29*, 389–412.

Stankiewicz, B.J., Cooper, E.E., & Hummel, J.E. 1994, November. *The role of attention in left-right reflectional invariance.* Paper presented at the meeting of the Psychonomic Society, St. Louis, MO.

Stehouwer, D.J., & Campbell, B.A. 1978. Habituation of the forelimb-withdrawal response in neonatal rats. *Journal of Experimental Psychology: Animal Behavior Processes, 4*, 104–119.

Stehouwer, D.J., & Campbell, B.A. 1980. Ontogeny of passive avoidance: Role of task demands and development of species-typical behaviors. *Developmental Psychobiology, 13*, 791–806.

Steinert, P.A., Infurna, R.N., & Spear, N.E. 1980. Long-term retention of a conditioned taste aversion in preweanling and adult rats. *Animal Learning & Behavior, 8*, 375–381.

Sullivan, M.W. 1982. Reactivation: Priming forgotten memories in human infants. *Child Development, 53*, 516–523.

Sullivan, M.W., Rovee-Collier, C., & Tynes, D.M. 1979. A conditioning analysis of infant long-term memory. *Child Development, 50*, 152–162.

Suzuki, W.A., Zola-Morgan, S.M., Squire, L.R., & Amaral, D.G. 1993. Lesions of the perirhinal and parahippocampal cortices in the monkey produce long-lasting memory impairment in the visual and tactual modalities. *Journal of Neuroscience, 13*, 2430–2451

Terwilliger, R.F. 1968. *Meaning and mind: A study of the psychology of language.* New York: Oxford University Press.

Teuber, H.L. 1955. Physiological psychology. *Annual Review of Psychology, 6*, 267–296.

Thomas, K.M. 1997. *A developmental study of implicit and explicit motor sequence learning.* Unpublished doctoral dissertation, University of Minnesota, Minneapolis, MN.

Thomson, D.M., & Tulving, E. 1970. Associative encoding and retrieval: Weak and strong cues. *Journal of Experimental Psychology, 86*, 255–262.

Thompson, R.F. 1990a. Discussion of J.M. Mandler, "Recall of events by preverbal children." In A. Diamond (Ed.), *The development and neural bases of higher cognitive functions* (Vol. 608, pp. 503–516), *Annals of the New York Academy of Sciences.* New York: New York Academy of Sciences.

Thompson, R.F. 1990b. Neural mechanisms of classical conditioning in mammals. *Philosophical Transactions of the Royal Society of London, 329B*, 161–170.

Timmons, C.R. 1994. Associative links between discrete memories in infancy. *Infant Behavior and Development, 17*, 431–445.

Treisman, A. 1988. Features and objects: The Fourteenth Bartlett Memorial Lecture. *Quarterly Journal of Experimental Psychology, 40A*, 201–237.

Treisman, A. 1992. Perceiving and re-perceiving objects. *American Psychologist, 47*, 862–875.

Treisman, A., & Gelade, G. 1980. A feature integration theory of attention. *Cognitive Psychology, 12*, 97–136.

Tuber, D.S., Berntson, G.G., Bachman, D.S., & Allen, J.N. 1980. Associative learning in premature hydranencephalic and normal twins. *Science, 210*, 1035–1037.

Tulving, E. 1972. Episodic and semantic memory. In E. Tulving & W. Donaldson (Eds.), *Organization of memory* (pp. 381–403). New York: Academic Press.

Tulving, E. 1983. *Elements of episodic memory.* New York: Oxford University Press.

Tulving, E. 1985. How many memory systems are there? *American Psychologist, 40*, 385–398.

Tulving, E. 1986. What kind of a hypothesis is the distinction between episodic and semantic memory? *Journal of Experimental Psychology: Learning, Memory, and Cognition, 12*, 307–311.

Tulving, E. 1987. Multiple memory systems and consciousness. *Human Neurobiology, 6*, 67–80.

Tulving, E. 1990. Memory and consciousness. *Canadian Journal of Psychology, 26*, 1–12.

Tulving, E. 1991. Concepts of human memory. In L.R. Squire, N.M. Weinberger, G. Lynch, & J.L. McGaugh (Eds.), *Memory: Organization and locus of change* (pp. 3–32). New York: Oxford University Press.

Tulving, E. 1993. What is episodic memory? *Current Directions in Psychological Science, 2*, 67–70.

Tulving, E. 1998. Brain/mind correlates of human memory. In. M. Sabourin, F. Craik, & M. Robert (Eds.), *Advances in psychological science. Vol. 2: Biological and cognitive aspects* (pp. 441–460). Hove East Sussex, UK: Psychology Press.

Tulving, E., & Bower, G.H. 1974. The logic of memory representations. In G.H. Bower (Ed.), *The psychology of learning and motivation* (Vol. 8, pp. 265–301). New York: Academic Press.

Tulving, E., Hayman, C.A.G., & Macdonald, C.A. 1991. Long-lasting perceptual priming and semantic learning in amnesia: A case experiment. *Journal of Experimental Psychology: Learning, Memory, and Cognition, 17*, 595–617.

Tulving, E., & Pearlstone, Z. 1966. Availability versus accessibility of information in memory for words. *Journal of Verbal Learning and Verbal Behavior, 5*, 381–391.

Tulving, E., & Schacter, D.L. 1990. Priming and human memory systems. *Science, 247*, 301–306.

Tulving, E., Schacter, D.L., & Stark, H.A. 1982. Priming effects in word-fragment completion are independent of recognition memory. *Journal of Experimental Psychology: Learning, Memory, and Cognition, 8*, 336–342.

Underwood, B.J., & Humphreys, M. 1979. Context change and the role of meaning in word recognition. *American Journal of Psychology, 92*, 577–609.

Ungerleider, L.G. 1995. Functional brain imaging studies of cortical mechanisms for memory. *Science, 270,* 769–775.

Ungerleider, L.G., & Mishkin, M.M. 1982. Two cortical visual systems. In D.J. Ingle, M.A. Goodale, & R.J.W. Mansfield (Eds.), *Analysis of visual behavior* (pp. 549–586). Cambridge, MA: MIT Press.

Uzgiris, I.C. 1981. Two functions of imitation during infancy. *International Journal of Behavioral Development, 4,* 1–12.

Uzgiris, I.C., & Hunt, J.McV. 1970. Attentional preference and experience: II. An exploratory longitudinal study of the effect of visual familiarity and responsiveness. *Journal of Genetic Psychology, 117,* 109–121.

Vander Linde, E., Morrongiello, B.A., & Rovee-Collier, C. 1985. Determinants of retention in 8-week-old infants. *Developmental Psychology, 21,* 601–613.

Vargha-Khadem, F., Gadian, D.G., Watkins, K.E., Connelly, A., Van Paesschen, N., & Mishkin, M.M. 1997. Differential effects of early hippocampal pathology on episodic and semantic memory. *Science, 277,* 376–380.

Victor, M., & Agamanolis, D. 1990. Amnesia due to lesions confined to the hippocampus: A clinical-pathologic study. *Journal of Cognitive Neuroscience, 2,* 246–257.

Victor, M., Angevine, J.B., Mancall, E.L., & Fisher, C.M. 1961. Memory loss with lesions of hippocampal formation. *Archives of Neurology, 5,* 244–263.

von Hippel, W., & Hawkins, C. 1994. Stimulus exposure time and perceptual memory. *Perception & Psychophysics, 56,* 525–535.

Vriezen, E.R., Moscovitch, M., & Bellos, S.A. 1995. Priming effects in semantic classification tasks. *Journal of Experimental Psychology: Learning, Memory, and Cognition, 21,* 933–946.

Wallace, J.E., Krauter, E.E., & Campbell, B.A. 1980. Animal models of declining memory in the aged: Short-term and spatial memory in the aged rat. *Journal of Gerontology, 35,* 355–363.

Warrington, E.K., & Weiskrantz, L. 1968. New method of testing long-term retention with special reference to amnesic patients. *Nature, 217,* 972–974.

Warrington, E.K., & Weiskrantz, L. 1970. Amnesic syndrome: Consolidation or retrieval? *Nature, 228,* 628–630.

Warrington, E.K., & Weiskrantz, L. 1982. Amnesia: A disconnection syndrome? *Neuropsychologia, 20,* 233–248.

Watkins, P.C., Matthews, A., Williamson, D.A., & Fuller, R.D. 1992. Mood-congruent memory in depression: Emotional priming or elaboration? *Journal of Abnormal Psychology, 101,* 581–586.

Watson, J.B. 1930. *Behaviorism.* Chicago, IL: University of Chicago Press.

Watson, J.B., & Rayner, R. 1920. Conditioned emotional reactions. *Journal of Experimental Psychology, 3,* 1–14.

Watson, J.S. 1984. Memory in learning: Analysis of three momentary reactions of infants. In R. Kail & N.E. Spear (Eds.), *Comparative perspectives on the development of memory* (pp. 159–179). Hillsdale, NJ: Lawrence Erlbaum Associates.

Weiskrantz, L. 1987. Neuroanatomy of memory and amnesia: A case for multiple memory systems. *Human Neurobiology, 6,* 93–105.

Weiskrantz, L. 1990. Problems of learning and memory: One or multiple memory systems?

Philosophical Transactions of the Royal Society of London, 329B, 99–108.

Weiskrantz, L., & Warrington, E.K. 1979. Conditioning in amnesic patients. *Neuropsychologia, 17*, 187–194.

Weizmann, F., Cohen, L.B., & Pratt, R.J. 1971. Novelty, familiarity, and the development of infant attention. *Developmental Psychology, 4*, 149–154.

Werker, J. 1990. Discussion of J.M. Mandler, "Recall of events by preverbal children." In A. Diamond (Ed.), *The development and neural bases of higher cognitive functions* (Vol. 608, pp. 503–516), *Annals of the New York Academy of Sciences*. New York: New York Academy of Sciences.

Werner, J.S., & Perlmutter, M. 1979. Development of visual memory in infants. In H.W. Reese & L.P. Lipsitt (Eds.), *Advances in child development and behavior* (Vol. 14, pp. 1–56). New York: Academic Press.

Wickelgren, W.A. 1972. Trace resistance and the decay of long-term memory. *Journal of Mathematical Psychology, 9*, 418–455.

Wickelgren, W.A. 1979. Chunking and consolidation: A theoretical synthesis of semantic networks, configuring in conditioning, S-R vs. cognitive learning, normal forgetting, the amnesic syndrome, and the hippocampal arousal system. *Psychological Review, 86*, 44–60.

Wilk, A., Klein, L., & Rovee-Collier, C. 2000, March. *Measuring infant recognition memory: Novelty preference vs. operant responding*. Paper presented at the meeting of the Eastern Psychological Association, Baltimore, MD.

Willingham, D.B. 1994. On the creation of classification systems of memory. *Behavioral and Brain Sciences, 17*, 426–427.

Willingham, D.B. 1997. Implicit and explicit memory do not differ in flexibility: Comment on Dienes and Berry (1997). *Psychonomic Bulletin & Review, 4*, 587–591.

Willingham, D.B. 1998a. A neuropsychological theory of motor skill learning. *Psychological Review, 105*, 558–584.

Willingham, D.B. 1998b. What differentiates declarative and procedural memories: Reply to Cohen, Poldrack, and Eichenbaum (1997). *Memory, 6*, 689–699.

Willingham, D.B. 1999. Implicit motor sequence learning is not purely perceptual. *Memory & Cognition, 27*, 561–572.

Willingham, D.B., & Goedert-Eschmann, K. 1999. The relation between implicit and explicit learning: Evidence for parallel development. *Psychological Science, 10*, 531–534.

Willingham, D.B., Nissen, M.J., & Bullemer, P.T. 1989. On the development of procedural knowledge. *Journal of Experimental Psychology: Learning, Memory, and Cognition, 15*, 1047–1060.

Willingham, D.B., & Preuss, L. 1995. The death of implicit memory. *Psyche, 2 (14)*, 1–10.

Willis, W.D., & Grossman, R.G. (1973). *Medical neurobiology*. St. Louis, MO: Mosby.

Winocur, G. 1990. Anterograde and retrograde amnesia in rats with dorsal hippocampal or dorsomedial thalamic lesions. *Behavioral Brain Research, 38*, 145–154.

Winocur, G., & Kinsbourne, M. 1978. Contextual cueing as an aid to Korsakoff amnesics. *Neuropsychologia, 16*, 671–682.

Wise, S.P. 1996. The role of the basal ganglia in procedural memory. *Seminars in the Neurosciences, 8*, 39–46.

Witherspoon, D., & Moscovitch, M. 1989. Stochastic independence between two implicit memory tasks. *Journal of Experimental Psychology: Learning, Memory, and Cognition, 15*, 22–30.

Woodruff-Pak, D.S. 1993. Eyeblink classical conditioning in H.M.: Delay and trace paradigms. *Behavioral Neuroscience, 107*, 911–925.

Woodworth, R.S. 1938. *Experimental psychology*. New York: Henry Holt.

Wright, A.A., Santiago, H.C., Sands, S.F., Kendrick, D.F., & Cook, R.G. 1985. Memory processing of serial lists by pigeons, monkeys, and people. *Science, 229*, 287–289.

Wyers, E.J., Peeke, H.V.S., & Herz, M.J. 1973. Behavioral habituation in invertebrates. In H.V.S. Peeke & M.J. Herz (Eds.), *Habituation I* (pp. 1–57). New York: Academic Press.

Zentall, T.R. 1973. Memory in the pigeon: Retroactive inhibition in a delayed matching task. *Bulletin of the Psychonomic Society, 1*, 126–128.

Zola-Morgan, S.M., & Squire, L.R. 1984. Preserved learning in monkeys with medial temporal lesions: Sparing of motor and cognitive skills. *Journal of Neuroscience, 4*, 1072–1085.

Zola-Morgan, S.M., & Squire, L.R. 1985a. Medial temporal lesions in monkeys impair memory on a variety of tasks sensitive to human amnesia. *Behavioral Neuroscience, 99*, 22–34.

Zola-Morgan, S.M., & Squire, L.R. 1985b. Complementary approaches to the study of memory: Human amnesia and animal models. In N.W. Weinberger, J.L. McGaugh, & G. Lynch (Eds.), *Memory systems of the brain: Animal and human cognitive processes* (pp. 463–477). New York: Guilford Press.

Zola-Morgan, S.M., & Squire, L.R. 1990a. The primate hippocampal formation: Evidence for a time-limited role in memory storage. *Science, 250*, 288–290.

Zola-Morgan, S.M., & Squire, L.R. 1990b. Neuropsychological investigations of memory and amnesia: Findings from humans and nonhuman primates. In A. Diamond (Ed.), *The development and neural bases of higher cognitive functions* (Vol. 608, pp. 434–456), *Annals of the New York Academy of Sciences*. New York: New York Academy of Sciences.

Zola-Morgan, S.M., Squire, L.R., & Amaral, D.G. 1989a. Lesions of the amygdala that spare adjacent cortical regions do not impair memory or exacerbate the impairment following lesions of the hippocampal formation. *Journal of Neuroscience, 9*, 1922–1936.

Zola-Morgan, S.M., Squire, L.R., Amaral, D.G., & Suzuki, W.A. 1989b. Lesions of perirhinal and parahippocampal cortex that spare the amygdala and hippocampal formation produce severe memory impairment. *Journal of Neuroscience, 9*, 4355–4370.

Zola-Morgan, S.M., Squire, L.R., Clower, R.P., & Rempel, N.L. 1993. Damage to the perirhinal cortex exacerbates memory impairment following lesions to the hippocampal formation. *Journal of Neuroscience, 13*, 251–265.

Zola-Morgan, S.M., Squire, L.R., & Mishkin, M.M. 1982. The neuroanatomy of amnesia: Amygdala-hippocampus vs. temporal stem. *Science, 218*, 1337–1339.

Zola-Morgan, S.M., Squire, L.R., Rempel, N.L., Clower, R.P., & Amaral, D.G. 1992. Enduring memory impairment in monkeys after ischemic damage to the hippocampus. *Journal of Neuroscience, 12*, 2582–2596.

Author Index

Locators annotated with *f* indicate figures.
Locators annotated with *t* indicate tables.

Subject Index

Locators annotated with *f* indicate figures.
Locators annotated with *t* indicate tables.

A

absolute information, infant memory and 182
accessibility, of memory
  context impact on 238-239, 245-246
  declarative/procedural 211-213
  explicit 10-11, 142-143, 212, 239
  implicit 11, 212, 238
active memory
  mechanisms of 37, 193, 207, 249
  priming with 233-234
    novel, retention effects of 242-245, 243*f*
    retention effects of 239-241, 240*f*
adenosine monophosphate, *see* cyclic AMP
adult memory
  capacity of 1, 3, 247
  experimental dissociations in 7-8, 127
  independence in 23-24
  independent variables in 143-186, 144*t*
  parallels with amnesics 128
  parallels with infants 139-141
  process-dissociation procedure for 19-20
  infant memory *versus* 2-3
  Jacksonian principle of, multiple memory systems and 73-74
  memory dissociations in 186, 188
    task comparisons with infants 137-141, 138*t*
    tasks for 127-129

priming in 232-233
affect, as dissociation variable 172-175, 173*f*
age and aging
  as dissociation variable 144-150, 146*f*-148*f*
  in Jacksonian principle 66-68, 71-73
    children's memory and 75-82, 80*f*-81*f*
    multiple memory systems and 73-82, 80*f*-81*f*
  memory performance per 17-18, 197, 234-235, 235*f*
  multiple memory systems and 73-82, 228
  priming latency and 141-143, 142*f*
agendas, in MEM memory system 222*f*, 223-224
alcoholic amnesia, *see* Korsakoff's syndrome
Alzheimer's disease 26, 74
amnesia
  adult memory parallels with 128
  alcoholic, *see* Korsakoff's syndrome
  anterograde 30, 38, 40-41
  conscious awareness with 8, 16, 21
  drug-induced temporary 14
  infant memory parallels with 115-126, 120*f*, 126*t*, 248
  infantile 73
  Jacksonian principle and 72-73
  memory dissociations with 3-4, 7, 128, 193-194

27. McMILLAN, John and Grant R. GILLETT: *Consciousness and Intentionality.* n.y.p.
28. ZACHAR, Peter: *Psychological Concepts and Biological Psychiatry. A philosophical analysis.* n.y.p.
29. VAN LOOCKE, Philip (ed.): *The Physical Nature of Consciousness.* n.y.p.